New Wine

New Wine

The Story of Women Transforming
Leadership and Power
in the Episcopal Church

Pamela W. Darling

COWLEY PUBLICATIONS
Cambridge ✦ Boston
Massachusetts

Library of Congress Cataloging-in-Publication Data:
Darling, Pamela W.
    New wine: the story of women transforming leadership and power
in the Episcopal Church / Pamela W. Darling
        p.   cm.
    Includes bibliographical references and index.
    ISBN: 1-56101-094-4 (alk. paper)
    1. Women in the Episcopal Church. 2. Episcopal Church—History. 4. Anglican Communion—United States—History. 4. Feminist theology. I. Title.
BX5968.5.D37 1994
283'.73'082—dc20   94-10734

New Wine was edited by Cynthia Shattuck, copyedited and typeset by Vicki Black. The index was prepared by Gardiner H. Shattuck, Jr., and the cover designed by Vicki Black.

The photograph on the front cover of bishops Barbara C. Harris, Jane Holmes Dixon, and Penelope Ann Jamieson was taken by Alexandra Dorr at Washington Cathedral on the occasion of the consecration of Jane Holmes Dixon.

This book is printed on recycled, acid-free paper and was produced in the United States of America.

Cowley Publications
28 Temple Place
Boston, Massachusetts 02111

This book is dedicated with profound gratitude to
Mary Abbot Emery Twing, Elizabeth Dyer,
The Philadelphia Eleven, Barbara Clementine Harris,
Pamela Pauly Chinnis, and all the other Episcopal women
who have dared to be first,
that Christ's body on earth might be made whole and strong.

Contents

Acknowledgments

This book arose from a dilemma shared by many Christian feminists. We find ourselves in the midst of religious institutions which have channelled God's grace in our lives, but which have also reinforced—even sanctified—age-old patterns that diminish women and limit the humanity of all people. It is a conflict which produces both controversy and acute personal suffering. As an Episcopalian involved in my church's wrestling with the "problem" of women's changing roles, I have found myself at times dismayed, elated, outraged, hopeful, and occasionally paralyzed by the contradictions and complexities of the process. To avoid the despair that drives many women from the church, I sought a sense of perspective in the history behind our present condition.

The project began in the heart of the tradition itself. The General Theological Seminary in New York City is as close to being representative of the Episcopal Church as any place I know, complete with all the tension and conflict, the impatience and resistance which characterize the church's life today. Its history and architecture epitomize the patriarchal church of old, as its efforts to incorporate women mirror the best and worst of that process in the late twentieth-century church. I am grateful to then-Dean James E. Fenhagen, the faculty, and trustees, whose support enabled me to live the Anglican tradition as I studied it. Professor Roland Foster was a most able guide through the thickets of academic history, and it is a pleasure to acknowledge his warm personal friendship and unfailingly helpful suggestions.

As a librarian, I know well that research is possible only with the generous help of colleagues who share information about resources, copies of elusive materials, and provocative ideas. Particular thanks go to the staff of St. Mark's Library in the 1980s, especially to Suzie McGlaughon, Matt Grande, and David Green; to Ruth Leonard, archivist of the Society of the Companions of the Holy Cross; to Mary Sudman Donovan, Sandra H. Boyd, Joanna B. Gillespie, and all their colleagues in the Episcopal Women's History Project; to Victoria Lee

Erickson and Susan Ware, whose knowledge of sociology and history was so cogently shared in classrooms at Union Theological Seminary and New York University, and whose enthusiasm and exacting standards were a powerful incentive to complete what sometimes seemed a quixotic task. Thanks also to Mary Lou Suhor and Sue Pierce for access to facts and files in the Pennsylvania office of *The Witness* magazine, and for good talk and constant encouragement.

To study the church is also to range well beyond *academe.* Staff of the Episcopal Church Center in New York answered countless questions and cheerfully provided materials. Thanks are due especially to Mary Ellen Fenn, Joanna Gajardo, Kathie Ragsdale, and Ann Smith in the Women in Mission and Ministry Unit; Julie A. Wortman, then of *Episcopal Life;* Jeffrey Penn of the Episcopal News Service, Barbara Braver of the Presiding Bishop's staff, and Donald Nickerson and Charles Scott of the General Convention Office, for responding to requests reasonable and unreasonable with timeliness and good humor; John Ratti of the Office of Communications, for crucial guidance through the publishing maze; and the Cornerstone Project of the Episcopal Church Foundation, for support and encouragement.

Historian and theologian Fredrica Harris Thompsett speaks compellingly about our need for a "community of accountability" to keep our work both rooted in the story of our forebears and open to the rich diversity of the present. Representative of that community for me have been those who shared in the work of the committee for the Full Participation of Women in the Church and its successor, the Committee on the Status of Women. With love for all, I thank most particularly my mentor Pamela P. Chinnis and the indefatigable Marge Christie, who believed in the usefulness of my work to our common task and who continue to inspire me as exemplars of wise and energetic lay leadership.

I have been blessed with the friendship of many participants in events described in these pages. Conversations with them over the years have influenced my perspective in ways impossible to acknowledge adequately. But I must record here my special debt to Philadelphia ordinands Carter Heyward, Suzanne R. Hiatt, Katrina Welles Swanson, and Nancy Hatch Wittig for sharing their experiences, documents, and wisdom about the effects of "women" on the old wineskins of the church. This work is a testimony to the courage and love of all the Philadelphia Eleven, and to their commitment to achieving wholeness in the life and ministry of the Episcopal Church. We are empowered by their faith and sacrifice.

Janet B. Campbell spent long hours spotting inconsistencies, typographical errors, and infelicities of style, and taught me what to expect from an excellent editor. What a pleasure, then, to fall into the most capable hands of Cynthia Shattuck, who saw the book inside the dissertation and helped me carve it free, and Vicki Black, who knew how to polish and make it shine. Sister Andrea of the Order of St. Helena prayed me through. Above all, I give thanks for the sustaining love of my family, who kept me fed, clean, and sane from start to finish.

Introduction

Jesus said to them, "Neither is new wine put into old wineskins; otherwise, the skins burst, and the wine is spilled, and the skins are destroyed; but new wine is put into fresh wineskins, and so both are preserved." (Matthew 9:17)

The traditional "wineskins" of church and society do not easily contain the new relationships between men and women developing today in Western culture. The age-old assumption that women are naturally inferior to men and thus belong in subordinate positions is being overturned, and the often radical changes in sex roles that follow call, like new wine, for fresh wineskins.

The effects of these changes can be dizzying and disorienting, as everything seems to be in flux: family patterns, ideals of community life, educational and employment opportunities, models of leadership, rules of access to positions of authority and power, norms of friendship, goals for personal and vocational accomplishment, behavioral and sexual standards. The institutional church, for so long arbiter of such questions, is perhaps most challenged by these developments, and its members most painfully divided. The old wineskins of religious tradition and social custom cannot hold women and men fired by a new gospel of mutuality, justice, and care. But fresh wineskins are not readily at hand, and much good wine is being spilt as our institutions struggle to respond to changing realities.

The Episcopal Church in the United States has not been protected from this painful process, which is by no means complete as the twentieth century draws to a close. Ethical issues, theologies of ministry, and the polity of this part of the world-wide Anglican Communion are all being reexamined in the light of evolving concepts of what it means to be "male and female," created in the image of God. In the search for appropriate new forms of ecclesial life for men and

women—equally beloved of God, equally saved by Christ, equally en-
livened by the Holy Spirit—an examination of what brought the old
wineskins to their bursting point offers both warning and guidance.
So this book explores women's changing roles and the effects of
those changes on the institution, in search of wisdom to inform the
next stages in the unfinished process.

This book is also an experiment in feminist ecclesiology. To describe something as "feminist" risks misunderstanding, as the term
has become invested with almost as many meanings as users. Yet
such a description is helpful, even in its fuzzy catch-all sense, because it signals that something different from a traditional approach
is being attempted here. For me, feminism involves the dual assumptions of the intended equality of men and women as creatures of the
one God, and the reality of millennia of inequality built into social,
cultural, and religious structures—which we are called to correct.
With these assumptions, I have set forth to study the *ecclesia*—the
church, and specifically the Episcopal Church in the United States of
America—using the tools of contemporary women's history and feminist social theory. The result is not conventional sociology or church
history, nor is it feminist theology, philosophy, or ethics. I have studied these disciplines, and have drawn freely from their insights in examining a set of developments affecting women in the life of the
Episcopal Church. But the purpose for this examination, and consequently the form that it takes, is more practical than theoretical. The
focus is on the church as a living organization: how it functions and
how people function within it.

I begin with the assumption that our understanding of the church
can be enhanced, and our responsibilities as leaders of the church
more effectively and righteously fulfilled, by asking new kinds of
questions. As historian Joan Scott has so provocatively suggested in
an article aptly titled "Gender: A Useful Category of Historical Analysis,"[1] using a feminist lens in the traditional investigations of history
and social analysis can bring into view what has long been hidden.
As old realities become newly visible, solutions to hitherto intractable problems may also present themselves.

Following a brief overview of the roles of women in colonial and
frontier America, the narratives comprising this book span the cen-
tury-plus from the 1870s to the early 1990s. They describe women's

relationships to the organizational structure of the Episcopal Church, their evolving roles, and the institutional mechanisms that have promoted or resisted these role changes. The primary focus of attention throughout is women's search for a voice, authority, and place alongside men within the church's leadership at the *national* church level—in the General Convention, the House of Bishops, the Executive Council, the Episcopal Church Center, and their predecessor bodies. Although most Episcopalians have little direct contact with these organizational units, the development and implementation of legislation and program at the national level establishes the framework in which all diocesan and local parish life takes place. It is my belief that a better understanding of the evolution of our national structures is essential if the atomizing tendencies of our era and the tensions inherent in a culture of ever-accelerating change are not to split the church apart.

These narratives are primarily a study of "women" and the Episcopal Church, not the stories of individual women. Women moved from auxiliary and unofficial roles into the official governmental structure and the ordained ministry of the church not through the heroic efforts of solitary leaders but through the sustained and shared efforts of many women across several generations. The church has accorded prominence to a few exceptional women who have served in conventional or subordinate roles in relation to its official structures. But individual women who challenged and sought equal access to those structures generally found themselves isolated, pressed into serving the institution's purposes, or disempowered. This is a natural defense mechanism of bureaucratic structures, and is particularly effective in neutralizing women, who have not been socialized to pursue individual achievement. Only as Episcopal women used their countervailing strengths—skills in sustaining relationships, nurturing groups, and building networks—did they slowly amass the power to be seen and heard by the institution. Thus what follows is chiefly an account of corporate development, not individual accomplishment.

Women's "place" in society and the church remained relatively stable throughout the colonial period of American history and in the early decades of the new United States and its Anglican counterpart, the Episcopal Church. But nation and church responded on very different time-tables to the "woman question" that arose in the mid-nineteenth century and led to the ratification of the woman's suffrage amendment to the Constitution in 1920.

The process of change in the Episcopal Church occurred in three discernible stages, with the ordination of women in the 1970s marking a critical turning point in the profound and prolonged transformation of both external and internal church structures. Up through World War II, changes in women's roles in the Episcopal Church occurred very gradually, with a minimum of explicit conflict or controversy. During this first stage, change took place in a separate arena of the church's life, not affecting the traditional male monopoly on either legislative control or the spiritual and organizational authority vested in the ordained leadership. Even during the secular peak of first wave of feminist activism in the 1910s and 1920s, scattered challenges to women's exclusion from national church governance were easily defeated and soon forgotten. The question of women's "place" simply did not engage most Episcopalians. This benign neglect made it possible for Episcopal women to develop powerful unofficial structures, both to minister in the world and to influence the official structures of the church.

Beginning in 1946, the "woman question" was no longer neglected. In this second stage of change in the roles of women, the "place" of women became a perennial issue for the General Convention and increasingly for the whole Episcopal Church. The growing controversy resulted in the dismantling of the constitutional and canonical barriers to women's participation in the governance and ministry of the Episcopal Church. The renewed campaign that culminated in seating women as members of the House of Deputies in 1970 opened the final door to women's participation in church governance, and six years later the male monopoly on ordained ministry was also voted away. These two actions had profound and far-reaching effects both on the institutional life of the church and on its theology and sense of corporate identity. The effects of women's entry into organizational and spiritual leadership positions, only partly anticipated by proponents and opponents alike and still by no means realized, raised the emotional temperature of the church to new heights.

The third stage of transformation began in the mid-1980s, when the intensifying controversy over women's roles expanded to include a broad agenda of theological and social issues. As the symbolic implications of ordaining women became clearer, conflicts over language, authority, and sexuality became the focal point. The effects of developments in the United States on other provinces of the international Anglican Communion, and vice versa, forced Episcopalians to broaden their ecclesiastical horizons and expand their sense of accountability. There were inconsistencies in the way institutional structures, particularly the House of Bishops as the apex of the church's hierarchy within the United States, responded to these new pressures. This organizational ambiguity revealed hidden connections between women's relationship to church leadership and broader issues of power, language, and sexuality. These new patterns of relationship between men and women began to place extreme stress on the old structure.

Each of these stages of change in the role of women was related to what had gone before in the life of the church, and to the surrounding secular culture. Each included, at least in some form, characteristics typical of organizational change processes: an ongoing cycle of challenge, response, conflict, resolution, adaptation, new challenge. The power dynamics that shape the institutional life of the church are thus a part of this study, for the interconnection between gender and power, and particularly the way it has evolved since the middle of the twentieth century in the Episcopal Church, can be instructive for the church in the future.

Good history can be like corporate psychotherapy: by understanding where we have been, we can make wise choices about where we are going. Good church history must also point to the action of God in the ongoing life of the community of the faithful. Like the biblical authors of old, we each tell the story from our own perspective, bearing witness to the grace that enables us to live and love in our own time and place. To the degree that we can articulate the truth of that presence in our own lives, so those coming after may recognize and be nourished by the gospel, the good news, of our story. Here, then, is a story of women in the Episcopal Church, told from the perspective of the late twentieth century.

Part One

Women's "Proper Place"

Every man should be master in his own house. (Esther 1:22)

I permit no woman to teach or to have authority over a man; she is to keep silent. (1 Timothy 2:12)

Where do women belong? From the Old Testament to the defeat of the equal rights amendment to the United States Constitution, from the First Epistle to Timothy to the religious right of the 1980s and 1990s, the "proper place" of women has been understood by many religious and secular authorities as separate from and subordinate to the place of men.

For most cultures and throughout most of recorded history, men have dominated women, although the particular social forms of this domination have varied significantly from one era to another. Examining women's place in America's history and how that place has evolved in the years since this country's beginnings provides the necessary context for understanding the dramatic changes in the place of women occurring in the church in our own time.

Chapter 1

From Colonial America to the First Wave of Feminism

T he religious and social lives of women and men in the first century of colonial America were significantly different from our own. Before the concepts of individual conscience developed in the late eighteenth and nineteenth centuries, deference to authority was the religious duty of *everyone* in a many-layered social hierarchy, with God (represented by kings and bishops) at the top and children, servants, and slaves at the bottom. Social and moral controls on behavior within the community were built into the deferential social system. Deference to one's superiors ensured harmonious social relationships, while obedience to law and custom promoted the smooth functioning of society.

Seventeenth-century colonists—men and women alike—brought to the new world a sense of themselves as occupying a specific place in a fixed social order. Though many shed allegiance to a particular secular or religious authority when they emigrated, the concept of a God-given hierarchy was strong, and new social rankings were quickly established.

Within this social hierarchy, tasks and roles were clearly assigned. Free adult men bought and sold property, ran farms, managed businesses, and were generally responsible for the financial and legal functions of church and society. Women might engage in public activities as agents of their husbands, but their responsibilities were primarily in the private domain: managing the household, raising the children, maintaining the social fabric of the community. Within the church, their activities were similarly hidden. Although women acting as deputies for absent husbands occasionally performed such vestry duties as engaging supply clergy, they were barred from vestry service in their own right, as from other formal leadership positions.

Hierarchies, and the power embedded in them, were necessary to maintain order. But the conditions of colonial life—high mobility, intense survival pressures, new circumstances to which former laws and customs did not apply, and the "equal opportunity" of hardship—worked relentlessly against the old hierarchies. As the deferential system lost power, informal networks of women became a strong social force as the guardians of reputation and morality in the community. Though often trivialized by those in the hierarchies as "gossips," women transmitted the community's behavioral values and provided pastoral care and intervention in domestic crises and community conflicts.

Women were essential to religious continuity in families and communities, therefore, both in Congregational New England and in Anglican Virginia. Because of their educational responsibilities for children and slaves, they were expected to be informed about religious matters, and were often accorded a high degree of respect for their religious opinions by both laymen and clergy. In one instance, a woman's disapproval of certain theological views expressed by a candidate prevented his being appointed to a parish, much to his outrage that the "opinions of a lady" should be sought on such a matter.[1]

Colonial women also played a key role in family denominational choice. The First Great Awakening reached Virginia in the mid-1740s, and revivals continued almost without interruption throughout the century. Wives and mothers often influenced male family members either to remain in the Anglican fold or to convert to another denomination. Some men switched more than once when a second wife's preference was different from that of the first. Whether we regard this as evidence of women's spiritual authority within the family or as an indication of men's relative indifference to religious matters, the fact remains that women's attitudes and commitment to the church were critical to its survival.

As the shift from an agricultural to an industrial economy deepened the division between public and private life, the practice of religious piety was increasingly identified with domestic affairs. Many religious activities were based in the home, where family prayers and the religious education of children were chiefly the responsibility of women. Baptisms, weddings, and funerals were usually conducted at home under a woman's direction. Some public worship services were held in homes and plantation chapels by clergy ministering in large rural areas, and women figured prominently in arrangements for such services.

Frontier Ice Cream Socials

In addition to being a moral and cultural force within colonial society, women also played expanding roles in establishing and building churches. From colonial New England and Virginia to the American West, women were the catalysts for establishing new congregations, from locating property and raising church buildings to calling clergy.

As historian Joan Gundersen discovered, for example, women who gathered in 1858 as the Ladies Social Circle in Northfield, Minnesota soon organized an Episcopal congregation, raised money, obtained ecclesiastical permission, recruited men to sign deeds and serve on the vestry, built buildings, organized Sunday school programs, and hired clergy, who did not stay long if they lost the women's support.[2] Men were permitted to join the Social Circle—one of the few respectable opportunities for social gathering—but had to pay double the regular dues. Some of the male deed-signers were not even church members, apparently signing the deed as a form of public service in order to help the women meet legal requirements. Not liking the location of the building lot the distant missionary authorities had chosen, the women of Northfield quietly purchased another and erected their church there, complete with gifts of a churchyard fence and altar linens from other women's groups "back home" in New York and Tennessee.

Such silent defiance was not without precedent in women's dealing with religious authorities. Almost two centuries earlier, in 1677, in Chebacco, Massachusetts, Congregational women had a building raised secretly, after male religious leaders had refused to authorize a new congregation. Although the women were fined for this presumptuous action, a minister was nevertheless soon sent to the new church, which was located near their homes so women with small children could walk to services.

In the nineteenth century, the financial power of women's groups and their informal family networks spanning the continent as settlers pushed the frontier westward played a foundational role in the spread of the Episcopal Church. While male clergy preached and lay-men had legal control of the financial and organizational business of the congregation, women served as nurturers and guardians of the religious life of the community. Frederic Dan Huntington, bishop of Central New York when it was still virtually the frontier, noted admiringly:

> Both the original Church life and the survival of it from year to year are owing to women. The first services were often called for and held, the places of worship provided, the comforts and decencies, and not merely the decorations, were furnished, the money was raised, the church buildings were put up...and the clergy have been paid by the ingenuity, zeal and toil of women.[3]

Missionary Bishop Jackson Kemper also admired the support of the women, noting during his 1856 visitation to Nebraska and Kansas that the "ladies have ice cream socials to build the Church."[4]

As agriculture gave way to a market economy and an expansive industrial system, women gradually followed men out of the home and into the public sphere. Women of the poorer classes found marginal employment as domestics, seamstresses, and laborers in the new mills. Some of their middle-class sisters found occupations, often unpaid, in the cultural, educational, and religious life of towns and cities. Yet as the lines marking the separate domestic sphere of colonial women faded, an ideology arose explicitly prescribing that women's separate sphere was in the home and not-so-subtly rebuking those who ventured forth. Many women remained so busy with domestic and child-rearing responsibilities that the home was quite enough to fill their time to exhaustion. But single women, women wealthy enough to have servants or slaves to care for their homes and children, and women old enough to have no small children at home all had time available for outside pursuits. Many cherished the companionship and opportunities for service they were able create in the church. Because religion was increasingly identified with the private world of home and family, these women were able to engage in many quite public activities without seeming, perhaps even to themselves, to have left their "proper place."

By the mid-nineteenth century, women's place in the church was increasingly ambiguous. The self-effacing behavior decreed as appropriate for women enabled them to play substantial roles in the very midst of a church that supported with its rhetoric and theology the increasing separation of the sexes and the isolation of women in a private sphere. Because men operating in the public sphere had less and less time for religious activities, women were increasingly the mainstay, the numerical majority, the active membership of the church—staffing its programs, shaping its piety, and existing in sometimes uneasy alliance with its male clergy.

In the society beyond the church, meanwhile, a movement for women's rights was slowly growing. The first women's rights convention in the United States was held in Seneca Falls, New York in 1848, and suffragettes were increasingly visible in American social and political life for the next seventy years, until the woman's suffrage amendment to the Constitution was finally ratified in 1920. Public debate about women influenced the awareness and self-consciousness of church members, so that changes affecting women in the church became more deliberate, less accidental. Out of such contradictions—the growing discontinuity between the religious ideal of deferential piety and a secular model of political activism—pressure arose to formalize the relationship of women to the church's institutional structure.

An Infant Bureaucracy

Like other Protestant churches in the decades immediately following the American Revolution, the Episcopal Church had no national administrative or financial structure. Bishops administered their dioceses under the authority of diocesan conventions made up of clerical and lay representatives from local congregations. Every three years a General Convention of all the dioceses met. This convention was a bi-cameral legislative body with a House of Bishops, which included all living bishops of the American church, and a House of Deputies, which was made up of clerical and lay representatives elected by each diocese and missionary district. Guardian of the church's constitution, canons, and prayer book, the General Convention authorized the consecration of new bishops and the formation of new dioceses, and provided a sense of national identity to the fledgling denomination within the international Anglican Communion. However, no national organizational unit existed between conventions, so there was room and need for special-purpose societies that could provide administrative support for religious programs between the periodic gatherings of church legislative bodies, as well as continuity and direction for program activities that transcended local boundaries.

These societies and associations were generally independent agencies. Managed by boards of committed individuals, they raised funds by subscription, organized volunteer labor, employed staff to conduct day-to-day business, and hired agents to carry out the society's work in distant places. Bible societies and Sunday school associations disseminated materials and trained teachers; missionary societies educated members about local and remote mission opportunities, collected supplies and materials to send to mission stations, and raised funds to train and support missionaries at home and abroad. Not all societies were specifically church-related, but those that were had considerable autonomy and flexibility to pursue the mission of the church as their leaders perceived it, without waiting for the approval or financial support of official denominational bodies.

In 1820, after several preliminary attempts to develop a support system for Episcopal missionary work in frontier areas of the country, the General Convention authorized the creation of "a general Missionary Society for Foreign and Domestic Missions." Bishops of the church were to be its president and vice-presidents; its managers, the Board of Missions, were appointed by and reported to the General Convention. Housed in Bible House in lower Manhattan, the Board of Missions was to hire staff, create auxiliary societies in each diocese under the leadership of the local bishop, and raise funds to carry out the mission of the church. Through this mechanism the Convention sought to harness the energies of an independent society within the ecclesiastical authority system. This process inadvertently created the core of today's centralized church bureaucracy, whose legal corporate name remains "The Domestic and Foreign Missionary Society of the Protestant Episcopal Church."

The early years of the Missionary Society were full of disappointments. Money did not pour in to the Society's coffers, and many bishops were reluctant to support their fundraising efforts because they seemed to compete for funds with local needs. Establishing auxiliary branches of the Society proved particularly difficult, and much depended on the particular personalities involved in each diocese. The societies upon which the Domestic and Foreign Missionary Society was modeled were typically founded and directed by male community leaders, often clergy. Groups called "auxiliaries" provided a forum for less influential members of the community—such as women and young men—to support Society programs. Since social custom severely limited the activities men and women could engage in together, when women wished to participate actively in religious, benevolent, or reform programs they were likely to create their own auxiliary organizations, and the term "auxiliary" gradually became almost synonymous with women's organizations. For example, at least eight of the eleven local auxiliaries represented at the first triennial meeting of the Domestic and Foreign Missionary Society in 1823 were women's groups.

Associations of women flourished in the early nineteenth century, their memberships composed chiefly of middle-class white women, engaged in everything from distributing Bible tracts to nursing the poor to campaigning against prostitution, often by publishing the names of customers in the local newspaper. Such activities gave these women opportunities to be active in the public sphere despite growing pressure to remain in an increasingly segregated domestic world. They learned organizational skills, developed communication networks, experienced the power of group action, had opportunities for public speaking (at a time when women were generally forbidden to speak to "promiscuous assemblies" of men and women), and became writers and publishers.

During the Civil War, northern white women brought these skills to the Sanitary Commission, providing support services to Union troops and working with freed slaves in some areas, while southern white women performed similar activities for the Confederacy. White and black women together played a major role during Reconstruction, establishing and teaching in schools for former slaves and supporting other recovery efforts. In the Episcopal Church, dozens of women augmented the work of a few clergymen deployed by the Freedmen's Commission (later the Department of Colored Missions) in various southern states.

In the process, some participants in reform activities became ardent proponents of women's rights. The various associations that provided so many middle-class white women opportunities for meaningful activity outside the home in the early and mid-nineteenth century formed a nurturing foundation for the women's movement. It is in this context that what came to be called "women's work" was organized in the Episcopal Church and other Protestant denominations.

The Episcopal Church as a whole was not hospitable to the passions and rhetoric of the burgeoning women's rights movement, but necessity led the Society's Board of Missions to ask the "woman question" within the church. Driven by the immense pressures of providing financial and human resources to support expanding missionary work, the Board sought a way to take advantage of the various local auxiliaries that were raising money and providing staff for benevolent programs in and beyond the church.

The opening wedge for women at the Board of Missions was, perhaps predictably, a program for children. To involve children in the church's mission through education and fundraising projects, the Secretary for Domestic Missions created a publication called *The Young Christian Soldiers*. Maria H. Bulfinch was hired as its editor, thus becoming the first woman appointed to the staff of the Board of Missions. The man responsible for this appointment was the Rev. Dr. A. T. Twing, who had joined the board in 1861 and became Domestic Secretary in 1866. Apparently a free spirit, he is reported to have said that the church was "more likely to die of dignity than of her duty,"[5] and among his innovations was a campaign to change the perception of women's proper role. Twing downplayed the prevailing notion that women, at least those of the "better" classes, belonged at home, elevated on a pedestal of moral superiority to rule the domestic sphere, using the back pages of the Board of Missions' monthly publication, *Spirit of Missions*, to report on women's benevolent works outside official church structures, while he encouraged Bulfinch's work on staff.

Twing's efforts opened the possibility that perhaps women *could* serve the church beyond the domestic sphere without abandoning their "proper place." In June of 1870, the lead article in *Spirit of Missions* was titled "Woman and the Mission Work," and held up an explicit model of "useful" women supporting the church's programs, proclaiming that "it is clear to reflecting minds that woman must erelong rise to a higher sphere of usefulness, and take a broader part in every department of work."[6] Redefining as opportunity the threat of women's activism encroaching on men's domain, the article sought to "incite inquiry and induce reflection" about the potential benefits of channelling the "general activity animating the women of the land" into the church's programs. Its careful prose sidestepped controversy and set a tone combining support for an idealized image of Woman with a rejection of secular feminism, a tone that was to mark the Episcopal Church's rhetoric about women for decades. This tone, deferential and respectful of existing church structures and authority, would have been reassuring to readers uneasy about what was "animating the women of the land," for there was apparently nothing revolutionary about its suggestions for harnessing women's energies for the work of the church.

The campaign was successful. The 1871 General Convention authorized the formation of "such Christian organizations as may consist with the government and rules of the Church," which was understood to mean that an official women's organization could be established. And so the Woman's Auxiliary was born.

Chapter 2

Separate and Unequal: The Woman's Auxiliary

T he Woman's Auxiliary began very simply. In early 1872 an energetic young woman named Mary Abbot Emery was hired by the Board of Missions as General Secretary of "The Woman's Association, Auxiliary to the Board of Missions," known for nearly a century thereafter simply as the Woman's Auxiliary.

Daughter of a New England sea captain, Mary Emery had moved to New York City a few years earlier. Her family members were all active Episcopalians, including two clergy brothers, one of whom served at Calvary Church, Gramercy Park, in lower Manhattan. At nearby Grace Church, Mary Emery became active in the Ladies Domestic Missionary Relief Association, and there came to the attention of Dr. Twing, who had helped to organize that association in 1868. Following her appointment to the Board of Missions, Mary Emery soon developed a network of women's organizations that were parish-based and linked within diocesan women's auxiliaries.

Mary Emery knew how to use the rhetoric of deference. She could describe a radical new program in pious language that seemed to affirm the status quo. In the March 1872 *Spirit of Missions*, responding to questions about the program that had been received following announcement of her appointment, she promised that the women of the Auxiliary would "do our duty faithfully, in whatever way the Church approves, and leave the future in His hands." Dismissing the prevailing pattern of societies with a common constitution and centralized control, Emery emphasized personal piety and loving cooperation:

> That which no rigid system can bring about must be done by the active, living power of Love. The tie which must bind together the

women of the church in their work for Christ, must be a personal ardent devotion to their common Lord and Master; a faithful sympa-
thizing fellowship with one another for His dear sake; a mutual
interest in the spreading of His Church.

According to Emery's vision of the Auxiliary, the women of the
church would be bound together through daily use of prayers distributed to all Auxiliary members and by regular communication—
through judicious use of the church press and personal
correspondence (parish secretaries all to be duly "appointed by their
Rectors"). Their efforts were intended to stabilize and enhance the
status quo: "Do what you can, and do it in just the way best suited to
your individual tastes, to the circumstances of your parish, to the
state of life in which God has placed you."[1]

Mary Emery assured her readers that the Woman's Auxiliary
would enhance, not compete with, existing church structures, for its
officers and programs would always be subject to the local clergy.
This was a prudent strategy in the midst of the emerging suffrage
movement: 1872 was, after all, the year in which Susan B. Anthony
was arrested for attempting to vote, and passions were running high
about women's "proper place." The Emery strategy of quiet infiltra-
tion rather than explicit confrontation was well suited to the conservative nature of the Episcopal Church. Within two years, the
framework of a national network was in place. In October 1874,
Mary Emery convened the first gathering of diocesan officers—sixty-
six women from five dioceses—to report on activities, exchange
ideas, learn first-hand about the Board of Missions' operations, and
build personal connections within the widespread Auxiliary.

A Family Enterprise
Mary Emery inspired many to embrace her vision of this new enterprise. Her own efforts were supported and multiplied by her sisters,
whose connections with the Auxiliary made it practically an Emery
family enterprise for decades. First Susan Lavinia Emery and then
Julia Chester Emery followed Maria Bulfinch as editor of the children's paper. In 1876, when Mary Emery "retired" after a whirlwind
four years to marry Dr. Twing, Julia took her place as General Secretary and yet another Emery sister, Margaret Theresa, joined the staff.

Julia Emery directed the Auxiliary for forty years after her sister's retirement to matrimony, with Margaret presiding over the expanding "missionary box" work, and Mary Emery Twing assisting from the sidelines as Honorary Secretary.

In her four years as General Secretary, Mary Emery had laid a firm foundation for the Auxiliary. She drew into a network both existing and new women's organizations, with parish and diocesan units all contributing to the national program of the Board of Missions. Brought to maturity by Julia Emery, the Auxiliary's enduring program was based on four elements. First, the Auxiliary provided education about the missionary activities and needs of the church. Second, it sponsored specific missionaries or projects in particular locations. Third, it provided the means for systematic giving by women, both in cash and through the making or purchase of needed clothing and supplies for "missionary boxes." And fourth, the Auxiliary offered a devotional program that both established the theological context for support of mission activity and involved the women personally in spreading the gospel through individual and corporate prayer.

From Mary Emery's appointment in January 1872, the back pages of *Spirit of Missions* were given over to Auxiliary concerns, providing monthly information to developing local groups. These stories about missionaries and the people among whom they served, ideas for educational and fundraising projects, inspirational poetry and prayers, and news of Auxiliary meetings, programs, and accomplishments around the country all served to stimulate local projects and encourage grassroots leadership.

For women who had previously been completely overlooked and excluded from the church's organizational life, the Auxiliary provided a welcome channel for involvement in all manner of worthy activities. The rubric of "missionary work" was a broad one, and the Auxiliary's agenda encompassed educational programs with speakers from exotic places, Bible studies and prayer groups, sewing circles and ice cream socials, as well as the occasional special service at which bishops and leading clergy would recognize and acknowledge the presence of women in the church. The Auxiliary was, in fact, a dramatically successful program:

The original policy as created by Mary Emery was simple, and being free from complexities needed no change even after fifty years. Following the general plan of the Church's government, no written constitution seemed necessary, and freedom of action made it easy and attractive to all to enter the ranks of this authorized society of Churchwomen.[2]

Organizationally, the Woman's Auxiliary was extremely flexible, varying in form and program emphasis from place to place. Like the extraordinarily successful Women's Christian Temperance Union and women's organizations of other denominations during that period, the Woman's Auxiliary was centrally coordinated but locally organized and controlled. No national constitution existed: the Auxiliary was simply an informal network of cooperating groups that could adapt to changing local circumstances. Any woman interested in the church's mission could consider herself a member, any group of women in a parish could call themselves a local branch. A diocesan branch consisted of all parish groups in a diocese, and all diocesan branches together formed the Woman's Auxiliary to the Board of Missions.

As a rule, the approval of the local priest was necessary for formation of a parish group. The bishop had to approve—and often appointed the first officers of—each diocesan branch. Given the church's authority structure, such endorsements served to legitimate the activity by signalling the auxiliary's subordinate status within the church hierarchy. In practice, however, most of the groups operated independently of the clergy, organizing their activities to suit local needs and interests, and looking for program guidance and resources to the Auxiliary network.

The Auxiliary's organizational structure was effective, in part, because it nurtured and mobilized the energy and imagination of thousands of women in a wide variety of situations. This form of organization was also effective because each group was perceived as primarily a local group, not following orders from some central headquarters, and therefore not challenging the authority of the official leadership—the priests and bishops—of the local church.

Transformation from Within

Thus, although it was established at the same time that the secular women's movement was stirring the social and political scene, the Woman's Auxiliary was not perceived as threatening to the status quo. It was authorized by the hierarchy of the institutional church and flourished for decades because it was consistently described as a system for capitalizing on the energy of the women's movement while safeguarding the dominant position of men within the church's program. The Auxiliary was described this way and it was perceived by many to function this way, yet at the same time it created opportunities for women to develop and exercise leadership skills that slowly but steadily undermined the male monopoly of church affairs.

To achieve this transformation of power from within required an ability to hold fundamental contradictions in tension. To read the 1870 article "Woman and the Mission Work" first proposing what became the Auxiliary (probably written by Dr. Twing, perhaps with Mary Emery's assistance), or Julia Emery's jubilee account of the Auxiliary in 1921, is to encounter writing which today seems almost double-talk. The language appears coded to reassure those frightened or scandalized by changes in women's place in society, while at the same time giving voice to women frustrated by traditional constraints and longing for ever greater opportunities.

Praising "love's low, small, benevolent voice" above "the forum's shrill treble," the early proposal of 1870 carefully reinforced a self-effacing model of feminine behavior and repudiated the suffragettes. Yet the proposal went on to present a vibrant, almost aggressive picture of the contributions of women, past and present, to the church. Its plea for an organization of women with "a simple plan of operation, held in loyalty to the Church, auxiliary to the Board," promised that such a "system of unpaid agents...would astonishingly swell the missionary revenues."[3] Dangling money as an incentive, and threatening no overturning of the status quo, the proposal was acceptable because it seemed merely to institutionalize for useful purposes the accepted subordination of women to men.

For decades, the Emerys and other Auxiliary leaders held up this image of submissive women. After administering the "simple plan" and its astonishing revenues for forty of its first fifty years, Julia Emery in her jubilee account of the Auxiliary in 1921 gently criticized "women in these later days" who complained about limitations on their participation in the church. She extolled the existing structure: "There can hardly be more privileged opportunities presented to the women of the Church in the future than those which officers of the Auxiliary of the past have already enjoyed."[4]

Yet there are striking contradictions in that jubilee account. Chronicling women's contributions to the work of the Board of Missions, Emery was meticulous in depicting the subordinate status of the Woman's Auxiliary to the (all-male) board while simultaneously suggesting that without the Auxiliary the Board of Missions would not have been able to carry out its work at all. Despite a demure avowal that the women of the Auxiliary were "indifferent that the Auxiliary should have credit for their work," she devoted four columns to detailing the funds raised, buildings built, salaries paid, and good works supported by the Auxiliary.

During these years rhetoric and action were in acute tension. The rhetoric conformed to the acceptable model of feminine behavior, submissive and dependent upon men and masculine authority structures, while reports of Auxiliary accomplishments held up a sharply contrasting model of female autonomy and independent action. Seen in a larger context, such apparent contradictions between actions and the ways those actions are described publicly signal the dynamics of a value system in flux.

A Proper, Powerful Lady

Julia Emery's ability to hold together the contradictions of her church and society concerning the role of women allowed the Auxiliary to develop an increasingly powerful position within the evolving national church structure. Her particular temperament seemed perfectly suited to the possibilities of the time, enabling her to accomplish great things within narrow limitations. Emery's manner disarmed people who might have resisted her programs and ideas. At her funeral, the president of the Board of Missions, Bishop Arthur S. Lloyd, commented on her inconspicuous demeanor:

> Never in all her life was she "aggressive"; always she was prone to
> think that she might be wrong and the other person right; and yet
> she held fast to what she believed to be right.[5]

In a later tribute, Lloyd discussed at some length Emery's character as facilitator and peacemaker, asserting that "in the fifty years of the Auxiliary's life there has not been one ugly page in the story of its growth," which he attributed to her "astonishing understanding and sympathy and self-restraint."[6] Such qualities were astonishing because they were not the ones generally thought necessary to handle the inevitable conflicts of organizational life.

Another revealing description of Julia Emery's leadership conveys both the flavor of the era in terms of women's "proper place" and the organizational—even revolutionary—genius that functioned within those confines:

> In undertaking this work she was of necessity pushed into public life, but she was never aggressive, never unduly prominent, but always self-effacing and more than generous in according to others prominence and credit where due.[7]

Thus while successfully organizing women to do what they had previously been forbidden to do, Julia Emery presented herself as a perfectly "proper" lady: quiet, submissive, devoted to the authorized structures of the church, and supportive of its leaders.

Julia Emery was shrewdly aware of the importance of appearances, refusing to play cards in public or to attend the theater until after her retirement. Her friend and colleague Margaret Tomes recalled that Emery "felt 'Caesar's wife should be above suspicion,' or, in other words, that the Secretary of the Auxiliary should give no ground for criticism."[8] Combined with her manifest faith and commitment to the missionary task of making Christ known throughout the world, Julia Emery's propriety and deferential manner made it easy for bishops and parish clergy to support the organization she managed.

Emery's style of leadership was quite unlike the aggressive, directive style of leading churchmen, yet it seemed to work. Bishop Lloyd's awed amazement, echoed in the comments of others at both her retirement and her death, arose from the common assumption that women could not lead. Julia Emery presented a contradiction between an earlier norm or ideal that associated "womanly" behavior with their absence from public life, and a new reality in which apparently traditional women were assuming very untraditional leadership

roles in church and society. Because she could hold these contradictions within her own person, Julia Emery was perfectly suited to
managing this particular stage in the expansion of women's roles in
the Episcopal Church.

She instinctively understood where the institutional limits were,
whether they could be pushed back, and how to describe possibilities
for change in a way that did not alienate or threaten the people in
power. Emery never clamored for women's rights, probably because
she did not consciously experience the lack of them. In describing the
formation of the Auxiliary, for example, she distinguished it sharply
from political movements claiming women's rights:

> The women of the Church did not have to go to Her representative
> body, urging a claim and begging for recognition; instead that repre-
> sentative body came to the women of the Church, asking their help,
> giving them an assured position, and the right to share in the respon-
> sibilities and activities of the Church's mission—privileges ever since
> continued to the auxiliary by a long succession of the [Missionary]
> Society's officers.[9]

It is indeed true that women did not ask the General Convention for
recognition: they could not have done so, because they had no access
to it. But by presenting the establishment of the Woman's Auxiliary
as strictly a male initiative, a tale of invitation and privileges bestowed, Emery created an atmosphere that protected women's work
from appearing to challenge the power of the male church.

Moreover, she may well have perceived events just as she described them. Her knowledge of the Auxiliary was shaped by her experience of the crusading Dr. Twing and the perceptions of her older
sister, who had been invited by the male leadership to join in an exciting new venture. So Julia Emery's initial experience of the church
was not that of one who was excluded and had to fight her way in,
but of one "given" a share of the responsibilities and privileges from
the start. Because she trusted this welcome, Emery's interpretations
of subsequent events always carried a kind of contradiction, the tension implicit in being both on the margin and at the center of power.
She knew that she had responsibilities and privileges; she also knew
that they were limited, and that to work from within to expand those

limits she would have to act with great circumspection. To this end, her words and actions were always chosen with care.

One particularly dramatic example of Emery's careful diplomacy is found in her formal comments about the Rev. William S. Langford, who had followed Twing as Domestic Secretary and attempted to assert control over the Woman's Auxiliary funds. Adroit maneuvering circumvented this effort, while assuring the Board of Missions of the Auxiliary's dedication and support for the total program of the Society. After Langford's death, Julia Emery had this to say about their early conflicts and relationship:

> For a time there was the lack of mutual understanding which makes combined effort harmonious and delightful. But...Dr. Langford came to know the Auxiliary, and the Auxiliary to recognize the manner of man he was...[with] his sunny presence [and] constant kindness and forbearance. Under his tutelage the lesson has been oft repeated of the welcome dependence upon the Board of Missions which the Auxiliary enjoys.

This statement is as rich in irony as in diplomacy, its contradictions made acute by the very next sentence:

> And if sometimes to the women of the Church the men of the Church seem slow in their wise caution, they remember gratefully the friend and leader who could effect so much with a sudden outburst of enthusiastic effort.[10]

Julia Emery knew the limits that were placed on women in the church, and she knew that to continue her work of expanding them from within the structures of the church she had best describe women's subordination as "welcome dependence" and a man's intransigence as "wise caution."

A Shadow Church Emerges

Under Julia Emery the Woman's Auxiliary became an essential if extra-constitutional part of the Board of Missions, recognized as "the very most potent factor in the American Church."[11] When the Society moved in 1894 from the cramped quarters at Bible House to its own building twelve blocks north, space for the Auxiliary was automatically provided, and it eventually occupied the entire second floor of what came to be called the Church Missions House.

During Julia Emery's tenure the United Thank Offering, begun at the Triennial Meeting in 1889, provided well over $1.5 million to support Episcopal mission work throughout the country and around the world—from many millions of pennies deposited daily in blue boxes in individual homes. This sum was in addition to money raised through the Lenten "mite box" program of the Junior Auxiliary and the funds and goods provided through local and diocesan Auxiliary projects. By the time of Emery's retirement in 1916, Woman's Auxiliary branches had been established in all ninety-two dioceses and missionary districts of the Episcopal Church.

Through dogged work, deferential rhetoric, and a manner of utmost propriety, Julia Emery acquired considerable power for women in the church. Individual bishops seeking support for missionary work in their areas, the Board of Missions, and the whole church had come to recognize the importance of the women's financial contributions to general programs, and Langford was not the last to attempt to wrest control of the Auxiliary's resources from the women. But the self-effacing Julia Emery, secure in her niche in the Church Missions House, steadily held together a growing empire—educating women and children in local parishes, developing organizational skills in hundreds of diocesan and national Auxiliary officers, training and supporting women missionaries, and financing countless projects.

Behind the screen of Julia Emery's nonthreatening rhetoric, in the Woman's Auxiliary a shadow church was forming. By 1880, the pattern was set for a triennial meeting of the Auxiliary to gather at the same time and place as the General Convention. The Triennial eventually included delegates from auxiliaries in every domestic and overseas diocese of the Episcopal Church, and came to be referred to as the "Third House" of the General Convention, along with the House of Deputies and the House of Bishops, although it had no canonical basis or legislative role.

Such nomenclature both revealed and obscured the relationship between the women's organization and the rest of the church. On the one hand, the Auxiliary and its Triennial gave women a parallel organizational structure, authorized by the church, where they could participate in aspects of the church's work. But the votes of women in the "Third House" were practically meaningless. Neither the Auxiliary nor the Triennial had a place in the church's constitutional structure, and only the votes of bishops and deputies (clergy and laymen representing each diocese) were needed for adoption of Convention legislation. The women's votes bound no one, and Triennial had no certain way to make its voice heard, even though the men were meeting just across the hall.

For decades this exclusion from the church's policy-making bodies seemed to trouble no one. For Julia Emery and countless other women, opportunities for ministry within their own separate sphere were evidently sufficient. Self-effacing rhetoric protected a growing enterprise which, being merely "women's work," could operate with considerable autonomy, and there was always the possibility of influencing official policy from behind the scenes. Woman's Auxiliary staff and officers had the ear of many influential churchmen in dioceses throughout the country, and they did not challenge the prevailing norm that women should not act or speak in public forums. They knew their "proper place."

Chapter 3

Outside Groups

Vida Scudder and the Companions of the Holy Cross

The majority of turn-of-the-century Episcopal women shared the Emery view of women's proper role within the church. There were others, however, who chose to exercise their religious commitments outside the official Auxiliary structure. Their experience expands our picture of women's "place" and sheds light on the political processes and institutional life of the Episcopal Church. One of the most remarkable of these women was Vida Dutton Scudder, a professor of English at Wellesley College during much of the time Julia Emery presided over the Woman's Auxiliary.

Julia Emery and Vida Scudder shared many characteristics. Their long careers as active laywomen in the Episcopal Church overlapped for almost four decades. Both were strong, dedicated, and immensely productive, and both wielded enormous influence over several generations of church men and women. Both were deeply committed to the Christian faith and passionate about promoting the church's mission in the world. Both were raised by their mothers in an extended family setting. Both remained single and blazed new trails for women in the public sphere, while shunning feminist rhetoric and distancing themselves from women's rights activists.

But they were also radically different women. Emery worked methodically in her office, week in and week out, leaving her desk tidy at the end of each day, while Scudder's work and life intermingled with all the irregular schedules, seasonal changes, and occasional chaos of the academic world. Emery was an organizer and administrator, a facilitator, a superb bureaucrat; Scudder was an educator and crusader, an orator, a provocative intellectual. Because of these differences, they played complementary roles in expanding the place of women in the Episcopal Church. Emery worked from within the national structure through the Woman's Auxiliary, while Scudder functioned on the margins, leading unofficial groups and lobbying the national structure. Emery explicitly sought to incorporate women into the institutional mission of the church, and her deferential manner enabled her to create a powerful organizational network, subsidiary to the church's central agency, that multiplied the roles women could play under the (often titular) direction of the clergy. Scudder's contagious enthusiasm for the church's witness to justice inspired men and women, clergy and laity, to implement a wide variety of social action projects and educational programs—from settlement houses and labor negotiations to essay contests for seminarians and summer schools for church leaders—outside the church's institutional structures.

Their contrasting relationships to the church's organization illustrate the options available to women of their day, and the advantages and disadvantages of working in dependent or unofficial positions. Emery chose to work through existing structures; Scudder believed a radical restructuring of society and the church was needed. Emery built a shadow organization within which women could participate quasi-autonomously in the official programs of the church. Scudder built unofficial organizations to do what the cumbersome official machinery could not do—some comprised exclusively of women who directed their own activities as a matter of course, and others in which women worked as near-equals alongside men. Emery worked methodically from within the church's developing administrative structure, while Scudder darted about on the periphery, working through a variety of unofficial groups to stimulate the church to action.

Scudder's labors toward the goal of social transformation were as wide-ranging and energetic as Emery's toward the goal of extending the church's mission and saving message throughout the world. Like Emery, Scudder explicitly promoted new roles for women in this process without ever involving herself directly in the contemporary feminist or suffrage movements. When Scudder called women "from the privacy of the hearth" to labor in the world, she employed acceptable rhetorical categories such as religious duty, Christian and civic responsibility, and concern for the poor. As the rhetoric of subordination enabled the Woman's Auxiliary to create an organizational role for women in the church, so the rhetoric of duty enabled Scudder to establish a model of women's active engagement in the affairs of the world.

Vida Dutton Scudder

Vida Scudder belonged to a distinguished Boston family of professional people in education, publishing, theology, and medicine who believed in educating their women as well as their men. Vida's education was the focus of her widowed mother's attention; family travels and living arrangements revolved around Vida's schooling during her rich but solitary childhood. On one visit to England, Vida's mother was exposed to the Christian socialism of Frederick Denison Maurice, and through it was attracted to Anglicanism. Back in Boston, the family came under the spell of the great Episcopal preacher, Phillips Brooks, and Vida was confirmed in the Episcopal Church in 1875, at the age of thirteen.

At Smith College her personal world began to expand as her intellectual gifts flowered. Vida studied literature and began to write, publishing a play and several short stories and articles. She discovered friends her own age, forming a close attachment to classmate Clara French. After graduation Vida and Clara, with their mothers, went to Oxford to study. "Privileges there were just being tentatively opened to women, and if I am not mistaken we were the first American girls to enjoy them," Scudder later recalled.[1]

Perhaps because of her mother's interest in her education, Vida Scudder seems to have regarded women's education as a matter of course rather than a "cause." She did confess in her autobiography to having entertained as a child "the private fairy tale when, disguised as a boy, she had crept into Harvard," but she kept this dream to herself.[2] Her mother's convictions on women's education had ensured Vida's own education, but Vida's concern was to inspire educated women to serve society, not to persuade society to educate more women. Just as the Emery sisters took for granted the church's openness to women won through the struggles of an earlier generation and concentrated their energies on consolidating women's place in the altered structure, so Vida Scudder took for granted women's right to be educated and went on from there to fashion a new model of active and responsible womanhood.

Through Edward Bellamy's Nationalist Club, Scudder met William Dwight Porter Bliss and became a charter member of his Society of Christian Socialists and of the frankly socialist Episcopal mission, the Church of the Carpenter, establishing a life-long pattern of energetic support for radical social causes. During those years she was also writing and studying: she published several essays and a selection of George MacDonald's poems she and Clara French edited, and in 1887 she completed a master's degree at Smith College. A family friend then urged Scudder to apply for a position on the English faculty of eight-year-old Wellesley College, and so, almost accidentally, she began a forty-year teaching career.

Scudder became an immensely popular and inspiring teacher who used her academic life as a base for social/political activity. With Smith friends and new Wellesley colleagues, she began speaking and writing about how college-educated women could make some difference for good in the world. They studied the English settlement house movement, which was trying to bring health, educational, and recreational services to overcrowded urban and industrial populations, and its emerging American adaptations.

With Scudder as spokeswoman, the idea for a College Settlement Association took shape. In the fall of 1889, shortly before Jane Addams and Ellen Gates Starr began Hull House in Chicago, the association opened a residence on Rivington Street in New York City, followed by houses in Philadelphia and Boston. For decades the association recruited women college graduates to finance and oversee these settlements, where other college women lived as residents in impoverished neighborhoods. Here they experienced first-hand the effects of economic exploitation, while bringing some assistance and cultural enrichment to their neighbors. A deliberate focus on consciousness-raising for middle-class women along with direct aid to the poor distinguished this approach from other settlement work. Philanthropy as such was disdained, and in its place was the conviction of women's responsibility to respond to the world's ills. "Women are called out from their seclusion," Scudder wrote, "from the privacy of the hearth, to meet life's deepest and most tragic issues."[3]

During this period, a tragedy of her own led to an important new contact. Scudder's closest friend, Clara French, died suddenly of typhoid fever in the summer of 1888. Grieving and in need of support,

Scudder joined the Society of the Companions of the Holy Cross. This religious society of young women met occasionally for study and observed a simple rule centered on daily thanksgiving and prayer for the poor and suffering. Emily Morgan had founded the society as an expression of her own deep social convictions: as a young child, she woke herself by the 5 A.M. factory whistle to pray for the poor women who had to go to work while she remained cozily at home. A year younger than Scudder and with less formal education, Morgan was a natural leader whose contemplative spirit and commitment to social issues were a counterpoint to Scudder's own more activist approach.

Scudder's sixty-five-year association with the Society of the Companions of the Holy Cross, which lasted until her death in 1954, was as important for the Companions as it was for her. It gave her both community and independence, offering support and challenge for her spiritual life, intellectual companionship, and comrades in many of the social struggles that occupied those years. Scudder gave the Companions an articulate voice, tremendous energy, and a vision and temperament that complemented Emily Morgan's. Organized outside official church structures and directed by strong-minded women, the Companions were to play a unique role in Episcopal Church politics in the years ahead. The clarity and personal conviction that Scudder and the Companions developed through years of disciplined prayer and study enabled them on occasion to instruct the men of the Episcopal Church, and to be heeded.

Quickening the Conscience of the Church

At the time that Vida Scudder began teaching at Wellesley, escalating economic and social crises were beginning to claim the church's attention. Urbanization and industrialization had cast their pall over American communities; the 1886 Chicago Haymarket riot made visible the violent tensions of mounting labor strife throughout the country. The network of religiously-motivated labor reformers was small but vital, and Scudder's Boston connections linked her to likeminded others. She later recalled of that time: "We enjoyed starting what was practically a branch of the English Social Christian Union....In true Boston fashion, our chief activity was the publication of pamphlets, some of them mighty good."[4]

To address the problems raised by the crises in the cities, reform- ers formed an organization known as CAIL, the Church Association for the Advancement of the Interests of Labor. CAIL was a feisty group of Episcopalians who supported labor while maintaining the trust of factory owners, combining direct action as mediators during strikes with education through the monthly *Hammer and Pen* and lobbying efforts in support of reform legislation. Prizing the respecta- bility and access to ecclesial power of the episcopate, the group sought bishops to serve as president and honorary vice-presidents, eventually signing up the majority of American bishops for these roles. But the real energy sustaining the organization for much of its history came from Harriette Keyser, a leading New York suffragette and member of the Companions of the Holy Cross, and her friend, Margaret Lawrance. An early member, Keyser was elected secretary of CAIL in 1896, a post she was to hold until her retirement in 1925 at the age of eighty-four.

In its heyday, CAIL's visibility, effectiveness, and financial support rested on a foundation of parish chapters organized by Keyser in a manner similar to that of the Woman's Auxiliary. Yet unlike the Auxil- iary, CAIL was an unofficial group, outside the church's organiza- tional structure. Its members were Episcopalians, lay men and women as well as priests and bishops, its work was consciously de- rived from church teachings, and it had the blessing of episcopal sponsors. But CAIL was neither authorized nor controlled by any par- ish, diocesan, or national church body. This freedom gave it great flexibility and the ability to act quickly in crisis situations. At the same time, after a dozen years of effort in what seemed to be a worsening situation, members grew convinced of the value and ap- propriateness of official church engagement and response to social needs. They hoped to be recognized officially in order to bring the moral weight of the church to bear against the increasingly exploita- tive conditions affecting American workers.

Persuading the church to act was not easy. When General Conven- tion met in San Francisco in 1901, CAIL sponsored mass meetings for bishops and deputies in the evening at the Alhambra Theatre, with speakers from organized labor alongside distinguished clergy. In re- sponse, the Convention authorized a Joint Commission on the Rela- tions of Capital and Labor to study the aims and purposes of labor organizations, investigate the causes of industrial disturbances, and be available to act as arbitrators in disputes—functions CAIL had been performing *outside* the church's structure. Such authorization signalled, members hoped, assumption of responsibility by the whole church for direct action previously left to individuals and unofficial organizations.

The Alhambra Theatre was also the scene of a dramatic (if little-noticed) demonstration of the opportunities and limits placed on women in the church at the turn of the century. At an evening meeting of Convention deputies, Harriette Keyser spoke on CAIL's organization and programs to the all-male bishops and deputies—a presentation that was possible because of her position in an unofficial church organization. In stark contrast, official reports from the Triennial meeting to the Convention itself were always presented by a male deputy on behalf of the Woman's Auxiliary. Keyser, and later Vida Scudder, were welcomed, off-hours, on platforms closed to Julia Emery and her Auxiliary officers. Unofficial groups could do what official groups could not; only women outside the structure might speak.

Ironically, the "official" Joint Commission on the Relations of Capital and Labor was virtually inactive during its first six years, deeply divided and powerless to take on the advocacy functions Keyser's association had been performing. Pressure from some other outside source was needed to overcome the disagreement and inertia that paralyzed it. The catalyst turned out to be organized women in the form of the Society of the Companions of the Holy Cross.

Harriette Keyser wrote to her Companions in the summer of 1907, reporting on the commission's inaction and urging the Companions "to consider some sort of action to force the Church to recognize its social responsibility."[5] Keyser could not attend the annual summer conference at the Companions' home, Adelynrood in South Byfield, Massachusetts, but her letter stimulated serious discussion. As founder Emily Morgan wrote to the full membership, "We had appointed a committee with Miss Dudley, head worker of Denison House, as chairman, to draw a plea to be presented at the General Convention, and our action was quickened by having Miss Jane Addams of Hull House with us for the evening when the matter was under discussion."[6] Vida Scudder also played a major role in these discussions, and the committee that drafted the petition consisted of Scudder, her Boston friends and colleagues, Helena Dudley and Florence Converse, and Hull House co-founder Ellen Gates Starr.

In their report to the Companions concerning the petition, Dudley noted the reluctance with which an organization of praying women moved into the church's political arena:

> In venturing so serious a step as bringing itself to the notice of the Church, the Society realizes that it has reached a new stage in its corporate life, but...our pledge to constant prayer for the reconciliation of classes inevitably led to this step, at a juncture when there seems a real possibility of quickening the social conscience of the Church.

The Companions' commitment to both prayer and action emboldened them to petition the General Convention:

> The Society of the Companions of the Holy Cross, a body of women pledged to intercessory prayer, and among particular objects, to prayer for the reconciliation of classes, voted...to beg the General Convention at its coming session to take some action which shall bring the Church to fuller knowledge and closer touch with the industrial and social problems of the day, and thus to remove the reproach of unconcern so often brought against the Christian Church.

The petition's rhetoric is both deferential (it voted "to beg" the Convention), and challenging ("remove the reproach of unconcern"). And after years of praying for the "reconciliation of classes," the society did not hesitate to inform the Convention of Christ's will or to provide specific suggestions for carrying it out:

> [To] enable the Church to work actively toward the reconciliation of classes, which we know to be the will of Christ, the Society...petitions the General Convention that the Committee on Capital and Labor...may this year be heard, its report acted upon, and its reorganization, with fuller and more definite powers for action, considered.[7]

Bishop Arthur Hall of Vermont, leader of the 1907 annual retreat, agreed to present the petition to the General Convention on the society's behalf. Communications of a similar sort were also sent by CAIL, the Christian Social Union, the Christian Socialist Fellowship, and the Eight-Hour League, all unofficial organizations with similar aims and overlapping memberships. Outside pressure tipped the balance within the commission and the Convention. "On the strength of a memorial on the subject from the Society of the Companions of the Holy Cross,"[8] the official church took another step toward active social engagement—in its own bureaucratic way. It created a permanent commission on labor relations with the same membership but a wider mandate that enabled CAIL members on the commission—particularly its activist president, Henry Codman Potter, bishop of New York—to move into action, with the unofficial staff support of the indefatigable Harriette Keyser.

Unofficial Networks

But Bishop Potter died in July 1908, and the movement toward coordinating programs and incorporating them into the official structures of the church was once again paralyzed. The critical importance of a key individual who could personally connect activist unofficial groups with the official church machinery was recognized in the next report of the Joint Commission on the Relations of Capital and Labor. To fill the void left by Potter's death and bring additional energy to the task, the report recommended dissolving the former commission and creating a larger Joint Commission on Social Service, to include five each of bishops, priests, and laymen—three of whom actually turned out to be lay*women*.

The 1910 General Convention approved this organizational strategy, but its implementation took an unanticipated form. Because final action on the resolution came so near the end of the Convention session, the then-standard procedure of making appointments during Convention was not followed. Instead, the new commission was "given power to fill vacancies and to add to their number between sessions of the General Convention."[9] Inadvertently, through this change in procedure the Convention had made possible the unprecedented appointment of three women to the commission: Vida D. Scudder, Deaconess Susan T. Knapp, Dean of the New York Training School for Deaconesses, and Mary K. Simkhovitch, director of New York City's Greenwich House settlement. Thus, although women would not gain voice or vote in the Convention itself for another sixty years, their importance to the emerging social service ministry of the church was tacitly acknowledged by these early appointments.

It also demonstrated the importance of the network of women's unofficial contacts and organizations. Personal and group contacts facilitated more than occasional lobbying. Membership in women's groups provided a base of experience and support for gaining access to previously male-only enclaves. Scudder and Simkhovitch had known each other since Simkhovitch's college internship at Denison House in Boston; Knapp had been set apart as deaconess by Bishop Potter, president of CAIL; Harriette Keyser and the Society of Companions completed the circle, and both Simkhovitch and Knapp became Companions within a few years of joining Scudder on the commission. Like the Auxiliary and the deaconess program, the Companions gave church women an organizational home not otherwise available; and like CAIL, its unofficial status did not carry built-in subordination to the rest of the church.

None of these women fit the contemporary ideal of feminine behavior. Scudder and Simkhovitch violated the model of the deferential, subordinate church woman by exercising leadership in their professional careers and by choosing independent channels for their ministries rather than operating within the Woman's Auxiliary. Knapp had transformed the deaconess training program in New York, and although deaconesses took a special vow of obedience to their bishops, Susan Knapp herself was an independent leader who did not hesitate to resist priests or bishops who tried to impose their ideas on her program. Despite their unconventionality, however, their professional accomplishments were in roles considered appropriate for women—teacher, settlement worker, deaconess—and their reputation for piety was reassuring to those threatened by women in leadership positions.

These unprecedented appointments of women to a national commission, however, had repercussions. The next Convention adopted a rule that all joint commission vacancies occurring between Conventions were to be filled by the chairman of the House of Bishops and the president of the House of Deputies—a practice that continues to this day. The unexpected appearance of women in positions of leadership apparently stimulated the church hierarchy to tighten up its borders and clarify its channels of authority—a pattern of response that was to recur again and again in the coming decades.

Prayer or Politics?

The 1916 summer conference of the Society of the Companions of the Holy Cross focused on the topic of social justice and was chaired by Helena Dudley. Interweaving monastic piety and radical politics, the Companions at Adelynrood prayed, kept silence, debated. Vida Scudder later wrote of this conference:

> Early Celebration or Prime preceded breakfast daily. During breakfast and throughout all the meals in Retreat there was the usual reading, the books being *Jesus and Politics,* and *Sons of Francis.* One morning, Miss Starr told in a thrilling way of her experiences in the Chicago strikes....At three, there was usually an informal gathering of some sort, when the Socialists invited those who did not approve of Socialism to tell them why; or the Pacifists and Militarists met in friendly intercourse; or Church Unity was presented and prayed for.[10]

As part of the program, Vida Scudder organized the drafting of a resolution on social justice that built on the "general adjurations" of the 1913 General Convention statement.[11] Although adopted by a majority of the Companions present at the conference, the resolution was also circulated to other members for a vote on whether to forward it to the General Convention because a deepening disagreement was developing within the Companions on the appropriateness of such action. The radical network had had strong representation at Adelynrood that summer and had outvoted those present who opposed such a public role in church affairs, and despite the growing opposition, the mail vote sustained their position.

Founder Emily Morgan was one of those opposed to taking a corporate public stand, though she bowed reluctantly to the majority view at the time. Morgan's concern was that such activity detracted from the Companions' dedication to prayer by channeling corporate energy into political activities, and that the taking of public stands by the organization on the basis of voting could alienate a minority who disagreed. For her, the struggle was cast in terms of a conflict between prayer and action. Morgan's 1918 letter to the Companions suggested that the society was "trying to do two incompatible things:

to provide a quiet place for prayer and refreshment and at the same time to seek a publicity, even in righteous causes, that will in the end destroy the spirit of both prayer and quiet."[12]

But beneath the prayer/action, conservative/radical split in the Companions lay another issue: that of religious authority and women's proper place in the church. Implicit in the Companions' struggle was an uneasy pair of convictions: that women are perfectly capable of exercising leadership in the world and the church, but that the less said about it the better in order not to invite opposition. Prayer was an acceptable activity for women, but in the atmosphere generated by the suffrage campaign many Companions felt it was inappropriate, perhaps even dangerous, for women to appear to be invading the male world of politics. To call attention to themselves by openly engaging in the church's political processes risked loss of support for its vigorous, though not public, ecumenical and social justice ministries.

Yet despite their retreat, the Companions' combination of prayer, education, and social action has had enormous, if usually hidden, influence on the larger church. Through public conferences at Adelynrood, through the speaking and writing of numerous Companions, and through the complex networks of personal relationships such as those involving the Social Service Commission, the society became an important channel through which women could serve. Offering what Emily Morgan called a "spiritual background behind a large amount of social work and movements,"[13] to this day it provides a shadow structure, similar in function to the Woman's Auxiliary but outside the official church organization, through which women have participated not only in the church's ministry of prayer and its mission in the world, but also to a limited degree in decision-making processes from which they were officially excluded.

Through the Companions of the Holy Cross, women's unofficial influence pressed against the male-only tradition of the church. In 1916, the Companions' resolution was adopted by the General Convention and eventually went to Lambeth, where in 1920 it formed the basis for a statement from the decennial world-wide gathering of Anglican bishops. Women's influence on the church's evolving sense of social mission had reached a new peak, but world events would soon dwarf its significance. The United States' participation in World

War I marked a dramatic transformation of the society surrounding the church. Under these new conditions, the Episcopal Church would demonstrate that it was by no means ready to incorporate women fully into its administrative and governmental structures.

Chapter 4

Will a National Church Include Women?

J n the pivotal period between the Civil War and the First World War, as America was transformed from a rural-agricultural society to an urban-industrial nation, the Episcopal Church redefined its sense of corporate relationship to the state. The image of the apostolic church, solid and unchanging as the rock of Peter, gave way to a dynamic, institutional image of a national church, a cathedral for all the people—and thus a corporate body engaged in a new kind of dialogue and interaction with the surrounding society.[1] The nineteenth-century belief that the affairs of the world were not the business of the church was crumbling away. With this shift came a new perception of the church's mission, of the way Christian values should be expressed and lived out.

The new identity also brought a broadened perception of who constituted "the church." The hierarchical, masculine, apostolic image began to yield to a populist image of a democratic nation gathering for worship, and in such a gathering women began to be visible. Though marginalized in auxiliary or unofficial organizations, women who had grown up in the larger American society with the "woman question" and the struggle for suffrage, many of them college-educated, were participating in church activities in wholly new ways. Their very existence challenged the framework of female subordination which had justified the creation of the Woman's Auxiliary forty years earlier.

As women became increasingly visible in positions of leadership within the church and society, resistance to changes in the old social and political order intensified. By 1916, opposition to the women's suffrage campaign in England and the United States had reached the point of violence. Divisions were deepening between workers and factory owners, capitalists and socialists, gradualists, revolutionaries, and anarchists. Rhetoric both about women's place in society and about competing economic and political theories was harsh, inflammatory, and intolerant. In this volatile context, many Episcopal women carefully avoided "feminist" issues and deliberately sought a middle way on social reform for women and workers. Writing in early 1917, when most Americans still believed it possible to remain apart from the Great War convulsing Europe, Vida Scudder outlined an active role for the church in support of a process of gradual but extensive social change:

> It is a pity that the Church should take controversial positions with which honest Christians can disagree, when there are so many positions out of the reach of legitimate controversy which are nevertheless quite revolutionary....Let the Church speak her own language. If bravely and consistently uttered, if faithfully obeyed, it will be found to correspond closely with economic theories quite at variance with those on which society now more or less uneasily reposes.[2]

Implicit in this statement was Scudder's belief that the gospel, faithfully preached and practiced, would bring about economic and social justice. Cast in typically Anglican ethical rather than religious language, her call to a "Social Gospel" was straightforward and non-partisan. Its hope rested on gradual transformation from within.

The United States' entry into World War I dashed the hopes of the gradualists, however. The rash of violent labor disputes as the unprepared American economy first geared up rapidly for wartime production and then abruptly geared down again, and the polarization within the national conscience over the imprisonment of many pacifists, precipitated a crisis for the American intellectual and religious communities. Widespread disillusionment with the strategy of gradual transformation was reflected in an article Scudder wrote before the 1919 General Convention:

> We were going to do such fine things....The Church was hard at work creating social service commissions....She was convinced that it was wrong to be impatient and that sudden change was dangerous. Gentle, gradual, should be our progress....No one need suffer and no hostile criticism need be incurred, but...all men of good will should be brought slowly into line through mild persuasion. That was the

Christian way; so we all thought. But history is apparently in a hurry....The Church has disappointed many different people lately, for she has neither led social change nor delayed it.[3]

Though disillusioned and disappointed, Scudder was not one to give up, and she did what she knew how to do best: she helped to form a new unofficial organization to work directly on social reform. The Church League for Industrial Democracy came into being, with Scudder as chair of its executive committee and with the goal of "bringing Christ to industrial society."[4] Schooled in bureaucratic strategies through years of experience in other social action groups, organizers of the Church League spent the summer of 1919 building momentum and recruiting new members for an encounter with the "official church": the General Convention gathering in October in Detroit.

Detroit: The Transformation of 1919

The General Convention of 1919, the first after the Great War, took place in a city wracked by violent labor disputes. The Convention introduced sweeping changes to the institutional life of the Episcopal Church that affected its organizational structure and leadership roles, financing and programming priorities, corporate self-definition, and the common vision of how the church ought to relate to the world around it. Still rolling on the tide of nationalism that the war had unleashed and buoyed up by the experience of unity in crisis which wartime efforts had brought to the mainstream of American society, in Detroit the Episcopal Church reconstituted itself as a "national church" with a new, centralized government to be financed by a "Nation-Wide Campaign." Urging support for the campaign, Alexander Mann, rector of Trinity Parish in New York and president of the House of Deputies, set the tone for this burst of religious nationalism: "It is an effort to lift all of us out of our comparative isolation to give us consciousness of the national life of the Church and consciousness of her responsibility to the nation."[5]

This new corporate self-consciousness led to sweeping changes in national church organization and governance. George P. Atwater of Ohio expressed the feelings of determination, even triumphalism, which brought many to support the new measures:

We have become a national Church in organization, and, what is better, in spirit and determination....A national consciousness has dawned. We are now the Church in the United States, and not a Church scattered through various geographical areas. National thinking, national action, and national cooperation will result in glorious national achievement.[6]

A sense of urgency gripped everyone in the church, radicals as well as conservatives. The readiness to try something new in 1919 was in part a response to the continuing sense of crisis and anti-anarchist hysteria following the war. Vida Scudder articulated the radical perspective, drawing out the themes of the 1916 social justice resolution:

Never did a General Convention meet in a graver crisis....The new order of industrial democracy is upon us; and it is for the Church to supply this order with its distinctive soul....Can the Convention not issue some sort of Encyclical, calling us all to social studies and to the systematic practise of social intercession? Good people are very much educated by saying their prayers; moreover the Convention surely believes that praying alters things.[7]

In Detroit, Scudder's Church League for Industrial Democracy and the Joint Commission on Social Service joined forces. The convention's opening service and the House of Deputies' meetings took place in Arcadia Hall, a cavernous dance hall able to seat over four thousand people. At noon and in the evenings that same hall was used for joint sessions and a series of "Open Forums," arranged by the commission with many speakers from the Church League. Not everyone approved, as humorously reported by a contemporary observer:

"Don't you think it is dangerous for the Church to allow that sort of thing under the auspices of the Joint Commission on Social Service?" said a clergyman to a group of men one afternoon. "Oh, I don't know," said another. "Those fellows are so full of hot air that they've got to have some place in which to blow it off. Let them amuse themselves if they want to. It's a good safety valve you know."

I have noted that the air has been so hot during some of the discus-

sion at the forum that many a dignified deputy...has had his arguments somewhat scorched. People who have had the temerity, for example, to cross swords with Miss Vida Scudder when those people
have not been well informed on social questions have found themselves decidedly worsted. Miss Scudder has been perhaps the most interesting person connected with the forum.[8]

Like Harriette Keyser in her 1901 appearance in San Francisco's Alhambra Theatre, Scudder could address the after-hours social service
forum in 1919, but not the legislative sessions that might have taken
action but did not.

In fact, the most significant Convention action affecting the social
service cause proved to be the administrative reorganization. It took
effect January 1, 1920, when a Department of Christian Social Service joined those of Missions and Religious Education in a new "national council" structure. While inclusion represented an important
step in the church's evolving attitude about engagement in social issues, it also signalled even greater bureaucratization, with a further
loss of spontaneity, flexibility, and engagement with ongoing events.

Reorganization—A New Era?

What the 1919 Detroit Convention could—and did—do was to reor-
ganize the church, with profoundly negative implications not only
for social service programs but also for the place of women in its
structures. The new structure was intended to provide a centralized
mechanism extending the oversight of the General Convention. The
National Council, headed by the Presiding Bishop (henceforth to be
elected, rather than simply the senior bishop in the House), would
have authority to act for the church between Conventions, and
would assume managerial responsibility over the three previously
separate and uncoordinated program units: the Board of Missions,
the General Board of Religious Education, and the Joint Commission
on Social Service. The Church Mission House was thus to become officially what it had long been in fact—the national headquarters of
the Episcopal Church.

The reorganization also brought a sharp rebuff to the Woman's
Auxiliary, which was entering a new and more formal era following
the retirement of Julia Emery in 1916 and the election of Grace Lindley as the new Executive Secretary. The informal, personal style of

leadership effective in the early years of the Auxiliary was giving way to more systematic group process and the creation of a National Executive Board comprised of elected representatives to share decision-making with Lindley. The formalization of leadership in the Auxiliary seemed to be an effective strategy, for women on the staff of the Woman's Auxiliary had been included in planning the reorganization of the church at the national level, and constitutional revisions proposed to the 1919 Convention provided for membership on the new National Council of eight women to be elected at the Triennial Meeting of the Woman's Auxiliary.

While the House of Deputies and House of Bishops debated this sweeping proposal, the Triennial women endorsed the reorganization plan and elected their eight representatives to serve in the new structure. They were proudly photographed as the first women to join a church governing body as full members. Many of the women attending Triennial returned home before the end of the General Convention, only to discover that when the final version of the reorganization plan was adopted the section including women was dropped and membership on the National Council was explicitly limited to men.

Thus barred once again from official church governance, Julia Emery's successors sought other ways to expand the Auxiliary's position within the church. Since they had been excluded from the council itself, the women asked to become auxiliary to the whole National Council rather than just the Department of Missions, a request granted at the first meeting of the council in February 1920. This relationship allowed an expansion of women's programs to embrace religious education and social service as well as missions, and ensured them a central, even if secondary, role within the expanding national structure. Deference was still the strategy of necessity, and Lindley described the Auxiliary's mode of relating to the church in terms explicitly drawn from Julia Emery's model:

> An organization trained by Miss Emery has been taught to be modest. This is why the Woman's Auxiliary never "blows its own horn."...It glories in its *auxiliary* position, for while it believes that women should have an ever-increasing opportunity to serve with men, it wants to work *with* them and not as an independent women's society.[9]

Vida Scudder, on the other hand, had never been "trained by Miss Emery." Her role in Detroit had been shaped both by limits on women's participation in the church and by the tension between what small groups want to do and what large organizations are able to do. Though widely respected as a well-informed and inspiring leader, she was nonetheless excluded from the church's decision-making processes and forced to work indirectly to influence its legislation. She supported the official Social Service Commission's primary obligation to educational work, and had contributed perhaps more than any other member to the development of its educational programs. Yet her life-long insistence on "doing something," her support of the Church Association for the Advancement of the Interests of Labor, her close relationship with Keyser and Lawrance, and her initiative in the establishment of the Church League for Industrial Democracy demonstrate a continuing frustration with the cumbersome machinery of the larger church, which seemed better suited to talk than to action.

Women Remain on the Margins

At Detroit in 1919 it seemed that the halting progress of integrating social issues concerning women and workers into the institutional mechanisms of the church had reached another milestone. Pressure from outside had succeeded in shifting the center of the institution, even as the radicals had moved further ahead. Scudder's role was central, and yet she herself remained on the margins. She electrified crowds at unofficial forums, drafted litanies and resolutions, and produced much of the educational material that undergirded the movement. She influenced its visible male leaders and its invisible female leaders. Yet she could not address the Convention itself, nor sit in its Houses or on the new National Council. In fact, the 1919 constitutional changes not only excluded women from the National Council but also inserted new language making explicit the traditional exclusion of women from *all* provincial and national church governance.

Responding to the ferment of the times, the church in 1919 focused its energies on strengthening its national administrative structures. The reorganization gave it valuable new capabilities and greater stability for dealing with contemporary challenges to the social and ecclesiastical order. But the accompanying bureaucratization also restricted access to power and leadership opportunities and increased resistance to change. The explicit exclusion of women as equal partners in the new structure strengthened male privilege in the church, even though such privilege was gradually eroding in American society.

For another half-century, Episcopal women would continue to be restricted to dependent or unofficial positions in the church. Some, like Julia Emery and her successors in the Woman's Auxiliary, used the rhetoric of dependence to give legitimacy to the creation of a powerful women's presence within the national organizations of the church. Others, like Vida Scudder and her Companions and fellow radicals, used official channels when they could but refused to depend on them. Instead, they created autonomous organizations to meet their own spiritual needs, to carry out the church's ministry in the world, and to challenge the institution to reexamine its traditional ways. Both strategies inspired and empowered countless disenfranchised churchwomen to prayer, service within the church and direct action to relieve suffering in the world.

Both Scudder and Emery demonstrated a deep ambivalence toward contemporary debates about the role of women. "I despise segregated discussion of women as women," Scudder wrote, although her own work frequently included such discussions.[10] Like Emery, she was uncomfortable with those who pressed noisily for women's equality for its own sake, but never hesitated to behave like an equal when working for other issues alongside male politicians, theologians, priests, and bishops. Like Emery, Scudder carried such contradictions within her own person, probably unconsciously, and out of that energizing tension came new models for the women who followed.

Sailing under a socialist rather than a feminist flag, Scudder gradually found access—limited but real—to areas of the Episcopal Church's life that had been closed to women, decision-making forums from which the Woman's Auxiliary was excluded by its organizational dependency. The long, slow process of persuading the Episcopal Church to accept some ongoing programmatic responsibility for issues of social justice, in which Scudder played a major though often hidden role, illustrates the way in which unofficial groups have given voice to the marginalized, and especially to women, within the official councils of the church. It also shows how the church's unthinking commitment to the existing social order was slowly undermined.

How long would women's "proper place" be restricted to marginal or dependent positions in the organization and governance of the Episcopal Church? Many believed that surely the ratification of the woman's suffrage amendment in 1920 would lead to the full enfranchisement of Episcopal women within a few years. A *Witness* editorial at the end of the 1919 Convention suggested that "equal rights for women in the American church" would probably be granted at the next Convention.[11] In the next chapter we will discover how mistaken such optimism turned out to be.

Part Two

Should Women Vote...Or Speak?

The 1919 General Convention signalled how unwelcome women were to those who governed the church. So long as women were content to remain outside of, or subordinate within, the governing structures of the Episcopal Church, their ministries were tolerated, their fundraising welcomed, and their peripheral presence acknowledged with benign paternalism. However, when they began to seek *equality* with the men of the church, the self-protective mechanisms inherent in structures of power began to function. Benign rhetoric was accompanied by bland refusal of requests. Parliamentary stumbling blocks appeared in every path. Persistence was met by rejection, even ridicule.

Resistance to changes in women's roles was a corporate phenomenon, an institutional process almost independent of the attitudes of individual church leaders, male and female. Constitutional provisions, parliamentary process, and bureaucratic structures took on a life of their own. Designed—as all organizational structures are—to promote stability and protect the goals and functioning of the institution as established by its founders, these impersonal forces guarded the church against the disintegrating effects of rapid change, and thus also bolstered the effective power of those resisting change even as a majority favoring it developed.

Thus we turn now from examining the experiences of particular women in the late nineteenth and early twentieth centuries to look at the way the national governing body of the Episcopal Church—the General Convention with its House of Bishops and House of Deputies—responded to initiatives for expanding women's participation in the leadership and decision-making councils of the church. Convention actions, of course, originate and are shaped by the attitudes and actions of individuals; yet patterns of institutional power and the dynamics of social change can often be seen more readily by focusing on corporate actions abstracted from the tangle of individual motivations. How did the church come finally to incorporate the contributions of women into its institutional structures? What can we learn about handling change in the future from examining this twentieth-century process? It is to these two questions that we now turn our attention.

Chapter 5

Double Messages and Rejection

During the General Convention held in 1913, bishops and deputies had listened to women speakers at the social service forums, recited a litany written by Vida Scudder and Florence Converse, and adopted a resolution that seemed to open a way to even greater participation of women in the Episcopal Church's life. The men attending the Convention had praised the dedication of women, their contributions to the church, and their moral influence in society, appearing to support an expansion of women's roles in the church without challenging traditional expectations of female behavior. The 1913 resolution described women in the familiar terms of moral superiority assigned to them in the domestic sphere:

> Exhibiting to a degree and in a manner unprecedented a heroic, self-sacrificing devotion of sex to the elevation of the race,...they represent both the bodies politic and the bodies ecclesiastic on the side of their most sensitive and most sacred functions of home and family, of education, and moral influence.

This lofty sentiment was combined with carefully worded support for women's activism:

> Convention puts itself on record as desiring to foster, to encourage, and as far as possible to inaugurate reasonable and legitimate means and agencies whereby the social and religious welfare of the women of this land may be promoted.... [It] commends works of a benevolent and philanthropic character... [and] refers with just pride [to the women's United Offering] as an evidence of the interest which women are taking everywhere in the extension of the Kingdom of God.[1]

Slipping in a near-suffragist phrase referring to "each and every member" as "equal representatives of a social order," the 1913 Convention also had pronounced it was "the policy of the whole Church to encourage the cooperation of women in all the activities of the Church, and to furnish all possible avenues for the expression of their zeal and devotion."[2] Thus the stage had been set for the first serious round in the campaign to admit women to a governing body—to the House of Deputies itself—in the midst of the final push for women's suffrage in the larger society.

At the next Convention, meeting in St. Louis in 1916, the House of Bishops took two actions quite contrary to the spirit of the resolutions of 1913. The promised "avenues for the expression of their zeal and devotion" would not soon lead women into the church's authority and decision-making structures. The first series of parliamentary actions involved women's eligibility for election as lay deputies to General Convention. Benjamin Brewster, bishop of Maine, presented to the House of Bishops a broad constitutional amendment "to accord to female communicants of the Church full rights, responsibilities and privileges." The Committee on Amendments to which it was referred divided the issue, declaring a sort of "local option" for diocesan conventions to establish eligibility rules for local and diocesan bodies, and leaving only election to the House of Deputies within the purview of the General Convention. It then offered a bland resolution stating that it "is inexpedient at this time to adopt a Constitutional amendment providing for the electing of women as members of the House of Deputies." The phrase "at this time" was deleted during debate, and the resolution passed. Women's participation in the House of Deputies was thus declared "inexpedient" for all time.[3]

The inexpediency argument was a powerful parliamentary device. The normal legislative process involves referral of proposed resolutions to legislative committees which consider the issues, hear testimony if appropriate, and report back to the Convention with recommendations for action. The "whereas" clauses of resolutions generally give the rationale supporting them, so favorable committee recommendations seldom provide additional reasons, while recommendations against a resolution typically include a rationale. An assertion of inexpediency gave the appearance of providing a rationale without actually saying anything about the issue. Use of this device implied an assumption that no real argument was needed, that the proposal clearly fell outside the reigning consensus about what was proper, suitable, and desirable. For many years the success of the inexpediency argument against proposals affecting women testified to a powerful consensus about the impropriety of allowing women a place within church governance.

While Brewster's measure was going through the legislative process in the House of Bishops, a similar proposal was on its way to defeat in the House of Deputies, introduced by Robert H. Gardiner, the deputy from Bishop Brewster's diocese of Maine. The deputies' Committee on Amendments reported "that with the highest appreciation of the work and influence of women in the Church, the proposed amendment is, in its judgment, inexpedient."[4] The measure was tabled without ever coming to a vote. This double message, of "highest appreciation" coupled with the inexpediency of full participation, set the tone for the next fifty years.

The second action affecting women taken by the House of Bishops in 1916 gives a glimpse into the underpinnings of the consensus on excluding women. The Conference of Women Workers in the missionary district of Hankow requested, through their bishop, a canonical change to allow women representatives on the bishop's Council of Advice. This time the committee recommendation spelled out the "inexpedient" factors. The report of the Committee on Canons noted that the Council of Advice was responsible for recommending candidates for ordination, granting dispensations, and "instituting enquiries in case of a charge of immoral conduct," and suggested that "all legitimate desires of this proposal would be satisfied by the formation of a consultative body of women with whom the Bishop might take counsel in all matters pertaining to the interests of *women* in the District."[5]

This argument demonstrated three important aspects of the consensus against women. First, women cannot judge men and should play no role in selecting and regulating the church's clergy. Second, despite their moral elevation in the domestic sphere, women must be excluded from the process of determining and judging "immoral conduct" in the church (disguised as a concern to shield them from exposure to immorality). Third, while their views may be useful in matters directly affecting women, they have nothing to contribute to the general work of the church. To the Committee on Canons in 1916 it was not necessary to argue these points; they were simply presented as self-evident reasons for defeating the proposal.

A tell-tale sign of the interconnections between racism and sexism also emerged. The bishops' votes affecting women occurred in the same legislative session as their approval of "a racial episcopate," a scheme first proposed in 1871, right after the Civil War, to create non-voting suffragan bishops to oversee black clergy and congregations.[6] While this idea made possible for the first time the elevation of blacks to the American episcopate (James Holly had been consecrated bishop of Haiti in 1874, and Samuel Ferguson as bishop of Liberia in 1885), theirs was clearly to be a separate and unequal status.

Like the suggestion for a consultative body of women to deal with "matters pertaining to the interests of women" in Hankow, the call for a racial episcopate demonstrated how thoroughly entrenched the white male norm was in the perceptions of the church's leaders in 1916. Nineteenth-century opponents to the suffrage campaigns for freed slaves and for women could not imagine white men sharing political power with anyone else. Similarly, to Episcopal bishops in 1916 it seemed appropriate for black men to minister to blacks and for women to consult about women, but only white men could exercise authority over the whole church.

How Should Women Participate?

Amidst the economic and political ferment preceding the next General Convention—the convention of national reorganization held in 1919 in Detroit—several different schools of thought emerged regarding women's participation in the Episcopal Church. One was based on traditional notions of women's subordination to men; a second reflected generations of campaigning for women's equality in the secular world; and a third combined the two with a scheme—not unlike the "racial episcopate"—for separate representation.

The traditional approach involved a deliberate reinforcement of male dominance in the church. It manifested itself in periodic flurries of "masculinist" enthusiasm, a recurring movement in many denominations that sought to counter a perceived "feminization" of the church by mobilizing men in special religious programs. Episcopalians had led the way with the establishment of the Brotherhood of St. Andrew in 1883, and in the next twenty-five years most Protestant denominations formed counterparts. They generally sponsored social service activities with a strong evangelical flavor, emphasizing the manliness of Jesus in opposition to the sentimentalized religion of the Victorian period. They were never successful on a broad scale, either in enlisting men for social service programs alongside those that women had already organized or in increasing men's participation in the churches. Nevertheless, the slogans of programs like the Men and Religion Forward Movement, which climaxed in the winter of 1911-1912 with little tangible result, echoed throughout the Episcopal Church for many years.

With powerful, often military rhetoric, women were both recruited for the task of attracting men and blamed for their absence. One cleric who had spent time in the west asserted that "when their wives compelled them to dress up, then the attendance of men began to slump." A prominent New York clergyman, perhaps ironically, titled his address at the annual service of the Churchwomen's Club, "How Can the Women Make the Church More Masculine?" and asserted that "two-thirds of the work done by the rector and curate could be done by the women," who should take it over in order to give clergy time to prepare good sermons to attract men to church. While preaching at the United Thank Offering Service during the General Convention in Detroit, a bishop charged women with the responsibility of solving the clergy shortage by sending their sons into the church, as they had sent them off to war: "Women must respond to the call of the church for its valiant sons."[7]

In the months before and after the 1919 Convention, the church press was filled with plans and promotional material about the "Nation-wide Campaign," an immensely ambitious, ultimately unsuccessful program to raise funds and stimulate church membership. Reflecting America's infatuation with the young advertising industry, the church established its own Publicity League which distributed copy for churches to run in local newspapers. These materials were explicitly addressed to a male audience, and combined high-pressure salesmanship with a subtly misogynist rhetoric. One bulletin began:

YOU FATHERS OF BOYS. As he sits by his good mother's side in God's House on Sunday, of whom is YOUR BOY thinking? Is it of her? NO!

It is of YOU—his father....The Church needs you—for without you
she cannot properly reach your boy.[8]

Rendering all the "good mothers" virtually invisible, such messages
charged with masculine bravado the atmosphere in which decisions
would be made about women's place in the church.

The goal of political equality for women in the church was in direct opposition to the "masculinist" tradition in the church, but that
goal found support both from the secular debate surrounding
women's suffrage in the United States and from developments in the
Church of England, where women were soon to be included in the
newly-established Church Assembly. Signed into British law on December 23, 1919, the Assembly Act extended to the church the principles implicit in the Parliamentary Reform Act of 1918, which gave
women equal political rights. Frankly pro-women news from the
English church appeared regularly in American church periodicals
during that period, extolling the ministry of women and discussing
their suitability for ordination to the diaconate and priesthood. A
widely-reported pronouncement of the Lord Chancellor of the British
Empire that he could not see "any valid reason" why a woman could
not become Chancellor or Archbishop of Canterbury cheered supporters of women's rights, while it raised for opponents the specter
of women turning ecclesiastical hierarchies upside down.[9] In the
months before the 1919 Convention, both American political developments and events in the "mother church" in England suggested
that women could no longer be completely excluded from governance or decision-making in either church or society.

In light of the finally successful secular suffrage campaigns in England and the United States, the franchise was very gradually being
extended to women in parish meetings, vestries, and diocesan conventions around the country. Missionary districts and dioceses initially formed on the frontier seem to have been more open to
women's participation in church business, as in other aspects of society. In some older eastern dioceses, action was urged by bishops and
other influential churchmen with experience of competent women in
unofficial church organizations, family ties to suffragettes, or previous experience on the frontier.

But at the same time, a reactionary movement developed to divert
growing support for women's participation away from the existing

decision-making structures into a new "House of Churchwomen." Begun in California, this approach gained momentum in the months leading into the 1919 General Convention: such bodies were proposed or created in California, Southern Ohio, Kentucky, the synod of the province of the Midwest, Kansas, Indiana, and New Hampshire. The May 1919 convention of the diocese of New Hampshire defeated a move to allow women seats in its convention, but established a commission to "consider the matter of a House of Women and report to the next Convention." Kansas boasted that its canon on a House of Churchwomen "really provides equal suffrage."[10] Was the "Third House" of the Auxiliary's Triennial Meeting about to be given equal standing within the Convention?

The brief popularity of the House of Churchwomen idea demonstrated widespread ambivalence about women's changing roles. A report from the first meeting of Southern Ohio's new House of Churchwomen presents the rationale and deferential rhetoric that surrounded this experiment:

> It seemed wise, almost self-evident to them [the men voting to create such a unit], that the women, who *for one reason or another* have the main burden of church work, save the financial obligation, and who manage all diocesan institutions and are nine-tenths of the workers in church schools and parish societies, should be *consulted* in regard to diocesan plans and policy.[11]

A forceful statement of women's essential roles within parish and diocesan operations appears to assert their equality with men, but is undercut by professed diffidence about the reasons for women doing nine-tenths of the church's work and by describing their proper role as consultation rather than assuming an equal share in decision-making. Such language robbed women of agency in the matter, making it "wise" for men to consult them, but not for women to initiate plans despite bearing the "main burden of church work."

The self-effacing rhetoric used by the churchwomen of Southern Ohio suggests that they might have been "trained by Miss Emery." The women's report included an explicit disclaimer of suffragist ambitions and a demure promise of support sure to allay any fears that women actually sought to exercise power within the diocesan structure:

The Suffrage side of the question is almost a side issue; the women in Southern Ohio neither demanded nor desired this movement. The men granted us the right almost without debate....It remains for the women to justify the men's faith in them. We must first coordinate our own work...and then stand ready to cooperate in every plan that the bishops and clergy and laymen advance.[12]

Clearly, many women still used this deferential language of submission in 1919. The careful reassurance, the eschewing of demands, the suggestion of humble gratitude for a privilege granted that characterize the Southern Ohio churchwomen's statement all follow the rhetorical style of Julia and Mary Emery. Yet another style of women's leadership within the church structures was beginning to emerge. Deaconess Helen M. Fuller offered a very different tone on the eve of the 1919 General Convention, when she decried the "Chaos in the Camp of the Church Women." Fuller stood more in the plain-spoken tradition of Harriette Keyser and Vida Scudder. Taking a dim view of the house-of-women idea, she described it as a way to avoid giving women equal representation:

In some places women are or are to be on vestries, leading logically and, as some hold, dangerously to partnership throughout the Church's organized councils. To avoid this danger separate Houses have been formed in some localities, rather hastily it would appear, since the women are unprepared.

Fuller's article discussed women's opportunities for mission and service within the church, and in a passage that might have been written today she deplored

the utter inefficiency of the Church in the matter of support. Will the Church now once for all remove the scandal of her sweated work?...A standardization of women's work and women's pay is a crying need in the Church and our house must be put in order if we are to speak with any right in matters of industrial conditions.[13]

Such frankness was an indication of the independence deaconesses could achieve despite their vow of obedience to a bishop, but it was unusual among women working inside church structures. Within the Episcopal context, expansion of women's roles was generally sought through insinuation, not confrontation, through the kinds of genteel arguments that implied that a change would actually strengthen the status quo. So, for example, a lengthy editorial in *The Witness* just before the 1919 Convention called for admitting women to the House of Deputies on the grounds that the church could not maintain its position in an increasingly secularized world without them:

> It is the part of wisdom and of simple justice to enlist the full powers of women in the efforts of the church to maintain the Christian principles through which must be solved the problems of home and family life, of public and private morality, of education which shall recognize God and His Church, of social and industrial relations, and of international peace and the orderly process of civilization.

This call for representation, however, was packaged in the most traditional images from the myth of domesticity, cajoling the church "to avail itself of their experience and devotion, their special knowledge of the women and children who need the message and help of the Church, their readiness to give all that they are, all that they have, for Christ and for His Church." Even the fear of women taking over at men's expense was countered by using nonthreatening stereotypes of self-sacrificing women responding to the church's needs. They would enter the legislative process, the editorial assured,

> not to displace men, but to supplement their work, to get them an example of devotion and sacrifice, to give them new hope and courage and confidence that, with God's help, the problems of the world can be solved. The great need of the Church is faith—faith that fears no difficulties, that counts no cost, and women have that faith.[14]

Such reassurances that expanding opportunities for women would not displace men bear a striking resemblance to those voiced about the new "racial episcopate." Edward Demby had been consecrated the first Suffragan Bishop for Negro Work in 1918. Early the next year, amidst preparations for the 1919 General Convention, *The Witness* ran a front-page story entitled "Great Things Predicted for Bishop Demby's Episcopate." Reporting on a meeting Demby had addressed in Arkansas, the story managed to praise Demby for his leadership, assure white readers that he knew his "proper place," and also remind others "of his race" of the behavior expected of them:

> While he has what would be termed a quiet, easy delivery, it is an unusually forceful delivery. He gave the Negroes good advice, declared his undivided allegiance to the Nation, and said that the condition of the American Negro was better than that of any other part of the race....He talked like a Bishop...[and] declared that the Episcopal Church was the first to attempt to help the Negro race....Personally, Bishop Demby is a good representative of his race so far as racial features and characteristics are concerned. Although splendidly educated and occupying a high position, he is as plain, and humble, and deferential, as any Southerner could desire or imagine.[15]

Like *The Witness*'s editorial support of suffrage for self-sacrificing women, its praise for Bishop Demby was double-edged, similar in tone to Bishop Lloyd's praise for Julia Emery's "non-aggressive" direction of the Woman's Auxiliary. Those who supported a more inclusive church leadership tended to perceive the change in terms that minimized the threat to existing structures—a fact which doubtless enabled them to be supportive. If Bishop Demby could "talk like a bishop" while remaining humble and deferential, women might take new roles in the church's governance without usurping male prerogatives. Or so many hoped.

Detroit 1919, Revisited

Heading for the General Convention in Detroit in September 1919 were those advocating the complete integration of women into the Episcopal Church's governmental structure, those completely opposed to it, and those seeking to create a separate but official legislative sphere for women. Individual memorials favoring women's participation were received from the Girls' Friendly Society, the dioceses of Lexington, Rhode Island, and Pittsburgh, Margaret L. Campbell of the missionary district of Southern Florida, and members of the Society of the Companions of the Holy Cross, but proposals relating to women's participation in diocesan and provincial councils did not fare well early in the Convention.[16]

A request in the House of Deputies for "the judgment of this House as to the desirability of making women eligible to representation in Diocesan Councils" was deflected with the comment that "such a question should and must be determined by the action of the several Dioceses themselves."[17] Commitment to such local option, moreover, proved to be a parliamentary tactic, not an expression of principle. A similar query about women serving on provincial synods seemed to meet with a favorable response when the Committee on Canons reported that the relevant canon allowed for such representation if any diocese wished to elect women. Indeed, the text of the existing Canon 51, "Of Provinces," referred simply to "lay deputies" chosen in a manner to be prescribed by each diocese. However, later that same day the House of Deputies approved a complete revision of the canon on provincial representation. Gone was the simple phrase "lay deputies," and in its place appeared language drawn from the newly-revised Constitution specifying "laymen, communicants of this church."[18] The loophole that would have allowed women to participate in provincial synods had been closed. A resolution to amend the new Article I, Section 4 of the Constitution to permit women to serve in the House of Deputies was reported out negatively by the Committee on Amendments, declaring they had "found women do not wish such representation."[19]

In the House of Bishops, a mixed picture emerged. The missionary district of San Joaquin which, unlike dioceses, did not have legislative independence concerning its own affairs but needed permission of Convention for an amendment to its constitution, sought to permit women to serve in its convocation. This request was opposed by the Committee on Amendments, even though it had previously supported such a local option. The committee's report argued that the measure "opens up the whole question of the rights of women to membership in the legislative bodies of the church...[which is] contrary to the previous usage of this Church."[20] The sanction of "previous usage" marked one of the limits of local option invoked repeatedly in years to come to resist expansion of access to the governance and spiritual leadership of the church.

The net effect of the various actions of the 1919 Convention was to strengthen the barriers against women's participation in the "councils of the church"—including the new National Council created to support the Presiding Bishop in administering the church between triennial conventions. "Departments" were to report to the new council, thus centralizing the administration of ongoing programs; each had authority to appoint up to twelve "additional members" with "seats and vote in the department, but without seats or votes in the Council." Women's eligibility for these additional seats was all that remained of the original plan to include eight Triennial representatives, and the gender-exclusivity of the National Council itself was explicit in the canons, even to the point of specifying that it could elect as its vice-president "one of its own members or any other male communicant of the Church."[21]

With the status quo protected by new canonical and constitutional bulwarks, churchmen could then safely pay tribute to church-women's traditional roles. Bishop James Wise of Kansas told the women of the Triennial Meeting that the church looked to them for its own rejuvenation as well as the rehabilitation of the American home, and—apparently oblivious to the irony of his comments—credited the organizational model of the Woman's Auxiliary with paving the way for the new structure being adopted by the national church.[22] Near the end of Convention a resolution was adopted noting that "the work of the women in this Church is of the highest importance and deserves our cordial support" and calling on the Presiding Bishop and new National Council to "recognize the Woman's Auxiliary and the Junior Auxiliary as indispensable allies."[23] The deputies then voted to establish a joint commission of "three Bishops, three Presbyters and three Laymen...to connote the whole matter of Woman's Work in the Church and the advisability of establishing a...House of Churchwomen."[24] The bishops immediately concurred, and so nine men were sent forth from Detroit to prepare recommendations on women for the next General Convention.

Chapter 6

The Tide Missed, A Movement Founders

A ttitudes and expectations can alter dramatically in three years. At the end of the 1919 General Convention, *The Witness* predicted equal rights for women at the next Convention in 1922, but by that time all momentum had been lost. In the United States the secular vote had finally been achieved and the visibility of women's issues disappeared along with the suffrage organizations. In the Episcopal Church, the proposed compromise of a separate house in Convention for women sank under the weight of indifference.

The "House of Churchwomen" was an attempt to embody within the church's government the doctrine of separate spheres that undergirded the rhetoric and practice of nineteenth-century women's benevolence and reform movements. Dressed in the legislative garb of a third house of Convention, the proposal gained initial support as a compromise both from those who welcomed it as a way of keeping women in a separate (and unequal) status and from those who regarded it as a way for women to achieve some official status. As Deaconess Helen Fuller had noted, some found the prospect of women's partnership dangerous and sought ways to strengthen the barriers between the sexes that cultural forces seemed to be weakening. From the perspective of some Woman's Auxiliary leaders, who often referred to their Triennial Meeting as the "Third House" despite its lack of legal standing, being transformed into a "real" house within the Convention structure could have seemed a major advance. But the separate spheres ideology was already waning as women of all social classes moved steadily into higher education, the professions, and the voting booth. By the time the General Convention of 1919 seized on the idea of a House of Churchwomen, its time had already passed.

In 1922, the men of the Joint Commission on Woman's Work in the Church made their report. To their credit, the report began by lamenting the "lack of woman membership," noting they had as compensation polled national and local Woman's Auxiliary officers, the Church Service League, and other organizations of women.[1] The commission was frank in admitting that, although four of its nine members were from dioceses that had already created separate houses for women in their diocesan conventions, its survey of opinion among bishops, dioceses, and women's organizations had found an "almost universal" feeling against such a compromise approach. Though no reasons for this opposition are advanced, one suspects that the wisdom of Deaconess Fuller's 1919 observations had become apparent to many, and the House of Churchwomen idea was quietly dropped.

The Joint Commission on Woman's Work, however, had defined its task broadly as that of ascertaining the "sentiment of our National Church" on the general subject of women's participation in church councils. In addition to canvassing respondents about the House of Churchwomen scheme, the survey also asked for opinions about admitting women to the House of Deputies, and about Resolution 46 from the world-wide Lambeth Conference of Anglican bishops in 1920, which stated:

> Women should be admitted to those Councils of the Church in which laymen are admitted, and on equal terms. Diocesan, Provincial or National Synods may decide when or how this principle is to be brought into effect.[2]

The commission's interpretation of responses to its survey suggests how difficult it was to hear any but the voices of those in power. Barely forty percent of the bishops supported the Lambeth resolution and only twenty-eight percent favored women as deputies. By contrast, substantial majorities of all the women's groups polled supported Lambeth and majorities of most also supported women as deputies. Yet from this data the commission concluded that "in many quarters the clergy and the laity, including the womanhood of the laity, have not yet made up their minds." The commission was therefore reluctant to make firm recommendations "in advance of the prevailing sentiment." It is possible that the commission also had data from clergy and laymen, but they presented only the responses of bishops (mostly opposed) and women (mostly in favor). Their report thus says, in effect, that the opinions of bishops represent those of all men, and that the views of the majority of women do not count in determining the "prevailing sentiment." It was an interesting example of clericalism, and a reminder that what those outside official positions of authority say is seldom heard unless it coincides with what those in power want to hear—a problem that would continue to plague the Triennial Meeting in dealing with the General Convention.

The survey results were followed in the commission's report by a lengthy section extolling equality between men and women while explicitly arguing for the continuation of separate spheres. In this section, decades of rhetoric opposing women's suffrage in the secular realm were distilled for application in an ecclesiastical world, where the retreating forces of patriarchy were still in control. With many literary flourishes, quoting Henry Adams and Shakespeare, among others, as well as the Bible, it set out an idealized, scripturally-based picture of "a normal diversity of spheres" and then sidestepped the whole issue of representation: "While clarifying this principle of 'equality without identity' this Commission does not try to anticipate just where it will lead us in its application to the question of admission of womanhood into full legislative power."[3] As a confusing *non sequitur*, the report ended by offering a resolution amending the constitution to make women eligible for election as deputies, which was promptly defeated.

When the General Convention met again in 1925, a constitutional amendment to allow women to serve as deputies was again defeated,[4] and by 1928 the threat of women invading masculine preserves in the church had been effectively contained. When the Convention met that year, no memorials, no petitions, no resolutions affecting "women" were presented. The Episcopal Church had survived the first wave of feminism with all its traditional structures intact.

Exclusion and Growth

The ramifications of this thorough reinforcement of the masculine monopoly of church leadership in the 1920s were keenly felt in the following decade. A fifteen-year struggle began in 1931, for example, to include women on the General Convention's Joint Commission on Holy Matrimony. Divorce was becoming an issue in the wider society, and the Matrimony Commission struggled to respond to the challenge it posed to the church's understanding of marriage. Despite traditional rhetoric extolling women as guardians of the family and upholders of the sanctity of the home, and in the face of repeated requests for inclusion from the Triennial Meeting and Woman's Auxiliary officers, the General Conventions of 1931, 1934, and 1937 deliberately and repeatedly excluded women from the study process and policy-making decisions regarding marriage.[5]

The Matrimony Commission's 1940 report revealed deep divisions among the church's male leadership and an inability to hear women's voices or respond to their perspectives on the issue. The report acknowledged meeting with a Woman's Auxiliary study committee, which was fulsomely praised:

> The Church is to be congratulated on having a group of women ready and able to do such a careful and thoughtful piece of work....It is a pleasure to append their report to ours.

But the commission was also quick to downplay the significance of the women's work:

> Of course their Report represents only the findings of the Committee and does not attempt to speak for the Woman's Auxiliary or for the whole Church.[6]

While that was technically true, the women were reporting on extensive surveys of Auxiliary officers and members, bishops, and seminaries around the country. By labelling it "only the findings of the Committee," the Matrimony Commission could ignore without comment the fact that in the two major areas of controversy—whether people could be remarried in the church after divorce and whether the sacraments should be denied to those who did remarry after divorce—the women's recommendations were diametrically opposed to those of the commission.

While the commission struggled to amend the rules in order to maintain discipline, the women argued for a compassionate approach to people in crisis. They recommended that remarriage in the church be permitted if the local priest judged it appropriate, stressing the uniqueness of each individual situation and the inadvisability of trying to legislate a uniform response. Their flexible approach reflected both pastoral sensitivity and awareness of the grave financial jeopardy experienced by divorced women, especially those with children, which often made remarriage a practical necessity. The commission's recommendation was that there be no remarriage in the church, but that a second marriage might be blessed after a year if the bishop found cause to nullify the first marriage. The women were adamant in declaring that the sacraments should never be withheld from remarried persons, but the commission's recommendation included loss of communicant status for at least a year, restored only with the bishop's permission.

The tension between the need to respond pastorally to individuals and the wish to impose "punishment" (the commission's term) to safeguard an ideal was acute. Whether the inability of the Matrimony Commission to incorporate women's voices into its decision-making contributed to the defeat of its proposed canonical changes cannot be known; but the differences between the two approaches to marriage foreshadowed the struggles over sexuality and authority that would preoccupy the church fifty years later. The exclusion of women from the development of church policy in the 1930s, even in issues of immediate and particular concern to women, also exemplified how thoroughly the first wave of feminism had been turned back in the 1920s.

Within their own sphere, however, women's voices were growing stronger in the years before World War II. The Woman's Auxiliary, led by Emery's successor, Grace Lindley, continued as a powerful communications network, providing educational materials, programming resources, training opportunities, and spiritual support for women in parish and diocesan organizations, tapping their time, energy, and financial support for the work of the whole church. Its publications illustrate both a breadth of programming and a gradual redefinition of "women's place." A Depression-era booklet entitled *The Woman's Auxiliary in the Life of the Church* offered a rationale and step-by-step guidance for establishing parish-based programs. It conjured up images of pious women shuttling between domestic duties and works of mercy, yet also presented a radical package of political and social reform. Lindley, its probable author, had been well tutored in the coded rhetoric of revolution from within.

The booklet begins innocuously with a recital of conventional women's activities and concludes with a pious exhortation:

> What does it mean to be a member of the Woman's Auxiliary to the National Council? Taking a mite-box, going to a meeting now and then, sewing for a missionary box, attending an occasional missionary service...group study, individual service to the community,...and assistance in the Church school....This is the reason for the existence of the Woman's Auxiliary—the reason for our meetings, our programs, our study, and our giving—not simply to raise a budget, but to bring Christ's kingdom upon earth.[7]

Twenty-five of its sixty-three pages were given to "devotional offices" for group and individual use.

Within this conventionally pious framework were dozens of very specific program ideas for local Auxiliary branches. Social service project suggestions laid out an agenda of activist, even radical, social reform of which Vida Scudder might have been proud:

> —Work with existing social service organizations to rectify any bad conditions found.
> —Influence women to use their vote intelligently and as a responsibility not to be shirked.
> —Help establish health centers and clinics.
> —Keep informed on legislation regarding public welfare and help arouse public opinion in support of good measures.
> —Be informed on: Marriage laws in your state; Child labor laws; Laws regarding landlords and tenants (especially sanitary requirements); Laws regarding race relations; Laws affecting workers; Hours of work, strikes, etc.[8]

From their auxiliary position, women were able to devise and promulgate a social program that included elements that could never have been endorsed by the whole General Convention. Committed to reform in health, education, child care, labor conditions, race relations, and even marriage laws, the Woman's Auxiliary of the 1930s stood firmly in the tradition extending from early nineteenth-century benevolent societies to late twentieth-century feminist politics. Precisely because they were auxiliary and packaged their radical ideas in devotional pamphlets, women could be witnesses to the gospel in society in ways closed to the official church, with its ponderous legislative process, complex bureaucratic structures, and often contradictory vested interests. But that very freedom may also explain why they were excluded for so long from official discussions, such as those about marriage.

Small Doors Begin to Open

While the participation of women in policy-making was being staunchly resisted, women were making inroads into the bureaucratic structure that was growing around the triennial legislative gatherings. After fifty years of exclusion from the Board of Missions, the Woman's Auxiliary could at last participate directly in its departmental-level deliberations, even though their representatives were appointed by the department rather than elected by the Triennial Meeting. Furthermore, the Auxiliary had successfully petitioned the National Council to extend its mandate to include education and social service as well as missions. By thus becoming auxiliary to the whole National Council, the women's organization was able to build staff connections and program links with all the church's national activities, while representatives on each of the department's policy boards began integrating women's perspectives into decision-making. Perhaps even more important, their participation steadily expanded the number of male church leaders accustomed to working directly with women. Bishop Arthur Lloyd had been awed by Julia Emery's competence, but such singular accomplishments might be dismissed as anomalies. As more and more women became involved, however, assumptions about what they could do gradually changed.

These minor successes meant that the question of women's participation in the National Council itself began to be raised again. The 1919 canon explicitly specified that council members were to be men, but after fifteen years, in 1934, a proposal was introduced to add four women to the twenty-four-member council. As in the original 1919 plan, the new proposal again specified that the women were to be elected by the Triennial Meeting of the Woman's Auxiliary, but this provision was bitterly contested by both bishops and deputies. It was eventually modified so that the Triennial nominated four women who were then to be elected by the General Convention.[9] Throughout the years this provision was in effect, the Convention never failed to elect the individuals nominated by the Triennial, but the insistence on reserving sole right of election demonstrated the Convention's continuing commitment to final control over the church's legislative process.

Nevertheless, women now had an opportunity to prove themselves in the top policy-making body outside the General Convention itself. Four women were nominated by the Triennial and elected by Convention to take their seats on the National Council in January of 1935: Elizabeth Matthews of Southern Ohio, Eva D. Corey of Massachusetts, Rebekah L. Hibbard of Los Angeles, and Isabelle Lindsay Cain of Upper South Carolina, all experienced leaders and officers of the Woman's Auxiliary. In 1937, Cain, Corey, and Matthews were reelected, and Mrs. Henry Hill Pierce of New York replaced Rebekah Hibbard. Though women were present on the National Council in only token numbers, their contributions were substantial and appreciated. When Isabelle Cain was reelected, Bishop Ernest M. Stires of Long Island, who was retiring from the council, observed: "I rejoice in your continuance on the Council. When you speak you invariably say something—a quality which does not always accompany speech in that room."[10] Some male leaders were beginning to hear women's voices, and the value of their presence was implicitly recognized in the council's recommendation to the 1937 Convention that appointments to a new Joint Commission on Strategy and Policy should include women. The first women appointed to this commission were Mrs. Henry Hill Pierce, Mary E. Johnston of Southern Ohio, Anne Patton of Los Angeles, Mrs. K. C. M. Sills of Maine, and Mrs. E. A. Stebbins of Rochester.[11]

But Where Are the Men?

As women gained strength in the auxiliary organizations of the church and began to make inroads into official governing structures in the 1930s and 1940s, another flurry of concern also developed about the apathy of men in the church. This search for the men was in part a reaction to the slight increase in women's visibility and in part a larger cultural emphasis on "masculinity" in the face of spreading world-wide warfare. Like the campaigns of the 1910s that climaxed right after World War I, the efforts a generation later also reflected the anxiety of church leaders that "ordinary" laymen were not participating in local parishes or providing adequate financial support for church programs.

A Laymen's League was established in 1932 in an attempt to create a national network similar to the Woman's Auxiliary, but efforts to produce "a revival of the man-interest in the church," proved both expensive and discouragingly ineffective. To enlist clergy support, promotional materials implied that establishing a branch of the league in a parish would increase men's participation and solve parish financial problems, as Auxiliary activities generally did. Yet reports attributed difficulties in organizing branches of the league to a lack of funds.[12] Evidently women's groups were accustomed to functioning on the proverbial shoestring, but men's were not.

Another approach to stimulating the "man-interest" was the Men's Thank Offering, authorized in 1940. Explicitly cited as a rationale for a Men's Thank Offering were the programs administered by the Woman's Auxiliary—the United Thank Offering, the Lenten Mite Box and Birthday offerings of children, and the United Youth Offering—which together had produced such substantial support for church programs (over $8 million from the Thank Offering alone by 1940), while educating participants about the mission of the church and their fellow Christians around the world. What worked with women and children, however, did not work with men: even less successful than the Laymen's League, the Men's Thank Offering disappeared without a trace before the next Convention.

The 1943 report of the Program and Budget Committee somewhat ruefully noted the contrast between the work of the women and children and the "whole Program of the Church." It credited women with having shaken off "the shackles of the depression...to point the way to courageous action" and noted that the United Thank Offering and the children's Lenten offering that year had totalled over $2 million. The tendency of male leaders to think of the church as including only other men is evident in the wistful comment: "If the parishes should follow the lead of the Woman's Auxiliary and the church's children, the primacy of the missionary enterprise would be established immediately."[13]

The Laymen's League and the Men's Thank Offering failed because separate programming for men was redundant: any man who wished could participate in all levels of church activity and governance. Such separate programming was necessary for women, however, because of their exclusion from so many areas of church life. The problem of men's underparticipation—a real and continuing issue—could not be solved by creating still more opportunities for men. But the failed effort to create parallel program structures for laymen and laywomen did bring to renewed attention the differences in the way men and women were treated in and by the church.

Chapter 7

Are Women "Laymen"?

The Campaign for Women Deputies Revived

W hen the General Convention met in Philadelphia in 1946, the House of Deputies was faced with a dilemma. World War II had opened many avenues for women's participation in society and the economy, and the diocese of Missouri had gone so far as to elect Elizabeth Dyer as one of its four lay deputies. Dyer's presence was the direct result of a campaign by the wife of the bishop of Missouri. Leah Scarlett had been astounded to discover, on attending her first General Convention as wife of Bishop William Scarlett, that there were no women in the House of Deputies. Before the diocesan convention met to elect deputies to the next General Convention, she gathered a group of leading clergy and, as her husband recalled in an affectionate memoir, "gave them a good fight talk on the subject: what an anachronism this is; how women are filling the highest posts in many fields; and considering how much Christianity has done in history to lift the status of women how ridiculous it is that a Church of Christ should in this day refuse the women the opportunity of serving."[1]

The choice of Elizabeth Dyer as a candidate was shrewd. She was a model churchwoman: an attractive young mother, active in her own parish where her husband served on the vestry, well known and liked throughout the diocese. She was also the niece of James O. S. Huntington, founder of the monastic Order of the Holy Cross (also a co-founder of CAIL and a long-time friend of Vida Scudder), and supporters counted on this connection to minimize opposition from Anglo-Catholics presumed to be resistant to changes in women's roles. The Missouri convention elected her with enthusiasm, and she went to Philadelphia as the second-ranked deputy from her diocese.

At the opening session on September 10, however, her presence was challenged when the roll was called. Augustus N. Hand, a judge from New York, responded with a supportive legal opinion that "interpretation of 'layman,' 'person' and 'man' in statutes was all inclusive," and moved that Dyer be seated. Several attempts to stall by referring to various committees were rejected, Judge Hand's motion carried, and Mrs. Dyer was seated as a member of the House of Deputies. When the chair of the Missouri deputation was appointed sergeant-at-arms for the House of Deputies, Elizabeth Dyer took his place, speaking on the floor of the House each time Missouri's votes were reported.

But the vote to seat her was by no means the end of the matter. The Committee on Amendments was directed to "clarify the term 'Layman'," and their report decisively contradicted Judge Hand's pronouncement on the inclusivity of the term:

> The meaning of the word "laymen"...is quite clear to your Committee. In our opinion, it means what it says. From time immemorial it has been construed to mean male communicants of the Church as distinguished from those in Holy Orders. So far as we have been able to discover not only has this construction never been questioned but it has always been accepted by the Church.

Having rendered its judgment on the proper interpretation of the existing constitutional language, the Committee on Amendments then offered a way to settle the question of women deputies through an amendment to Article I, Section 4 of the Constitution eliminating the gender limitation on eligibility for the House of Deputies. This amendment lost on a close vote, 256 to 263: despite Mrs. Dyer's presence, a slender majority preferred her not to come again.

The women of the Triennial Meeting were quite aware of these developments, and tried to make their views known to the deputies the next day. Triennial messages to the men of the Convention had usually been of the courtesy sort, only rarely attempting to influence action on substantive issues. This message, however, made clear the dismay of the great majority of Triennial delegates at the deputies' rejection of women's participation. By a vote of 236 to 126, the Triennial asked that distinctions between laymen and laywomen be eliminated in the Episcopal Church:

We request the General Convention so to interpret the word *layman* in the Constitution, Canons and other official documents of the Church, that it will be understood to include lay women as well as laymen...and we call upon the women of the church to prepare themselves to cooperate with the fullest devotion in all types of work open to the laity of the Church.

The message from the Triennial further cited the needs of the church's mission, examples from other denominations, and the growing consensus of the Episcopal Church's own women as rationale for the change:

The Work of Our Lord and His Church require the full strength of the membership of the Church, and...an extensive study shows that women in all Christian Communities are sharing in increasing numbers in important responsibilities in parishes, regional groups and legislative assemblies, and...the women of the Episcopal Church in Triennial assembled in 1937 went on record as supporting the participation of women in parish vestries and diocesan conventions.[2]

The women had spoken through the Triennial again and again, but the men could always choose not to hear. The General Convention had no obligation to respond to the women's message, and it was merely "received" by the House of Deputies. Initially the bishops seemed more responsive. At a convention dinner, the Archbishop of Canterbury, Geoffrey Fisher, expressed amazement at the controversy, noting that women had been part of English church councils for years, and the House of Bishops seemed to look favorably on a motion incorporating the "resolved" clauses of the Triennial message, which was referred to their Committee on Canons—but once there it disappeared.[3] Insofar as the constitution and canons were concerned, the Episcopal Church continued to consist of ordained and lay men, and women did not have the power to change the rules that excluded them. Missouri's quixotic attempt to test the interpretation of the rules by electing Elizabeth Dyer yielded only a reaffirmation of the traditional exclusion; likewise, the protests of the women's Triennial fell on deaf ears. Doors that had seemed to be opening during wartime were firmly closed again to those who presumed to take "men's places" in the church, just as the movement to exclude women from the secular work place was intensifying to make room for returning servicemen.

Courtesy—and Silence

That Elizabeth Dyer's seating in Philadelphia was indeed a parliamentary fluke and not the beginning of a new era became apparent three years later. Three additional dioceses had been emboldened by the relatively close 1946 vote, and four women were elected lay deputies to the 1949 Convention: Alice H. Cowdry of Missouri (Elizabeth Dyer had moved away), Elizabeth Davis Pittman of Nebraska, Dr. Ruth Jenkins of Olympia, and Mrs. Domingo Villafane of Puerto Rico (who was not able to attend the Convention in San Francisco). Once again, as soon as the opening roll had been called, a resolution to bar these women deputies from participation was raised, and this one passed with a very solid majority of 321 to 242 votes.[4] Opposition to women's presence had increased during the intervening years, and was now well organized and influential. As Ruth Jenkins recalled many years later:

> Long lines of clergy and lay deputies formed on both sides of the room awaiting their turn to speak. The arguments against the seating of women seemed incredible to me. It was hard to believe that so many were so unenlightened.... [It] was for me both disgusting and heartbreaking to see our great church still failing to recognize what women had done and could do for the well-being of the church.[5]

Missouri's Bishop William Scarlett wrote:

> It was a shocking bit of buffoonery.... The debate was on a low level, both of intelligence and sensitivity. It was amazing, and depressing, revealing one of the reasons why it is so difficult for our Church to take a forward step. Bishop [Angus] Dun [of Washington] and I listened for ten or fifteen minutes; then, indicating utter disgust, we walked back to the House of Bishops. It was difficult to take the House of Deputies seriously after such a performance.[6]

At the opening of the next session, what Jenkins described as "a sop" was offered, inviting the four women deputies "by courtesy" to sit in the House of Deputies without voice or vote. They rejected this offer, sending a message whose full text displays the kind of double-speak that women so often used to gain any kind of hearing in the male institution, cloaking their pain and anger in careful expressions of thanks and regrets, packaging their sharp critique in the most polite, even deferential, terms:

> We, the three women who were elected members of the House of Deputies and who were refused seats at the opening session, thank the House for its permission, accorded to us yesterday, to be seated without voice or vote. But we regretfully wish to inform the House that we believe such action is irrelevant to the main issue. We were elected by our Dioceses, not as women, but as lay Deputies. We feel that the real issue has not been met by this Convention. The question is not one of courtesy to women, but that of the right of women to represent, in its councils, the Church they are proud to serve. We, therefore, decline the courtesy offered to us.[7]

The women having been silenced, their message was read into the record by a male deputy from Missouri.

The Triennial Meeting of the Woman's Auxiliary once again petitioned the deputies to eliminate distinctions between laymen and laywomen. Their vote was not unanimous, with most southern delegates opposing representation, citing the perennial fear that if women participated men would withdraw, and reasoning that "men, and especially clergy, dislike women, that it is best that women conceal their real power and influence from men, and that the continued existence of the Woman's Auxiliary might be threatened." The majority voted to support the women deputies who had been excluded, but the Triennial message as a whole seemed to reflect the desire "that women conceal their real power," focusing attention on the needs of the church and conjuring up a reassuring image of traditionally devout women:

> Whereas, The Church is today facing great opportunities for advance at home and abroad which demand the consecrated and united efforts of every member, and...we believe that a fuller participation of women in the whole program and planning of the church would further this effort, therefore be it
>
> Resolved, that we, the women of the church assembled in Triennial Meeting, reaffirm our resolution passed in 1946 and submit it once more to the House of Deputies.[8]

As in earlier years, their message had little immediate effect. Shortly after it was read, on a vote by orders the deputies voted overwhelmingly against admitting women as deputies by amending Article I, Section 4.

The inability or unwillingness of the Convention to take women seriously was underscored in reports about the debate. Although *The Living Church* had repeatedly taken an editorial position supporting women's admission to the House of Deputies, its report of their exclusion trivialized the issue by its use of humor. "Reporters for the daily press were much amused by the proceedings," it began, and highlighted in a box in the middle of the page this example of resistance to women's voice:

> When a resolution offering women deputies a voice but no vote was defeated some suggested that it would have stood a better chance the other way around—a vote but no voice.[9]

The explicit refusal to hear what women had to say and the humiliation such jokes inflicted on women present in San Francisco stand in stark contrast to the strained dignity of the women's formal responses to rejection by their church's governing body.

Thus in 1949, the Convention had once again reaffirmed that the church was a male institution. Women could not represent in its councils the church they served and could speak only through men who agreed to bear their messages. Local dioceses could not exercise freedom of choice in electing representatives, and "layman" was definitely not an inclusive term. On the same day as this reaffirmation, the $2 million United Thank Offering was presented by the Triennial. Their money was accepted with effusive praise, but their participation in governing the institution that spent it was not welcomed, an irony not lost on observers:

> When the women sought permission to present the convention with an offering of $2-million...[the] money was welcomed in while the women were being locked out....The juxtaposition of these two events...provide[s] churchwomen across the land with an occasion of impatient criticism.[10]

The church did seem to acknowledge that this contradiction presented a problem, though it had trouble defining it. A Joint Commission on Women in Legislation was appointed to make recommendations to the next Convention. Its charge, as finally adopted, was "to consider the problem of giving the women of the Church a voice in the legislation of the General Convention," but the original wording, to study "the problem of women's voice," reveals the deeper ambivalence, even hostility, that continued to characterize the attitude of many church leaders.[11] No matter how polite or deferential, women's voices raised in the public forum were seen as a problem to be solved. As a courtesy women might on occasion be seated, but they must agree to be silent.

Anxiety about the potential effectiveness of even a few women's voices contributed to the ultimate composition of the commission. To the proposer's credit, the original resolution called for the inclusion of three representatives of the Woman's Auxiliary, along with three bishops and three deputies. A substitute resolution increased the male representation by specifying three presbyters and three laymen in addition to the bishops, with the result that the women on the commission (Leila Anderson of New York, Ruth Jenkins of Olympia, and Mrs. Edward G. Lasar of Missouri) were outnumbered three to one.[12]

The effect of all this maneuvering was not lost on leaders and staff of the Woman's Auxiliary, now led by Margaret Marston Sherman, who had succeeded Grace Lindley in 1940. The reforming zeal manifest in the Auxiliary's 1934 pamphlet had shifted its focus from the larger society to the church itself. Their 1951 program booklet dropped "Auxiliary" from its title, becoming *Women in the Life of the Church*, with a revealing subtitle: "A program of fellowship wherein the whole womanhood of the church may work on the whole program of the Church." Leaders in the Auxiliary no longer described their relationship as one of "welcome dependence" on the male leadership of the church. The introduction voiced growing ambivalence about the place of "women's work" in the church, increasingly recognized as restricted in contrast to opportunities for women elsewhere in society:

> As the program of women's work has expanded it has become increasingly evident that to be fully effective it must be integrated into the life and work of the Church itself. This conviction is shared...in the report on the Life and Work of Women in the Church given to the

[1948] Amsterdam Assembly of the World Council of Churches: "The general judgment is that women's organizations should be integrated into the total structure of the Church, even though certain emphases in program and leadership projects may be the special concerns of women. It is felt that it is not good enough for women to have parallel voluntary organizations."[13]

Clearly, a sense of grievance about women's place in the church was growing. The handbook disclaimed any separate role or programming for women, asserting that the "program of the Woman's Auxiliary is the program of the Church." Eleven of its thirty-three pages were devoted to a chronology of the "development of women's work," including numerous references to women's requests for inclusion in the regular policy- and decision-making bodies of the church, and the creation of several study commissions to "re-evaluate the scope of the work of the women of the Church." Although worship was still defined as central, the program booklet did not include a single suggested prayer. The inspirational quotations were not from Scripture or the church fathers but from Mary Abbot Emery Twing, Julia Emery, and Grace Lindley. An "interpretation of the Woman's Auxiliary" was offered in the form of a creed: "I believe in the Woman's Auxiliary as a central unifying power among the women of the Church."[14]

Attitudes had changed dramatically since Mrs. Twing and Miss Emery carved out a domain for "women's work" through piety and submissive rhetoric about its "auxiliary" status. Twentieth-century women who had been voting in civic elections for thirty years were increasingly restive at their exclusion from the church's legislative bodies, and they were beginning to chafe at the subordination implicit in being confined to auxiliary organizations. They were even appealing to the authority of their own foremothers, rather than citing the fathers of church tradition. A profound shift in human relationships within both church and society was in process.

History Repeats Itself

Each time the Episcopal Church authorized a study of women's place in the church, the resulting report urged that barriers be eliminated in order to promote fuller participation, and each time the General Convention failed to take such action. This pattern, begun in the

1850s, was repeated when the commission directed to study again "the problem of women's voice" reported to the Convention in 1952. Concluding that there was "no basis of distinction in principle between men and women as laypersons in the Church," the Joint Commission on Women in Legislation strongly recommended amending the constitution to allow women to serve in the House of Deputies. As before, the Convention refused. Those responsible for the defeat were the people most threatened by such a change—laymen who would have to share lay deputy seats with women. As *The Living Church* had predicted: "The men, who have found their masculine prerogatives invaded so much that they fight blindly for the few they have left, will probably be hard to convince."[15]

The debate exposed the range of rationalizations employed to continue the male monopoly: biblical and scientific arguments about different roles for men and women, assertions that only "career women" sought such roles, and frank admissions that women would take places away from men. Some clergy and bishops shared the latter concern, which tapped into their own recurring anxiety about the participation of lay men or women in the church, but when the vote came, it was only the lay deputies who defeated the measure in 1952. In the coming years there would be consistently less support for women deputies among laymen than among the clergy. Even in 1958 and 1961, when opposition in both orders significantly increased, there was still more support among the clergy than among laymen.

As the 1950s unfolded, the conservative mentality of the country was reflected in the leadership of the Episcopal Church. An idealized middle-class notion of the nuclear family was enthusiastically embraced as postwar baby-boomers and their parents flooded suburban parishes. The nuclear family model of strict gender division of responsibilities was even professionalized within church staffs, as theologically-trained women were hired to care for children in religious education programs, while men with such training were ordained for liturgical and administrative leadership. Middle-class expectations about proper behavior and roles for both men and women became more rigid as the decade of the suburban mother taxiing children to after-school activities and the "man in the gray flannel suit" dashing to the commuter train wore on.

Like the defensive reaction in church and society in the 1920s following the passage of women's suffrage, the resistance to new roles for women in the church increased in the face of the new threat to the male monopoly symbolized by Elizabeth Dyer's 1946 appearance in Philadelphia. Changing women's roles in the church as well as in society destabilized familiar patterns and upset traditional power arrangements. The issue of women as deputies—especially to the laymen whose positions were most directly threatened—served as a lightning rod for a whole constellation of anxieties provoked by the changing relationships between men and women. Sexual innuendo crept into the debate in the 1950s, a sacristy version of locker-room humor that served both to trivialize women and to strengthen bonds of complicity among men in opposition to women.

Commenting on the 1955 General Convention, for example, *The Living Church* noted with asperity that the debate "was conducted at a humorous, almost ribald level, with hearty laughter at every occasion of discovering a double meaning in some innocent remark of a speaker....It was not the importance, intelligence or competence of women that was on trial in the debate." The trivial nature of the debate and men's anxiety about being displaced were also noted:

> The possibility that the Convention might be a body that made serious decisions affecting people's lives, that people ought to have a chance to speak and vote on serious discussions affecting their lives—all these never seemed to enter anybody's head. It was just whether we liked this group in our club, whether they might take over and squeeze us out.[16]

Women's changing behavior sorely tested men's sense of themselves and their place in the world, triggering a reassertion of their "masculinity," often in crude forms. Documenting recorded examples of sexual innuendo in debates about women is difficult, since they were generally considered unprintable, but from eyewitness accounts it is clear that this method of opposing women's interests was common, frequently taking obscene forms in late-night Convention strategy sessions. As we shall see, this sexual agenda became more and more explicit as women moved beyond traditional, subordinate roles to assume leadership in the church.

The links between racism and sexism were also visible again at the 1955 Convention. It was held in Honolulu instead of its originally-chosen site of Houston because many hotel and restaurant facilities in Houston were racially segregated. This issue had been repeatedly raised by the planners of the Auxiliary's Triennial Meeting even before Houston had been chosen in 1952, and it was a coalition of liberal, black, and female leaders who eventually pressured Henry Knox Sherrill, the Presiding Bishop, to change the location.[17] In multicultural Honolulu, the Convention issued a strong statement opposing racial discrimination in the church as well as in society, but support for the statement was by no means unanimous.

At this same Convention, support for women deputies, which had grown slightly since the previous Convention, began a long decline: for the next two General Conventions efforts to make women eligible for election as deputies were defeated with clear majorities not only of the lay deputies, but also for the first time of the clerical deputies as well.[18] Overtly racist behavior was no longer to be tolerated within the national Episcopal structure, but women could still be excluded and demeaned with impunity. The challenge to white male hegemony on the issue of race appears only to have added incentive to the men's defensive behavior regarding gender. Like the timing of votes on women and the "racial episcopate" in 1916, the declining support for women's participation in the Episcopal Church in the civil rights era of the 1950s and early 1960s points to the complex and continuing interaction between racism and sexism.

Chapter 8

Out from the Shadows

By the end of the 1950s, the shadowy world of "women's work" was rapidly losing its appeal. Exclusion from membership in the House of Deputies had been especially bitter because it stood in increasing contrast to women's inclusion in other areas of church life and national governance, including subunits of the Convention itself. Beginning with the church's reorganization in 1920, women participated in policy-making at the department level of the new National Council, in addition to their staff roles. They began serving as assistant secretaries, facilitating the flow of business in the House of Deputies, in 1922. Women were added to the National Council in 1935, and were slowly but steadily being appointed to commissions, committees, and other interim bodies of the Convention. In 1940, the women of the Triennial were invited to join a joint meeting of the House of Bishops and the House of Deputies—an informational program, not a legislative session—and Triennial officers were seated on the platform along with officers of the Convention itself. In 1952, half a century after Harriette Keyser had addressed deputies after hours in San Francisco, Cynthia Wedel (later to become president of the World Council of Churches) became the first woman to address a joint session of the General Convention.

Dismantling the Separate Sphere
This increasing inclusion as advisors within the official church structure contributed to the collapse of the separate sphere. By the 1950s the Woman's Auxiliary staff and officers were committed to the abolition of women's separate, auxiliary programs in favor of complete integration as the equals of laymen within the church's structures. Though powerless to force their way into the Convention by constitutional means, since they lacked direct access to the legislative proc-

ess, they were steadily burrowing further into the National Council structure that ran the church between General Conventions. In a dramatic move in the spring of 1958, while pursuing the goal of complete integration, the Auxiliary transformed itself into the General Division of Women's Work of the National Council, and local units were encouraged to rename themselves Episcopal Church Women.

Much more than a change of name was involved. The staff and leaders of the organization understood the change—from being auxiliary to the National Council to being a division of it—as an improvement in status, believing they would no longer be subordinate but equal partners. The rhetoric of the decade had been that of working together, men and women sharing in the total program of the church. This partnership seemed to be acknowledged by the 1958 Convention in a courtesy resolution of greetings to the first Triennial Meeting of the Episcopal Church Women, which cited the change as "recognition of the fact that women are an important and integral part of every aspect of the Church's life."[1]

Nevertheless, women were not to be an integral part of the church's governance at that Convention. The day after the Triennial presented almost $4 million from the United Thank Offering, the deputies resoundingly voted against women joining them. The courtesy resolution greeting the new Episcopal Church Women must have had a hollow ring to the women's ears. They were eager to give up their separate sphere of operations, but Convention seemed less eager than ever before to welcome women into "every aspect of the Church's life."

In 1960, Margaret Sherman retired and was replaced as head of the General Division of Women's Work by Frances Young, who shared the commitment to total integration of women's programs within church structures. Young's previous experience had been in religious education rather than "women's work," and her appointment completed the break with the Woman's Auxiliary tradition. The Women's Division inherited and tried to maintain the Auxiliary's network of diocesan contacts, but the focus of programming deliberately shifted. Through subsequent reorganizations and budgetary shifts, the unifying umbrella of communication, coordination, and a separate national identity was gradually lost along with the subordinating "auxiliary" name.

Few anticipated this result, but it marked a critical turning point in defining women's place in the national church structure. Coming at the end of the conservative 1950s, the decision to rename and re-orient the Auxiliary manifested the impatience of many church-women over their continuing second-class status. Support for admitting them to the House of Deputies had declined steadily while a generation of educated women—including alumnae of graduate church training programs—were rapidly diversifying and profession-alizing "women's work." In the face of men's resistance, women sought to improve the situation by exercising the only power they had—over their own organization. They claimed equality with men, and sought to express this in a new organizational structure, but they could not control the rest of the church.

Stalemate, Crisis, First Approval

The conflict between these aspirations for complete integration and the exclusivity of the House of Deputies came to a climax in the 1960s. The 1961 Convention met in Detroit, and House of Deputies President Clifford P. Morehouse invited the women of the Triennial to visit the deputies during a regular business session, with their Presid-ing Officer, Frances Turner, to be seated on the platform and make an address.

Turner expressed the women's "appreciation to the House of Depu-ties for the gracious invitation to visit,"[2] but two days later it was made crystal clear that this "gracious invitation" had been for a cour-tesy visit only, with no implied commitment to women participating in the House's business. Immediately after receiving a message from the Triennial urging amendment of Article I, Section 4, the deputies defeated it by the largest margin ever, and the women were furious. They composed a new message, reiterating the polite whereas's of the first one and adding two rather testily-worded clauses:

> Word has come to us that the House of Deputies does not understand the expressed desire of the Women of the Church...for a reinterpreta-tion of the word "laymen"...[and] the Women of the Church do not feel that the interpretation...would adversely affect the nature of the Triennial Meeting.[3]

Designed to counter the familiar assertion that "women do not want such representation" and predictions that if women could be deputies none would want to participate in Episcopal Church Women or Triennial activities, this message also capitalized on a new enthusiasm then sweeping the church. Theories of "total ministry" involving both men and women had become very popular with the National Council and staff, and Women's Division Director Frances Young was a leading exponent of the "total ministry" concept.[4] The Triennial's second message reminded deputies that "a major emphasis of the 60th General Convention is a better understanding of the ministry of the lay person in the total ministry of the church," and "lay person" was explicitly intended as an inclusive term in this context.

This appeal, coupled with the poignancy of repeated attempts to have "the expressed desire of the Women of the Church" heard by the male leadership, apparently had some effect, because this time the Triennial's message was referred to the Joint Committee on the Structure and Organization of General Convention—a body more likely to deal directly with the substantive issue than the Committee on Amendments. The vote on the referral—250 to 121—also suggested that the subject was finally beginning to be taken seriously. At the same time, the vote indicated that a significant number of the deputies still wished the issue would just go away.

Thirty years of women's participation in the National Council had brought the inner circle of national church leaders to the point of rejecting the exclusion of women from church government. In the spring before the next Convention, President Morehouse appealed to his fellow deputies for an end to the exclusion of women, an address which was later published in *The Episcopalian*, the church's quasi-official publication. Dismissing the perennial argument that letting women in would drive men away as "an unwarranted slander upon the loyalty of the men of the church," Morehouse drew the connection between the church's treatment of women and the issue of racial discrimination:

> The truth of the matter is that men and women are equally loyal communicants of the church and the practice of segregation by sex is no more admirable than that of segregation by race or color.[5]

When the Joint Committee on Structure reported to the Convention meeting in 1964, it drew on the rhetoric of the spreading civil rights movement, cleverly combined with a states' rights analogy, to press the issue:

> The time has come to face squarely the fact that equality of opportunity is being denied the women of the church to be members of its legislative body. Furthermore, a substantial number of dioceses now seat women delegates in their diocesan conventions; yet...these same dioceses are restricted in their right to choose the representation they wish in the General Convention.[6]

The report unanimously recommended amending the constitution to admit women as deputies.

The third day of the Convention, October 14, 1964, was a point of crisis. Despite adoption of the "Mutual Responsibility and Interdependence" document from the 1963 Anglican Congress espousing principles of partnership and equality before God, the amendment of the "layman" clause was once again defeated. President Morehouse's leadership notwithstanding, the laymen whose seats would have to be shared once again blocked the way to women's participation.

Reaction was swift, and from an unprecedented quarter. At a joint session the next morning, Presiding Bishop Arthur C. Lichtenberger condemned the action of the House of Deputies, calling it a "travesty" in relation to the Convention's adoption of the mutual ministry principles and its acceptance of almost $5 million from the United Thank Offering. A visionary liberal and much-beloved leader who was about to retire early because of Parkinson's disease, Lichtenberger was circumspect, not presuming to dictate to the House of Deputies, but he made his views quite clear:

> I know I must speak, and I shall try to speak the truth, as I see it, in love. When I heard yesterday of the action of the House of Deputies about the women of our Church I was greatly disturbed. It is not my own personal feelings that are involved here, but my deepest convictions. Then today, after the Eucharist this morning, and now in our commitment to Mutual Responsibility and Interdependence in the Body of Christ, the contrast between what was done yesterday and today is very great.

Does this mean that what we did this morning, in offering ourselves to God, and after the women presented with grateful hearts
their United Thank Offering of prayer and gifts and joyful service,
that our declaration of mutual responsibility—that all this is a travesty? No, it was quite the other way. What we did this morning and
what we do now is reality—the other is, I believe, the unwillingness
to face the fact that women are members of the Body of Christ, that
they are of the laity and members of the Body of Christ.[7]

Never before had a Presiding Bishop taken such an action. When the
deputies convened that afternoon, Morehouse directed that the Presiding Bishop's statement be read again, and the House then went
into executive session. It was Morehouse's hope that the amendment
would be reconsidered, but many were incensed by the Presiding
Bishop's "interference," and the deputies refused.

From the high moral ground of defeat, the women of the Triennial
then put the leadership of the church on notice that they would not
let this issue rest. Cynthia Wedel set the tone:

What has happened here—the action by the House of Deputies and
the very strong reaction to it in this Triennial Meeting—makes it
clear that the Episcopal Church had better come to grips with this
problem....We hear the attitudes of our Church laughed at around
the world.[8]

The Triennial adopted a resolution, which was read into the deputies'
record. It articulated the connections between mutual responsibility
and interdependence and the full participation of women in the
church's legislative life within the context of a theology of obedience
and service, and announced their determination to achieve equality
in the church. The resolution expressed cool resolve and impeccable
dignity, but behind that facade the voices of women were rising.
Seminary professor Marian Kelleran minced no words in her address
to the Triennial, widely reported afterward:

I have listened to the debate on this subject in three conventions, and
I may say it is a scandal, and not in the sense in which the Gospel is a
scandal; it is trivial...ill-informed and platitudinous, full of such
stereotypes as that men are rational and women are emotional, or

that when you disagree with a man you have an argument but when you disagree with a woman you have an enemy.[9]

The women's unmistakable response, on the heels of the Presiding Bishop's scolding, completed the shift in the psychological balance of power. Opposition to women carried the day at the 1964 Convention, but it lost its respectability in the process. Disapproval of opposition to women deputies became the norm, expressed in a 1966 report from yet another study committee, appointed by the House of Bishops to consider women's roles—lay *and* ordained: "The Commission is disturbed by the scorn, the indifference, the humorless levity, that is occasioned by the question of seating women in the House of Deputies, let alone their admission to ordination."[10]

The 1967 General Convention met in Seattle, as the smoke of that summer's urban rioting still hung in the air. John Hines, the charismatic new Presiding Bishop, galvanized the opening assembly—a joint meeting of bishops, deputies, and the Triennial Meeting—with a challenge to set aside business as usual in order to respond to the urban crisis. The Triennial voted to abandon its agenda for several days of intensive study of poverty, racism, and injustice, which were followed by tense legislative sessions to hammer out a concrete response: $3 million from the United Thank Offering to a new General Convention Special Program that would provide financial support for locally-controlled civil rights and urban development projects. Aileen Rucker, staff executive for the Thank Offering at the time, recalled the drama of the moment:

> When the women of the church voted the three million...everybody got up and sang the doxology....There was such a feeling of excitement that day. You could look up [to spectators in the balcony] and hear all these men and women whose lives were going to be touched by this.[11]

When word came through to the House of Deputies that the Triennial had approved this massive redirection of its funds, the deputies voted to allocate or raise the rest of the money (Hines had asked for $9 million over the triennium), making the Episcopal Church the first and only major Protestant denomination to support so tangibly the powerless of the nation's cities.

It was a convention of high drama, immense controversy, and a widespread feeling that sacrifice and radical action were the only possible Christian response to a grave social crisis. And it was a pivotal convention for the place of women in the church. The leadership exercised by the women of the Triennial in supporting the Special Program, and the women's financial influence, gave the final impetus to the decades-old struggle to seat women in the House of Deputies. As the Triennial women observed from the gallery, by invitation, the amendment to Article I, Section 4 was passed easily by the deputies on a voice vote, and the House of Bishops immediately concurred. Its passage was almost anticlimatic.

Yet opposition to women as deputies, though no longer overtly respectable, could still function covertly through a bland insistence that the technical requirements be strictly observed. A Special General Convention was called for the summer of 1969 in South Bend, Indiana, and several dioceses sent women deputies, precipitating a final nasty episode. Technically, women could not serve until the amendment approved in Seattle in 1967 had been ratified by the next regular Convention in 1970, but many people felt this to be a formality that might be overlooked. At the opening session in South Bend, the deputation from the diocese of Los Angeles sought unsuccessfully to have Mary Eunice Oliver seated with the rest of its lay deputies. Caucusing at noon, the excluded women deputies and their supporters decided that to press the issue further at that Convention would detract from an urgent race relations agenda, and male alternates took their seats for the rest of the meeting.

Years later Mary Eunice Oliver recalled the bitterness of that experience, in which she found herself not only excluded, but also the object of scorn and ridicule:

> Being identified as "the last woman not to be seated in the House of Deputies," I became the object of abuse from those who opposed women as full participants in our Lord's service....Only by God's grace was I able to endure the humiliation, sexist remarks and laughter...[knowing] that everything I had to bear would make it easier for women who would follow.[12]

Only a profound antipathy to changing women's roles can account for this prolonged and hostile battle against admitting women to the

House of Deputies. Even the final ratification vote was not quite u-
nanimous. The measure came up at the beginning of the Convention
in Houston, on October 12, 1970. A roll call vote by orders was
called, not because the outcome was in doubt but "because of the
historic nature of the issue." All deputations in both orders voted in
favor of the constitutional amendment (meaning at least three of the
possible four deputies in each supported the change)—except the lay
deputation of Rhode Island. It asked to be polled so individual deputies' votes could be recorded. Two voted "no" and one voted "yes,"
resulting in a "no" vote from that deputation in the lay order. The
fourth Rhode Island lay deputy was Elizabeth Briggs, who was not
eligible to sit or vote until after the Convention had approved the
measure.[13]

Mary Eunice Oliver, who had chosen in South Bend to endure one
more year of exclusion, played an important role in shaping the reception the church finally gave to women in the House of Deputies:

> I was determined this moment would not be betrayed as just another
> agenda item with a pound of the gavel and the proceeding of busi-
> ness as usual. I had written weeks before to Dr. John Coburn, Presi-
> dent of the House, that we had to proceed penitently for all the years
> the church had excluded women. As women deputies went forward
> to be welcomed for the first time, Dr. Coburn called the church to re-
> pent. I began to cry. It was as though all of the rejection, agony and
> frustration of women poured out from me. I was blessed to have been
> sustained by the women...in that heavy moment of joy, relief, absolu-
> tion and sister solidarity. I was at peace.[14]

The Vote Does Not Equality Make

When American women gained the right to vote in 1920 after a sev-
enty-year struggle, the women's movement collapsed because many
believed its support was no longer needed. Too late, they discovered
that being able to vote did not contribute nearly as much to their
status and power in society as they had expected, in part because the
nature of electoral politics in America had changed significantly, and
in part because the franchise was only one element—more symbolic
than substantive—in the structures of domination through which
their patriarchal culture maintained the subordination of women.

Episcopal women made a similar discovery after their almost six-decade struggle to enter the House of Deputies, but by then it was too late to preserve their powerful women's organization. Many hopes that had seemed to be fulfilled when women were seated in the House of Deputies at the 1970 General Convention were to be disappointed.

Women finally gained a voice in the councils of the church because its institutional structures, including the women's programs, had themselves been changing. In the ferment of the 1960s many forces contributed to altering the Episcopal Church's sense of itself and of women's roles within it. In 1961, the entire church staff in New York City had moved uptown, from the Church Missions House at 281 Park Avenue South to the new Episcopal Church Center on Second Avenue at 43rd Street. Built in part with United Thank Offering funds, this modern office tower symbolized both the cheerful affluence of the postwar religious boom and a new phase in the bureaucratization of the church's national administration, in which women were appointed to many professional positions outside the General Division of Women's Work.

In this new environment, churchmen and churchwomen struggled to redefine the nature of "women's work" and its relationship to the rest of the national structure. The General Division of Women's Work was structurally within the hierarchy of the Episcopal Church Center staff in a way the Woman's Auxiliary had never been. Margaret Sherman, the last Auxiliary Secretary, had been elected by the Triennial Meeting, but Women's Division head Frances Young was appointed by the Presiding Bishop. This raised anew the issue of control over funds—those raised annually through the United Thank Offering as well as an accumulation of bequests and trusts that the Woman's Auxiliary had received over the years. Escalating tension was manifested in a decision by the women of the 1964 Triennial Meeting to phase out the support the United Thank Offering had been providing to the general budget of the church—twenty-eight percent of the offering, an impressive $1.2 million in that triennium.

And the women's concerns were not limited to financial matters. The 1964 Triennial also appointed a committee to analyze the organizational structure of the Episcopal Church Women at all levels, including the national coordinating role of the General Division of

Women's Work. Buoyed by the promise of inclusion in the next General Convention and sharing the sense of national urgency surrounding the Special Program, women participated in planning for the new church structure. The Women's Division itself was abolished in May 1968, leaving only the United Thank Offering officer, Aileen Rucker, and Executive Officer Frances Young.

In the new structure, Young and the programs she represented had been downgraded in a more complex hierarchy: she no longer reported directly to the Presiding Bishop or prepared budget plans to present directly to the Executive Council. Throughout the next year, as a conservative backlash against the General Convention Special Program preoccupied the church, Young and her committee sought to plan the next Triennial and chart the future course for women within the church's changing structure. Disagreements over goals and uncertainties about funds undermined planning; no consensus had been reached about "women's work" in a new era. It was a tense time, when the hopes of those who favored complete integration of women in church programs collided with a century-old tradition of separation.

As the women took their seats in the House of Deputies in 1970, hope of equality returned for a moment, but after that Convention another staff restructuring transformed Young into "Lay Ministries Coordinator," a position even further down the church organizational ladder. When Rucker retired as United Thank Offering officer at the end of 1970, her replacement was transferred into the new Program Group on World Mission. Many felt betrayed, as Frances Young recalled years later:

> We, under our plan, had really provided for a place for women, a staff person to be related to the women, and so forth. We thought we had [women's interests and representation] really protected,... all adopted by the Triennial Meeting. But then, when we came back to New York, again,... [we found there would be] no standing Committee on Lay Ministries.... The thing that we had thought was so good, so good, was just *phht*, thrown out the window.[15]

Disappointed, worn out, and frustrated, Young took an early retirement in 1972. She was replaced by a man as Coordinator of Lay Ministries, and a staff person "for women" was appointed within his section. The only support remaining for what had once been the Woman's Auxiliary's vast network was now reduced organizationally to a planning committee for Triennial Meetings. Even that committee was plagued with financial uncertainties because the funds previously administered by the Women's Division had been reallocated for "lay ministry" in the new administrative structure. Major programming shifted to "total ministry," with a focus on redressing the imbalance of clerical/lay power, and then an ordained man succeeded the layman in the position that had first been created for Mary Abbot Emery. What little remained of programming explicitly by and for women had been buried deep within the bureaucracy still headed by men.

The goal of integration had apparently been realized. Women could participate in the church's legislative body and were no longer confined to a separate program structure. But within the church bureaucracy men had taken most of the decision-making positions formerly occupied by women. Women had lost their parallel organizational structure and found themselves virtually without visibility or power in the new organization, though the reality of this power exchange had been obscured by exciting new theories about ministry. Many women shared these theories, but their vision of its implementation, in which men and women would truly work side by side, was apparently not shared by those exercising actual power in the institution—the men on the national staff and Executive Council who made the final decisions.

Church historian Mary S. Donovan has suggested that the fundamentally different concept of "lay ministry" held by men and women accounts in part for these developments.[16] They had experienced completely different spheres of activity within the church. Excluded from ordained leadership or a share in lay governance, women had created numerous community-building and social action ministries, but the experiences of laymen were chiefly confined to vestry service, ushering, or the occasional men-and-boys communion breakfast. During the restructuring period, most of the planning about lay ministry was done by groups in which the women were necessarily laywomen and most of the men were ordained. They may have used the same words when they spoke about "lay ministry," but they did not mean the same things. The clergy tended to focus on ways to increase participation in the church, especially among men, while the women were intent on supporting already-committed church members, mostly women, to expand the church's witness in the world.

By giving up their separate organization, women had unwittingly lost the necessary structure and power to implement their vision of lay ministry. Women saw a future in which women's activities and men's activities would be combined; men saw a future in which women's activities were no longer necessary because women would be allowed to participate in most men's activities. Because the positions of power and control in the church were still occupied exclusively by men, it was their vision that prevailed. Aileen Rucker described the frustration of women who thought they were expanding their work to encompass the previously impoverished programming for laymen, but instead found themselves swallowed up by programs dominated by men:

> This was the trouble with doing away with the General Division of Women's Work...that they thought that we had just dropped it instead of enlarging it to take in men and women both....I always [said] we are not doing away with women's work but enlarging it. But that never came through.[17]

As Frances Young remembered, "it was a very hard time...because it didn't develop the way we had planned. We had a good plan, but it did not work, it was not put into practice."[18]

Few people were prepared to recognize the implications of this process at the time. The rhetoric of equality is powerful, and no one wanted to admit that the men of the institutional church found it easier to welcome women in dependent positions than to share leadership with them. Julia Emery had employed a rhetoric of submission while creating a parallel organization that moved toward equality. Fifty years later a rhetoric of equality set women on a collision course with the structures of domination, and although women finally won their seats in the House of Deputies, in the process most of the structures that had previously supported women's ministries were destroyed.

Part Three

A Question of Ministry

Sir, a woman preaching is like a dog's walking on his hind legs. It is not done well, but you are surprised to find it done at all.

—Samuel Johnson

C hanges in women's roles in the Episcopal Church went hand-in-hand with changing theories about ministry in the mid-twentieth century. The Offices of Instruction in the 1928 Book of Common Prayer had defined ministry in terms of the traditional "holy orders" requiring ordination:

> What orders of Ministers are there in the Church?
> *Answer:* Bishops, Priests and Deacons; which orders have been
> in the Church from the earliest times.

The prayer book revision process which culminated in the approval of the 1979 Book of Common Prayer began during the 1960s when ideas about "total ministry" blurred distinctions between ordained leaders and other "ministers" of the church. The new catechism manifested this fundamental shift:

> *Q.* Who are the ministers of the Church?
> *A.* The ministers of the Church are *lay persons*, bishops, priests, and
> deacons.

Since the great majority of active laypeople were women, inclusion of the laity among the church's ministers in this foundational teaching document was a significant statement in the growing public debate about women in the church.

By 1970, when laywomen finally began voting in the House of Deputies of the General Convention, the focus of conflict about women's proper roles had already shifted from leadership in church governance to leadership in liturgical worship and the sacramental and teaching functions of the ministry. The new consensus that women and men were equal members of the laity and that the laity were also ministers of the church cast into sharper relief women's traditional exclusion from the ordained ministry.

Chapter 9

What Can Women Do?

Testimonies to women's roles in establishing and maintaining Episcopal congregations typically focus on the material aspects of buildings and furnishings, rather than on women's spiritual leadership. The legendary ability of women to raise funds for the church—through frontier ice cream socials, suburban Christmas bazaars, thousands of great and small personal bequests, and a century of the United Thank Offering—is acknowledged in occasional parish reports, convention journals, memorial plaques, and stained glass window inscriptions. Churches of the establishment in England were tended by male vergers and sacristans, who generally worked alone and for pay, but the care of buildings and sanctuary in the United States has been in the hands of volunteer women: altar guilds, sewing circles, kitchen committees. Here women were allowed to exercise behind the scenes, and in concrete ways, the leadership which was denied them in the public spiritual life of the congregation. Within a traditional patriarchal framework which assumed the subordination of women to men, it was appropriate for women to take care of such mundane and non-remunerative matters, freeing the (all-male) clergy to attend to the more highly-valued matters of the spirit.

The history of women's spiritual leadership, being neither official nor tangible, is hard to trace except by inference. Despite their actual leadership in forming and sustaining congregations, often motivated by deep religious commitments and experience, women necessarily yielded to clergy who were trained to teach and preach, authorized to administer the sacraments, and paid to provide spiritual care. Women built and maintained the churches, and hired men to lead them—because women could not be priests, they could not lead, exercise spiritual authority, administer the sacraments, or represent Christ to the faithful. St. Paul had said women were to be silent in church, and could not teach or have authority over men (1 Corinthians 14:34; 1 Timothy 2:11-12), and for centuries, despite other New Testament evidence of contradictory church practices, both men and women accepted this prohibition.

Can Women Read?

Since women were to be silent in the churches, they were necessarily excluded from reading Scripture aloud in church. Lay readers in the Episcopal Church are appointed or licensed by the bishop to conduct certain nonsacramental services in the absence of an ordained person, and to assist the clergy by reading the lessons, leading psalms, and (since 1967) administering the chalice during Holy Communion. Developed during the colonial period in response to an acute shortage of clergy, the office was first regulated in 1804 by a canon which, apparently reflecting common practice, assumed that all lay readers were male candidates for holy orders. A century later, the canon was revised to exclude women explicitly: "Such a license shall not be granted to any but a male communicant."[1] Part of a major revision of the canons proposed in 1901, this rewording reflected growing concern that the spreading women's rights movement might affect the church.

The question of women as lay readers rose again briefly in the context of the ill-fated efforts to open the House of Deputies to women in 1916, 1919, and 1922. Acknowledging that, with the achievement of secular voting rights, "women have taken larger place in the world's life and work," the 1922 General Convention appointed a commission to consider the "enlargement of the Ministration of Women in the Church." In 1925, its recommendation to license women as lay readers (though under more stringent limitations than men) was adopted by the House of Deputies, but the House of Bishops had independently rejected it even before word of the deputies' actions had arrived. Although the proposal required that "in every case the Bishop shall determine the conditions and manner under which the work of such women in his jurisdiction shall be done," and contained an explicit disclaimer against opening "the subject of the ordination of women, the office of the Deaconess, the House of Church Women So-called, the holding by women of office in Parish, Diocese or Church,"[2] this was evidently not adequate reassurance for the majority of bishops. As arbiters of the church's liturgical traditions, the bishops were unwilling to authorize women for the kinds of liturgical leadership roles that were open to laymen. They thus demonstrated the same opposition to women's intrusion into "their" domain that deputies had shown in keeping women out of the General Convention. Clearly, protection of territory and a reluctance to share power with others were intertwined with the issue of gender in the arena of ministry as well as governance. The 1925 defeat of the proposal for women lay readers coincided with the decline in overall interest in women's issues, and the exclusionary canon remained unchallenged for many years.

When the matter finally reappeared in the 1960s, its progress through the legislative process demonstrated the continuing ambivalence of male church leaders about women's place. The General Division of Laymen's Work (short-lived successor to the Laymen's League of the 1930s) proposed a major revision of the lay reader canon in order to "improve training and standards." Brought to the 1961 Convention, where the House of Deputies defeated the proposal for women deputies by the largest margin ever, the revised canon specified that a lay reader must be "a competent male person." After adoption by the House of Deputies it went to the House of Bishops, which deliberately amended it to read "competent lay person." A conference committee met and developed a compromise accepted by all: "in isolated areas, when no ordained clergyman or male lay reader is available, the Bishop may license a competent woman as lay reader."[3]

This compromise proposal was even more restrictive than the proposal which had failed in 1925, and clearly implied that women's service as a lay reader would be inferior, but its acceptance of women as better than nothing in "isolated areas" did indicate that the absolute prohibition on lay women exercising liturgical leadership had been broken. A few years later, after heated debate, a new section was added permitting lay readers—and thus some women—to administer the chalice, a function previously reserved to deacons. Finally, the Special Convention of 1969, citing Galatians 3:28 that "in Christ...there are no more distinctions between Jew and Greek, slave and free, female and male," struck the word "male" from the lay reader canon altogether, making women eligible to read lessons, lead certain nonsacramental services, and administer the chalice on the same terms as men.[4]

The Episcopal Church was slowly adapting its structures to changing attitudes about what women could and should do. In 1952, the study committee on the "problem" of women in the church had declared, "There is no basis of distinction in principle between men and women as lay persons in the Church."[5] The 1969 action making women fully eligible to serve as lay readers, together with the 1970 ratification of the constitutional change admitting women to the House of Deputies, brought the legal documents of the church finally into conformity with that principle. In so doing, they led to a final legislative confrontation with the Galatians text, the question of whether there was a "distinction in principle between men and women" as ordained persons—deacons, priests, and bishops.

Deaconess or Deacon?

The question of women deacons was hardly new. The nineteenth century saw not only the emergence of professional "church workers" (women employed in various capacities under the direction of the clergy) and the revival of Protestant sisterhoods, but also the revival of the "primitive Order of Deaconesses" as another avenue to professional church work for women. In 1855, two women began working with the poor in Baltimore, calling themselves the Order of Deaconesses. Within three years their number had grown to seven, and William Whittingham, the bishop of Maryland, agreed to legitimize their ministries in a service of "setting apart."[6] Like the women who were reviving the religious life in the Anglican Communion, these deaconesses were single women in search of a corporate framework to support full-time ministry. They were influenced by a few English and European models, most notably the Lutheran community of nursing deaconesses at Kaiserswerth in Westphalia, as well as by the example of New Testament women who shared in the diaconal ministry of service.

The early American deaconesses, with the support of sympathetic clergy and bishops, adapted available models to local needs and temperaments. They were unmarried; some lived in groups but most served individually in parishes, charitable institutions, and mission stations. They usually wore a simple dark dress, often with a short veil and cross but deliberately not elaborate enough to be mistaken for a nun's habit. Daily devotions, sometimes in common, under-girded their labors, and most of them understood their dedication to be a life-long commitment, although they did not take formal monas-tic vows. Their work and style of life was, in fact, similar to that of single clergymen, except that they could not perform sacramental functions and received minimal financial support. Many clergy were eager to secure the assistance of deaconesses, and bishops from Long Island to Nebraska, Alabama to Massachusetts "set apart" women for parish work, social service, and missionary ministries.

From the start, ambiguous terminology signalled the ambiguous status of these women in the church. Was the order of deaconess one of the holy orders of deacon-priest-bishop, or a religious order like nuns and monks? At the time, no one spoke of ordaining deacon-esses, and the visible sign of consecration was generally a hand-clasp similar to monastic vow-taking rather than hands laid on the head. But in 1862 the bishop of London "ordered" Catherine Elizabeth Fer-ard as a deaconess, apparently with the laying on of hands, and in the 1880s bishops in New York and Alabama also used the laying on of hands to order deaconesses. A statement by English bishops in 1871 that a deaconess was "a woman set apart by a bishop, under that title, for service in the Church,"[7] gave a certain legitimacy to the movement; but little definition.

The American church was not ready to go even that far. At the General Convention of 1871, the Committee on the State of the Church was asked to develop a national plan for women workers, but begged out of the task, citing anti-Roman Catholic bias—"preju-dice which identifies every such movement with the false and perni-cious system of the Church of Rome"—as an insuperable obstacle. Its report and resolutions contained the broad language about "Chris-tian organizations" which authorized formation of the Woman's Aux-iliary. But the attempt to authorize deaconesses, and to provide training programs for women church workers who would "in no case [take] vows of perpetual obligation," ran into heavy opposition.

Since the standard Episcopal response to unpopular new ideas is a call to study them, the 1871 Convention created a Joint Committee on Reviving the Primitive Order of Deaconesses.[8] Despite the appeal to the early church model, it took six more General Conventions—

eighteen years—before the church was ready to give canonical status to "women set apart by a bishop." In the meantime, groups of deaconesses continued to form. Some believed they were better off without the regulation that would come with canonical status, but most thought their ministries would be enhanced and their positions made more secure through official recognition, so legislative efforts continued.

Mary Abbot Emery Twing, by then Honorary Secretary of the Woman's Auxiliary, became a special advocate of the deaconess canon, which she regarded as a key to authorizing all women's ministries in the church. After several defeats, Twing realized that so long as sisterhoods with their "papist" overtones were tied to deaconesses, the chances of passage for the canon were slim. So in the 1880s she orchestrated the removal of sisterhoods from the proposal and a campaign of support among influential clergy, and finally achieved success with the adoption of a canon for the setting apart of deaconesses in 1889. Yet in a classic example of the way women are rendered invisible in institutional records, the church's official account of the development of the canons credits passage of the deaconess canon to William Reed Huntington, "who brought the matter before convention after convention until he secured [its] enactment." Mrs. Twing, of course, could not bring any matter before Convention except through the cooperation of church*men*, and Huntington was one of her allies. Twing's behind-the-scenes role has since been uncovered, as evidenced by a letter to Twing in which another ally, CAIL's Henry Codman Potter, who introduced the canon in the House of Bishops, wrote: "I shall be very glad to move the necessary Resolution which I would suggest that you draw, yourself, as no one else can know so well precisely what you want to say."[9]

Obedience is Different for Women

Implicit in these developments and explicit in the 1889 canon which authorized deaconesses was the unmarried status of women church workers. Although clergymen were able to combine marriage and family responsibilities with work for Christ, women were considered appropriate for church work only if they were single. This distinction was not on account of women's disproportionate responsibility for homemaking and child-rearing, since it excluded *all* married women, including those with no children at home and/or enough servants to give them ample leisure for other activities. Rather, it stemmed from the twin notions that a woman's highest calling was as a wife and mother, and that a married woman owed obedience to her husband. Consequently, many believed that God would not call a married woman away from her family to any additional service, and that no married woman could be obedient both to her husband and to the bishop or clergyman who directed her work.

The original canon authorizing deaconesses specified that a woman would cease to be a member of the order of deaconesses if she married. Dropped in 1931, it was reinstated at the next General Convention in 1934 on the strength of arguments from deaconesses themselves that "the work of a Deaconess is so exacting that it cannot be reconciled with the responsibilities and claims of marriage." A report calling for restoration of the celibacy requirement cited a survey showing sixty-one percent of deaconesses favored it. A minority report subtly appealed to anti-Roman Catholic sentiment, arguing that "our communion has taken for centuries the ground that the question of celibacy in the ministry is one to be settled by the minister himself," and rejected the notion that marriage made women unfit "for the only order of the Christian ministry in which she is permitted to serve."[10] This conflict epitomized the opposing views about what deaconesses were: members of a kind of religious order, in which celibacy was normative, or members of the clergy who, in Anglican tradition, were free to choose either marriage or celibacy. In 1934, the majority view among deaconesses themselves seemed to reject the female clergy model, recognizing that the responsibilities and claims of the prevailing model of marriage did not allow women the same freedom to pursue ministry that married men could take for granted.

At issue was not what deaconesses would do, how their ministries would be supported, or what the spiritual dimensions of their vocations within the church might involve, but rather the question of how their ministries would be controlled. All clergy vow obedience as part of the ordination rite, but it is the last in a series of promises; for deaconesses, obedience to the bishop was the first vow. Churchwomen were still seeking to define their own ministries within a system which reserved to men the power of definition, and historian Mary Donovan has aptly analyzed this continuing tension:

> The clergy saw the deaconess as a religious extension of the ideal of true womanhood—a woman who would be pious, pure, submissive, and domestic, who would simply substitute obedience to the priest or bishop for obedience to a husband. Contrastingly, the women saw the deaconess as a professional church worker—trained in Scripture and theology as well as housekeeping and nursing—who would exercise a vocation of service to the Lord Jesus Christ through the institutional church. The deaconesses were trained (generally by other deaconesses) to be initiators; the clergy expected them to work as directed.[11]

This persistent concern about authority and control in the debate over deaconesses, and the fact that the canon failed repeatedly until sisterhoods were excluded from it, reflects this broader anxiety about authority and changing gender roles.

For decades, the Woman's Auxiliary had provided training for the missionaries it was supporting. After the deaconess canon was approved, additional training programs were established to prepare women for professional ministries in education, health care, and social service in various church settings. By the 1920s deaconess recruitment was on the wane (in part due to continuing ambiguity and conflict over the nature of their ministry), but the need for trained church workers in proliferating types of mission continued. The Bishop Tuttle School in Raleigh, North Carolina prepared black women for work in rural parishes from 1925-1940. A deaconess training program in Berkeley, California became St. Margaret's House, and Windham House in New York City succeeded the deaconess training programs in New York and Philadelphia. Both eventually offered graduate degrees in religion and religious education. The Bishop Payne Divinity School, established in 1878 to prepare black men for ministry, also offered a program for women from 1945 until its closing in 1949 prior to merger with Virginia Theological Seminary.

As time passed, distinctions between educating women and preparing male seminarians became fuzzy. The graduate programs at Windham House, St. Margaret's, and the National Training Center for Deaconesses in Evanston, Illinois developed cooperative arrangements with nearby seminaries (General Theological Seminary, the

Church Divinity School of the Pacific, and Seabury-Western Theological Seminary, respectively) as their curricula became more and more like that of men preparing for the ordained ministry. Cooperative arrangements took various forms. At a joint reunion of Windham House and St. Margaret's House graduates in the summer of 1990, one woman recalled that "the men came from General Seminary at night to teach us because of course we weren't allowed at GTS."[12] Later, women from Windham House were permitted to take courses at General, but only by sitting in the hallway outside the classroom, apparently so as not to distract the young men.

Gradually, a new category of paid professional ministry was emerging. Alongside clergy in the cities and on their own in remote mission stations, women were creating and staffing religious institutions, ministering to the physical and spiritual needs of urban factory workers and Appalachian miners, nursing, teaching, and praying with people in parochial and missionary settings from New York to China. Many were set apart as deaconesses, canonically linked to their bishops and personally supported through the network of other deaconesses, while others had less formal connections to the church. Increasingly, deaconesses and other women church workers were professionally trained and well equipped to function as the peers of the clergy. A perennial shortage of clergy, especially in remote places, facilitated their acceptance, and deaconesses were formally authorized to conduct services decades before the 1961 canon permitted other women to be licensed as lay readers in "isolated areas." Education and experience were bridging the gap between what men and women could do, the gap which had been the justification for women's subordination.

Furthermore, the confusion over the difference between a deaconess and a deacon persisted. The church had trouble defining what the difference was, but it was clear that deaconesses were not female deacons: "They are not alike and never can be alike." The 1920 Lambeth Conference declared that deaconesses *were* in holy orders, but in 1930 Lambeth decided they were not. Despite an impassioned minority report declaring "we must stop treating Deaconesses as only half-way in the ministry, as immature and unfitted for responsibility,"[13] the 1934 General Convention rewrote their duties, saying that deacons could preach but deaconesses could only "deliver addresses." The relationship of these women to the church, as well as the responsibility of the church for their well-being, was endlessly debated, while the number of deaconesses continued to decline; by 1961 there were only eighty-one deaconesses left, from a high of more than two hundred, and of these only thirty were under the age of sixty-five.

In 1964, with little fanfare, the recommendations of the deaconess committee's 1934 minority report were finally heeded: amendments to the deaconess canon again dropped the phrases requiring that deaconesses be unmarried or widowed, and changed the term "set apart" to "ordered."[14] Only three new deaconesses had been set apart since 1961, and the first change was intended to improve recruitment possibilities by opening the order to married (or divorced) women. The change of terminology to "ordered" proved to be the beginning of the end of the ambiguous treatment of women in ministry.

This revision of the deaconess canon precipitated the first major crisis in the Episcopal Church over the ordination of women. In the diocese of California there was a new deaconess named Phyllis Edwards and a bishop named James E. Pike, both active in the civil rights movement and both aware of its implications for women's equality. They reasoned that the revised canon's use of "ordered"—the term used for deacons and priests—meant that deaconesses were henceforth ordained to the diaconate in the same way that men were. In the spring of 1965, to celebrate that change, Pike announced his intention to recognize and vest Edwards as a deacon—an announcement that generated intense opposition within and beyond the diocese. Bishop Francis Lickfield of Quincy, president of the Anglo-Catholic American Church Union, "urgently requested Pike to defer the contemplated ordination." Pike agreed to delay until the matter was discussed at the next meeting of the House of Bishops, at Glacier Park in early September—at which complaints of heresy were brought against him for his opinions about the Virgin Birth and other doctrines.[15]

Pike made a statement at Glacier Park that was understood as conciliatory, so no action was taken on the charges of heresy. However, the doctrinal controversy colored the whole discussion of women and the diaconate, and the ambiguity at the heart of the matter remained. The bishops at that 1965 meeting decided that deaconesses were "ordered" and received "an indelible character," but differed from male deacons in that they were not to distribute the bread or wine at Holy Communion. The bishops also approved a liturgy for "making deaconesses" very similar to the prayer book service for "making deacons." On September 13, 1965, using portions of that liturgy in Grace Cathedral in San Francisco, Pike recognized Edwards's ministry, investing her with the traditional deacon's stole and copy of the Gospels, and thereafter listing her as a full member of the clergy in diocesan records—a move that further infuriated opponents.[16]

"Proper" Ministries for Women

But was Deaconess Phyllis Edwards a deacon or not? Was there a difference between those previously set apart, and those henceforth to be "ordered"? Was the term "deaconess" merely the feminine form of "deacon" or did it imply some other (lesser) role? Were the holy orders of deacon-priest-bishop eternally reserved for men, or could women be admitted to one of them? If to one, why not all three? Once again, the call-for-study strategy was employed to deal with a controversial issue: a Committee to Study the Proper Place of Women in the Ministry of the Church was appointed to report on this perplexing matter to the 1966 House of Bishops' meeting, and John Hines, the Presiding Bishop, was asked to raise the issue at the next Lambeth Conference.[17]

The study committee made a progress report in the fall of 1966, at the same meeting in which the House of Bishops seriously considered a presentment seeking a heresy trial against Pike, who had just resigned as bishop of California. Although complaints centered on his theological views, indignation over Pike's provocative manner and extensive press and television coverage fueled the bishops' opposition to him. After days of debate, they decided against a trial, but adopted a harshly-worded statement of censure.[18] The Edwards recognition service had been a critical example of the type of behavior which so offended Pike's brother bishops, and it clearly linked the issue of women's ordination with questions of authority and collegiality, a connection that would reappear again and again.

It was in this context that the study committee boldly opened up the question of admitting women to *all* the orders of the church's ministry. Calling for a "fresh and unprejudiced look at the whole issue," they pointed to the relationship between changing attitudes about laywomen and the shift in focus to ordination, with the ambiguity of deaconesses serving as the bridge:

> The place of women in the Church's ministry demands the facing of
> the question of whether or not women should be considered eligible
> for ordination to any and all Orders of that Ministry. No one would
> deny that women are part of the lay ministry of the Church, and the
> Committee does not think that another examination of the status of
> Deaconesses alone would do justice to the matter.[19]

Sidestepping the immediate question of deaconess/deacon, the report plunged directly into the broader ordination issue. It suggested several factors which favored ordaining women to all orders: their widening roles in secular life, the potential women could bring to the church's expanding and more specialized forms of ministry, and positive ecumenical considerations (chiefly but not exclusively on the Protestant side). In summary fashion it also answered the major objections, such as "the alleged mental and emotional characteristics of women [which] are said to make them unsuitable," the marriage vs. ministry argument, theological positions based on biblical texts and traditions about the image of God, and "emotional and psychological pressures," among which they included "magical notions of priesthood and Sacraments that linger on in the most sophisticated minds."

This brief progress report not only touched on all the topics to be endlessly debated in the decade to come, but also set up a framework for the debate which made sociological considerations a touchstone. Declaring that the burden of proof now rested on those who opposed ordaining women, the report's central argument rested on two assertions by Vatican II theologian Hans Küng "that there are no dogmatic or biblical reasons against it... [and] that there are psychological and sociological factors" in favor of it. In an interview with study committee member Elizabeth Bussing, Küng had asserted, "The solution to the problem depends on the sociological conditions of the time and place. It is entirely a matter of cultural circumstances." Adopting Küng's approach, the study committee set the terms for the ensuing conflict between religious tradition and contemporary culture:

> To oppose the ordination of women is either to hold that the whole
> trend of modern culture is wrong in its attitude toward the place of

women in society, or to maintain that the unique character of the ordained ministry makes that ministry a special case and justifies the exclusion of women from it.

Although in its cheerful efficiency the 1966 report gravely underestimated the depth of the resistance, it did accurately identify many of the issues. Momentum for change in the roles of laywomen and deaconesses had carried the larger question of ordination into the political arena, and the question of women in the diaconate paled by comparison, disappearing temporarily into organizational limbo.

The change implicit in the 1964 deaconess canon was made explicit six years later. The shift in interpretation epitomized in the Edwards/Pike affair and endorsed by the Lambeth Conference in 1968 made women in the diaconate a *fait accompli*. Lambeth recommended that "those made Deaconesses by a laying on of hands with appropriate prayers be declared to be within the Diaconate," and encouraged member churches to adopt appropriate canonical legislation to this effect.[20] In compliance, the General Convention of 1970—including the church's first women deputies—repealed the old deaconess canon, eliminated all distinctions between women and men as deacons, and made female deacons subject to the same canonical provisions—and eligible for the same ordination process and ceremony—as male deacons. Finally, in a "grandmother clause," it approved a resolution that "those made Deaconesses by the laying on of hands, with appropriate prayers, be declared to be in the Diaconate."[21]

After almost a hundred years, Mary Abbot Emery Twing's campaign for the authorization of "women church workers" had reached a milestone she could never have anticipated. Women could be ordained to the first of the three "holy orders" of the church's ministry, and the process for admitting them to the other two was well underway. Their inclusion in the diaconate was the result of a long, slow process of adaptation, in which deaconesses and other women church workers accepted their subordinate status and operated within the bounds of accepted feminine behavior. But this style was to be rejected by key participants in the next phase of the struggle for women's ordination.

Chapter 10

Breaching the Sacred Barrier

For when there is a change in the priesthood, there is necessarily a change in the law as well. (Hebrews 7:12)

Women deacons are one thing; women priests are something else again. The diaconate is understood as a servant ministry, so it was possible for many to accept women as deacons without disturbing age-old concepts of women's "proper place." Deaconesses were in helping roles in church and society, serving the poor and sick, assisting at the liturgy. Their subordination to male priests and bishops was an explicit aspect of their formal identity. Priests, on the other hand, are the designated leaders of congregations—liturgically, pastorally, theologically, canonically. They bear the full authority of the church at the local level, have power to administer the sacraments, preside over corporate worship, organize the programs and fellowship of the community, instruct, exhort, teach, and proclaim the gospel. To accept women as priests meant to overturn centuries of socialization and religious traditions which presume that women are not, should not, and cannot be leaders, possess authority, exercise power, preside over mixed gatherings of men and women, or represent God within the human community.

Overcoming this conditioning is immensely difficult, for it involves personal conversion and corporate transformation. The transformation of the Episcopal Church signified by ordaining women as priests began in the 1970s, but will probably continue well into the twenty-first century—a long process of stretching both attitudes and organizational structures.

The first woman priest in the Anglican Communion was not an American. In a curious parallel to the seating of Elizabeth Dyer in the House of Deputies in 1946, the upheaval of wartime had also made possible the 1944 ordination of Florence Li Tim-Oi by Ronald O. Hall, the bishop of Hong Kong, to provide priestly ministrations to Chinese Anglicans under the Japanese occupation. When word of the ordination reached England, Bishop Hall was roundly denounced and Li Tim-Oi agreed to suspend her sacramental ministry to protect Hall from punitive action. Her subsequent disappearance throughout the years China was closed to the West made it easy for the Anglican Communion to resist dealing with the implications of her ordination, just as the American House of Deputies resisted women's representation throughout the 1950s and early 1960s. But Li Tim-Oi's ordination reminds us that the issue was by no means an American invention of the 1960s. In fact, women's ordination to the priesthood had been urged by women's rights activists on both sides of the Atlantic since the turn of the century, and was first alluded to in a Lambeth Conference report of 1920.[1]

Women had slipped into the diaconate through a side door of ambiguous terminology, but their campaign for admission to the priesthood involved a frontal assault on the portals—ecclesiastical, theological, and political—of the Episcopal Church. The period of formal political engagement, of an active movement for the ordination of women *within* the institutional church, was barely a dozen years. Beginning with the aftermath of the Edwards/Pike controversy over the diaconate in 1965, through the first authorized ordinations of women to the priesthood (and the "regularization" of those previously ordained) in 1977, the campaign included about eight years of conventional politics, three years of escalating confrontation and ecclesiastical disobedience, and a final period of institutional reaction and adjustment. The struggle generated intense distress, pain, and anger for proponents and opponents alike, an institutional and personal trauma whose effects are still being worked out within and outside the church.

The Limits of Conventional Politics
Talk precedes action, especially for Episcopalians, and extensive study, debate, and educational activities of many sorts launched and

sustained the movement for women's ordination. The 1966 report from the Committee to Study the Proper Place of Women in the Ministry of the Church stimulated widespread discussion, particularly within seminaries that had begun to admit women students to their regular divinity degree programs as well as to special religious education courses. In 1958, the Episcopal Theological School in Cambridge, Massachusetts had been the first to admit women to the B.D. program, followed by Virginia Theological Seminary in 1963 and the Church Divinity School of the Pacific and the Episcopal Theological Seminary of the Southwest in 1964. As a result, demand for separate training declined and the remaining programs for professional women church workers launched by the Woman's Auxiliary and the deaconess movement were forced to close—St. Margaret's House in Berkeley, California in 1966, and New York City's Windham House the following year. Henceforth, women would have access to the same theological education available to men preparing for ordination.

Study may be a prelude to action, but it can also be a delaying tactic. The 1968 Lambeth Conference had endorsed the principle that deaconesses were part of the diaconate, but referred the question of priesthood back to the provinces for further study. Responding promptly, the 1969 Special General Convention (the last at which no women served as deputies) appointed a joint commission to study "the question of the ordination of women and the licensing of women as Lay Readers."[2] The following spring—April 1970—at a meeting organized by the Episcopal Peace Fellowship at the Graymoor Conference Center, sixty Episcopal women prepared a statement criticizing the church for its racism, militarism, and sexism, and calling for acceptance of women in every church position and office, including the ordained ministry. After the Graymoor meeting some participants learned that the study commission appointed by the Special Convention had not yet met and would submit a "no progress" report to the regular convention that fall. Incensed over what seemed another delaying tactic, they persuaded commission members to meet and prepare a report for the October General Convention in Houston.

There women made their first appearance in the mainstream of Episcopal Church leadership. The first women deputies were seated, and the final canonical changes making women eligible for the diaconate on the same terms as men were adopted. The new commission endorsed the 1966 House of Bishops' study favoring the ordination of women to all orders, cited the 1968 Lambeth Conference and memorials from the dioceses of Central New York, Maryland, and Ohio in support of ordaining women, and proposed immediate action: "Open the priesthood and episcopate to women without delay... [through a process] of interpretation (rather than amendment) of the Constitution and Canons and Prayer Book Ordinal."[3] The Triennial Meeting endorsed this report by a very large margin, 222-45. Like the 1946 resolution of the Triennial Meeting asking Convention to reinterpret the word "layman," this approach appealed both to those committed to the equality of women and their partnership with men in ministry, and to those who held that masculine terminology could be interpreted as generic for all human beings. In the House of Deputies a modified version of the proposal was put to a vote by orders, where it passed with a comfortable margin in the lay order. But the clergy defeated it—defending their territory just as lay deputies had for so long defended theirs.[4] Proponents, however, were less disappointed than delighted by the closeness of the vote, and left Houston confident that the next Convention would approve the ordination of women as priests and bishops.

Meanwhile, momentum gathered on the international scene. Following the 1968 Lambeth declaration about women deacons, Canada, Hong Kong, Kenya, and Korea began to ordain women to the diaconate along with the United States. Lambeth had also voted to create an Anglican Consultative Council, an advisory body of clergy and lay representatives from each national province, to deal with communion-wide issues—such as ordaining women—between the decennial meetings of bishops. In February 1971, the first meeting of the council responded to a query from Bishop Gilbert Baker of Hong Kong and Macao (the jurisdiction in which Florence Li Tim-Oi had been ordained priest in 1944) by stating that it would be acceptable for bishops to ordain women priests if their provinces (or synods) did not object.[5] Later that year, in November 1971, with the approval of his synod, Bishop Baker ordained deacons Jane Hwang Hsien Yuen and Joyce Bennett to the priesthood.

The statement of the Anglican Consultative Council galvanized the opposition to women's ordination in the United States. Bishop Stanley Atkins of Eau Claire launched a campaign, quickly picked up by the traditionalist American Church Union which he then served as president, challenging the authority of the Anglican Consultative Council to give such permission to provinces and threatening schism if women were ordained. A Committee (later Coalition) for the Apostolic Ministry, based at the flagship Anglo-Catholic parish, St. Mary the Virgin in New York City, was organized to oppose women's ordination in the United States. The Society for the Preservation of the Book of Common Prayer (later the Prayer Book Society) was formed to resist prayer book revision, divorce, abortion, homosexuality, and women's ordination.

While those in opposition organized, American supporters of women's ordination also stepped up their activities. Graymoor conference veteran Suzanne (Sue) Hiatt, a 1964 graduate of the Episcopal Theological School who had been ordained deacon under the new canon in June of 1971, was an experienced community organizer and she toured the midwest to establish contacts and build a network of support for women in the priesthood and episcopate. In October of 1971, with the sponsorship of the Board for Theological Education, Hiatt and seminarian Nancy Hatch Wittig organized a conference on women's ministries at Virginia Theological Seminary. Meeting right after the House of Bishops had voted to appoint yet another study committee, the women assembled at Virginia wrote to Presiding Bishop John Hines protesting further study as a delaying tactic, warning that none of them would serve on another study committee, the time for study being long past. They also called on women to refuse appointment to the committee—a boycott which proved successful.[6]

From the Virginia gathering emerged the Episcopal Women's Caucus. This organization of seminarians, new women deacons, veteran lay women leaders, and male clergy and lay supporters dedicated to opening the priesthood and episcopate of the Episcopal Church to women immediately began forming networks around the country, stimulating discussion and working for passage of favorable resolutions at many diocesan conventions. In tandem with the work of the Caucus, more conferences on women in ministry were sponsored by the Board for Theological Education, and Sue Hiatt visited seminaries as part of a research project on women in theological education supported by the United Thank Offering. This provoked a loud protest from the American Church Union against use of national church funds to lobby for women's ordination, but the Thank Offering committee firmly defended its decision.[7] Women's organizational and financial power, so long kept on the margins of the institution, was being exercised in important new ways.

The fall of 1972 brought both an encouraging development and increased opposition. The House of Bishops received the report of its 1971 special committee (consisting solely of bishops, since no women agreed to serve), listened to a presentation by deacon Carol Anderson and two postulants for holy orders, Carter Heyward and Barbara Schlacter, and after lengthy discussion voted 74 to 61 in favor of the principle of ordaining women to the priesthood and episcopate.[8] Describing the debate, John Walker, then suffragan bishop of Washington, was widely quoted as saying "most of the arguments against women priests were in past days advanced against the full humanity and rights of black people."[9]

More organizations for and against sprang up. The Committee for the Apostolic Ministry launched an ad campaign in church periodicals, threatening schism if women were ordained and soliciting funds and signatures. Priests for the Ministry of Women formed to counter that movement, while a subcommittee of the American Church Union, the Anglican Women's Alliance, collected women's signatures on a petition opposing women's ordination. A Coalition of Concerned Churchmen (later the Fellowship of Concerned Churchmen) was set up as an umbrella group to coordinate opposition strategy for General Convention, while supporters of women's ordination gathered, at the invitation of the bishops of Washington, D.C., to plan convention strategy under the leadership of deacons Hiatt and Anderson.

Going into the 1973 Convention, supporters felt optimistic. Forty diocesan conventions had taken action on women's ordination, with a solid majority of twenty-seven supporting it and the rest divided between wanting further study and outright opposition. Forty-two women had been ordained to the diaconate since the 1970 canonical change, and many attended the Convention in their clerical collars to give personal reality to the theoretical debates.

But sharp disappointment awaited them in Louisville. Presiding Bishop John Hines, a strong supporter of women's ordination, had announced his intention to retire early, and on the fifth day of the 1973 Convention an election was held for his successor. Seeking a mediator to deal with the divisions and severe financial crisis symbolized by the General Convention Special Program, the House of Bishops chose the conservative bishop of Mississippi, John Allin. In an unprecedented conflict reflecting the dissension which had marked the closing years of Hines's tenure, the House of Deputies came close to refusing consent to his election—an action which gave an uneasy, combative tone to the convention and probably strengthened the resolve of the various conservative factions. In executive session, the deputies debated confirmation of Bishop Allin for almost three hours, not breaking for lunch until 2:30. When they resumed at 3:55, Allin was introduced and announced he would withdraw for a day "to consider in prayer whether he would accept or decline the election."

Only then could the deputies turn to women's ordination, which they debated for two long hours. The vote by orders on the majority report to authorize ordination of women to the priesthood and episcopate was as follows:

Laity (57 needed to pass)	Clergy (57 needed to pass)
Yes: 49	Yes: 50
No: 37	No: 43
Divided: 26	Divided: 20[10]

Just as the opposition to women deputies had organized in the interval after Elizabeth Dyer's seating in 1946, so the opposition to women priests had rallied to prevent change. It was a stunning defeat, and brought the first phase of the campaign, when everyone played by the rules of the conventional political game, to an end.

Just a Technicality?

The intricacies of voting in the House of Deputies played an unusual role in the movement for the ordination of women. The timing of events often has as much to do with the outcome of political processes as the actual merits of a cause, and it happened that the first consideration of ordaining women in 1970 coincided with a renewed attempt to amend the rules governing a vote by orders in the House of Deputies. Because of this coincidence, supporters of women's ordination had certain expectations about how the voting would be done in 1973 which influenced their analysis and strategy. The constitution provides that for ordinary votes, each deputy casts his or her vote individually, but on a vote by orders—which is required for certain kinds of actions and may be requested on controversial issues—each diocesan deputation may cast only one lay vote and one clerical vote. If the four lay or clerical votes in a deputation are evenly divided, the deputation vote is reported as "divided." This has the effect of a "no" since it does not count toward the majority of all deputations voting which is needed for passage of a measure. Under this system, it is quite possible for a proposal to be defeated even though a majority of deputies favor it; it is even theoretically possible for a proposal to be adopted which a majority opposes.[11]

The Houston Convention in 1970 had given first passage to an amendment which would have changed the constitution to count divided votes as half in the affirmative and half in the negative. Along with many others, organizers of the campaign to ordain women assumed that it would be ratified at the 1973 convention. Analyzing the relatively close 1970 vote on ordaining women, they quickly determined that it would have been approved had this other way of counting votes already been in effect, and so were reasonably confident of success at the next Convention. However, the change in the vote by orders was defeated early in the Louisville Convention, thus retaining the more conservative method of counting votes. As in 1970, the proposal on women's ordination would have passed in 1973 if the other method of counting votes had been used, and this significantly increased the level of frustration among supporters at Louisville, who felt they had been defeated by a mere technicality.[12]

It is interesting, if futile, to speculate on how events might have transpired if the method of voting had not been an issue at the time. An admittedly conservative method, it is defended as a useful curb on precipitous action. Because it requires far more than a simple majority, it ensures that controversial steps are not taken until very widespread support has been gathered. If this voting method had not been in question in the early 1970s, it is possible that more supporters of women's ordination might have remained committed to the conventional political process, even with its protracted time-tables. But such was not the case. Frustration over the voting process, together with John Allin's election as Presiding Bishop (a conservative who opposed the ordination of women), contributed to a sense of futility about the political process, and to the decision by some to give up the legislative route and seek—as their campaign buttons read—"Women's Ordination Now."

The Heart of the Matter: Women or Authority?

In the period of most intense controversy, 1973-1976, changing attitudes about women collided head-on with venerable notions of order and authority in the church. This collision was evident in the theological debates, in which a contemporary rejection of the subordination of women was set against an "authoritative" tradition of an all-male priesthood. It was also evident in the political processes, conventional and otherwise, that surrounded the theological debates. Carter Heyward notes that "in raising the issue of women's ordination, we must be careful always to raise the issue of authority which rests at the heart of the matter."[13] At critical moments along the way, questions of order and authority took precedence over the substantive question of whether women could or should be ordained, and key participants in the conflict cited opposing sources and interpretations of authority to justify their actions. Changing assumptions about women's "proper place" collided with the authority system of the Episcopal Church in a traumatic encounter, to be epitomized in the irregular ordination to the priesthood of eleven women in Philadelphia in the summer of 1974.

This event galvanized the church because it dramatically upset the balance of power. The movement for the ordination of women had many male supporters, but it was fundamentally a movement of women. Following the 1973 legislative defeat in Louisville, one group of those women chose to reinterpret the source of authority and power in the church by claiming them (in the form of the sacramental ministry), rather than waiting for them to be bestowed by institutional consensus. Sociological theory articulates what advocates of the oppressed have known for centuries, that systems of power do not voluntarily dismantle themselves: "The idea of women's priesthood had been set forth by a few...clergymen for many decades, but it was not until sufficient numbers of women...found it a possibility that it was accomplished."[14]

It took some time for sufficient numbers to find priesthood thinkable. The ordinations in Philadelphia were the climax of this process, but it had begun months before, when the defeat in Louisville radicalized many people, causing them to turn away from the conventional political process. Carter Heyward describes this transformation of attitude:

> I [began] to see that "women's ordination" is not a matter which belongs in the arena of a general convention. *A vote is to be taken when one is faced with viable alternatives, such as old and new prayer books. Whereas prayer book revision is a matter of taste, women's ordination is a matter of justice.*...In Louisville, it occurred to me that, on this issue, we have no business attempting to win favor with man and votes from him. People seldom vote for justice until it is too late.[15]

Supporters were motivated by a conviction that legislative approval of the ordination of women would be delayed for another generation, at least, as had the approval of women deputies. The parallel between the deputy struggle and the move for ordination had a powerful effect on Sue Hiatt:

> After the defeat in Louisville I had run into an older woman friend wise in the ways of the church who had remarked that she guessed the ordination of women would now become a perennial issue for general conventions, just as allowing women to vote as delegates had been from 1946 to 1970. Instantly I realized she was right and that my vocation was not to continue to ask for permission to be a priest, but to be a priest.[16]

Hiatt was known as "bishop to the women,"[17] and her perceptions of the situation were very influential with the expanding group of activists.

Immediately after the legislative defeat in Louisville, Carol Anderson, Carter Heyward, Sue Hiatt, and others began working on a rationale for proceeding without the approval of the General Convention. This rationale, developed with the help of legal experts Henry Righter of Virginia Seminary and William Stringfellow, included the following key points: the canons did not explicitly prohibit the ordination of women; in other places in the constitution and canons male references are plainly intended as generic, so interpreting those referring to ordination generically would be legitimate; and if the measure had been posed in reverse in 1970 and 1973 it would have failed because the majority vote, though not large enough to win, demonstrated that it was not the will of General Convention to exclude women from ordination.[18] These convictions strengthened the resolve to take action, and supporters were encouraged by the October 1973 ordination of Pauline Shet Wing Shuet to the priesthood, the third woman so ordained in Hong Kong.

A pivotal event occurred at the end of November 1973, when some of the new women deacons and their bishops met for an overnight strategy session to discuss the possibility of ordaining women without waiting for General Convention approval. Present at the meeting in New York were: deacons Carol Anderson, Merrill Bittner, Emily Hewitt, Carter Heyward, Sue Hiatt, Marie Moorefield, Betty Bone Schiess, Barbara Schlachter, and Julia Sibley; bishops Paul Moore of New York, Robert Spears of Rochester, Robert DeWitt and Lyman Ogilby of Pennsylvania, and William H. Mead of Delaware; Harvey Guthrie, dean of the Episcopal Theological School; and Thomas Pike, rector of Calvary Church in New York (where the brother of the Emery sisters and Dr. Twing had both served a century earlier). Everyone present supported the ordination of women, but many hours of discussion about whether individual dioceses and bishops could legally proceed before the next Convention did not persuade the bishops to act. Resenting being "told by (male) church politicians to be polite and patient and to 'let us do it for you girls,'" the women deacons found themselves no longer willing to accept or trust such promises of assistance, and walked out of the meeting in frustration.[19]

Everyone was angry and shocked by this unanticipated rupture of vital connections. Both the personal relationships each woman had with her diocesan bishop and the alliances between those seeking authorization by the institution and those already holding authority within it were badly damaged. The women felt betrayed because the bishops refused to use their institutional power to achieve a mutually agreed-upon goal; the bishops felt betrayed because the kind of support they felt they could offer was spurned. To the women, this rupture symbolized the loss of the last hope of achieving priesthood for women in the foreseeable future through conventional means, and led some to a commitment to unconventional tactics. To the bishops, as anxious to minimize institutional conflict as to promote the ordination of women, the walk-out was a signal that the process of dealing with the issue was slipping out of their control.

The November 1973 meeting marked a dramatic turning point in power relations within the church: a few strong women stopped being deferential to male authority figures. They stopped accepting the institution's analysis of what could and could not be done; they stopped asking permission and started making demands. They stopped being respectful toward their "fathers in God" as sole interpreters of divine will, and claimed access to God through the authority of their own consciences within a faith community of other women. There were only a few of them, and their behavior scandalized many otherwise sympathetic women; but it proved to be one of those moments after which nothing is quite the same again.

At a diocesan-wide ordination service on December 15 in the Cathedral of St. John the Divine, deacons Anderson, Hewitt, Heyward, Schlachter, and Sibley deliberately challenged Bishop Paul Moore of New York to do what he had said he could not do: they were presented by their parishes for ordination to the priesthood alongside male deacons. When Moore hesitated, and then refused, women again responded to the inaction of male supporters by walking out. The fact that many in the congregation joined them in this protest testified to the shift in the balance of power regarding this issue. Even the bishop's chaplain at the service joined in the walkout, which occurred as the Kiss of Peace was to be shared.[20]

The next month, during a visit of Archbishop of Canterbury Michael Ramsey, Anderson, Heyward, and Schlachter assisted in administering the chalice wearing armbands to protest women's exclusion from the priesthood. A young priest received the wine from Heyward and then scratched her so deeply that her hand bled, saying "I hope you rot in hell." At the end of the service, two bishops (J. Brooke Mosely, then dean of Union Theological Seminary, and Edward R. Welles of West Missouri) joined the women deacons in a silent protest, and afterward Anderson was verbally assaulted by an opponent of women's ordination. Polarization and confrontation had joined study and political action in an accelerating campaign.

Tensions grew. In a February 1974 meeting, leaders of the Episcopal Women's Caucus identified three differing strategies: education, traditional political organizing, and symbolic protests and dramatic action to try to force the issue—including the possibility of an "irregular" ordination. A group of women deacons met with John Allin, soon to be installed as Presiding Bishop, who made clear to them his deep opposition to women in the priesthood. William H. Mead, Mosley's successor as bishop of Delaware, indicated his willingness to ordain Sue Hiatt; when he suddenly died soon afterward, supporters felt an added surge of grief, frustration, and sense of urgency. Ordinations of men to the priesthood in Minnesota in March were the scene of silent protests involving deacons Jeannette Piccard and Alla Bozarth-Campbell. More and more people were responding favorably to these symbolic actions, further challenging the authority of individual bishops, and of the church, to exclude women from the priesthood. Yet the situation seemed deadlocked.

In June, John Allin was installed as Presiding Bishop; within weeks three prominent churchmen called publicly for the immediate ordination of women to the priesthood. Harvey Guthrie, dean of the Episcopal Theological School, announced at graduation that he would resign if the seminary did not appoint an ordained woman to the faculty. While preaching in Syracuse, Harvard professor Charles V. Willie, the vice-president of the House of Deputies, called upon "brave bishops" to ordain women priests. Edward Harris, dean of the Philadelphia Divinity School, reiterated the challenge in an ordination sermon, and the next day serious planning began.

Sue Hiatt met with Harris and Robert DeWitt, who had just resigned as bishop of Pennsylvania, to organize an ordination. On July 10, twenty-two people, including six women deacons and five bishops, met at Dewitt's home outside Philadelphia to make final arrangements for an "irregular" ordination on July 29. Word reached the new Presiding Bishop, who telegrammed each woman, "I beg you to reconsider your intention to present yourself for ordination before the necessary canonical changes are made,"[21] and telephoned the bishops asking them to cancel the service. But the die was cast.

The Philadelphia Eleven

Because of the powerful symbolic importance of ordination, great care was taken with arrangements for the event and how it would be presented to the rest of the church. The ordination service itself was not regarded as a protest or demonstration, and the original plan called for a relatively private service. Each woman notified her bishop confidentially, inviting him to participate; but to minimize the possibility that opponents might prevent the service from taking place, there was to be no advance publicity until the day before the service. The liturgy was scrupulously planned, using the 1928 Book of Common Prayer rather than the "trial use" version then authorized, to preclude any questions about the proper form of the sacrament.

Attention was also give to press strategy: Betty Medsger, an investigative reporter from Philadelphia who coordinated press relations for the ordination, later described the factual approach chosen for materials to be distributed to key journalists:

> Act as though the event is the most natural and appropriate thing in the world, and achieve that by explaining the situation fully. Point out that there will be opposition and outline what the theological and canonical basis of the opposition is likely to be....Have ready a thorough and comprehensive description of the coming event.[22]

In this way, the story would be presented on the women's own terms, with the focus on women and priesthood, minimizing the danger that the service would be interpreted to the public as the radical act of a few extremists.

Timing was an important element in this strategy, but the original plan of no advance publicity had to be modified. Bishop Lyman Ogilby of Pennsylvania, who had been present at the July 10 planning session, decided not to join or authorize the service in his diocese, apparently in response to Presiding Bishop Allin's efforts to prevent the service from taking place. The organizers learned that Ogilby intended to issue a statement objecting to it. Medsger described the "red alert" this caused:

> It was crucial that we be the first with the news. If anti-ordination forces preceded us to the press, the condemnation of the event would

make the first and most memorable public impression. We had to announce the news so as not to be put in a defensive position.[23]

On July 19, key journalists were contacted. On July 20 the story ran in major newspapers throughout the country, and statements by the eleven ordinands and the four bishops were released. In a forthright statement, the women wrote:

> God willing, on Monday, July 29th, the Feast of Saints Mary and Martha, three retired or resigned bishops will ordain to the priesthood eleven women deacons from eight dioceses of the Episcopal Church. We know this ordination to be irregular. We believe it to be valid and right....We are certain that the Church needs women in priesthood to be true to the Gospel understanding of human unity in Christ. Our primary motivation is to begin to free priesthood from the bondage it suffers as long as it is characterized by categorical exclusion of persons on the basis of sex. We do not feel we are "hurting the cause," for the "cause" is not merely to admit a few token women to the "privilege" of priesthood. We must rather re-affirm and recover the universality of Christ's ministry as symbolized in that order.
>
> We do not take this step hastily or thoughtlessly. We are fully cognizant of the risks to ourselves and others. Yet we must be true to our vocations—God's irresistible will for us now. We can no longer in conscience answer our calling by saying "Eventually—when the Church comes around to accepting us."
>
> We welcome your support; we earnestly request your prayers. Above all, we urge you to continue the best way you know how in the struggle to bring closer to reality the Pauline promise that "there is neither male nor female for we are all one in Christ Jesus."[24]

Because of the advance publicity, the crowd on July 29 vastly exceeded expectations and a large, well-informed contingent of print and broadcast reporters and technicians was on hand to cover the ordination. Reflecting on the process ten years later, Betty Medsger articulated both the communication strategy and the sense of prophetic hope and risk-taking that characterized the event:

> Press strategy helped the event to be perceived as a significant historical moment...[righting] a longtime injustice. These women and bishops were not kooks; they were wise and committed individuals

willing to take a risk...to obey what they thought faithfulness to justice, truth and the church demanded....Feminist concerns [at that time] were reduced to funny front-page stories about "bra-burning women's libbers." Women were downplayed and trivialized. But in Philadelphia we were not trivialized. The eleven women were articulate spokespersons for what they believed in. It was a story of dignity and courage and a symbol of hope for women everywhere.[25]

On July 29, 1974, the Feast of Saints Mary and Martha, eleven women deacons became priests in the Episcopal Church. In an inner city black parish, the Church of the Advocate in Philadelphia, Merrill Bittner, Alla Bozarth-Campbell, Allison Cheek, Emily Hewitt, Carter Heyward, Suzanne Hiatt, Marie Moorefield, Jeannette Piccard, Betty Bone Schiess, Katrina Welles Swanson, and Nancy Hatch Wittig were ordained by three retired or resigned bishops—Daniel Corrigan, Robert DeWitt, and Edward Welles—in the presence of one active bishop, Antonio Ramos of Costa Rica. Hosting the event was the Advocate's rector, Paul Washington, a crusading civil rights activist. The warden, Barbara C. Harris, led the procession; the preacher was Charles Willie, the first black man elected vice-president of the House of Deputies. Black and Hispanic men, women of all colors, and bishops without jurisdiction gathered from the margins of the institutional church to claim a place in the center. They were joined by a congregation of two thousand, and extensive newspaper and television coverage of the event brought it into homes nationwide.

The Philadelphia ordinations sent shock waves through the Episcopal Church. Women had presented themselves for ordination and bishops had agreed to ordain them without waiting for legislative approval, in the absence of required canonical consents, and in defiance of direct appeals from other bishops. In doing so, they followed the model of the civil rights movement, appealing to the "higher" authority of conscience informed by the Holy Spirit, accountable to a community which valued the full humanity of women above the claims of ecclesiastical tradition. Intrinsic to their claim of legitimacy was a judgment that the rest of the church was opposing God's will in regard to women. Consciously adopting a prophetic stance, participants in the Philadelphia ordinations said, in effect, that ordaining women was more important than orderly process, and that restoring equality between men and women as symbolized in the priesthood was a greater good than traditional church discipline.

Such claims were anathema to the all-male episcopal leadership of the church, the bishops canonically responsible for maintaining the good order and discipline of the church. They were a dramatic challenge to those who believed that the stability of the larger society always takes precedence over the interests of particular groups, or that women's role is naturally supportive and subordinate. They threatened those clergy whose sense of personal identity was tied to their membership in an exclusively male profession. They were upsetting to those who felt that successful change could occur only through due process, or that the ecclesiastical function of the priesthood was incompatible with a prophetic overthrow of tradition.

Most shocking of all was the fact that—unlike the campaign to seat women in the House of Deputies—women had taken it upon themselves to act within the church without permission. The ordinations had to be performed by male bishops, but it was women who had laid the groundwork, raised the money, gathered the support, and persuaded them to participate. Although the official reaction focused on punishing the ordaining bishops and male priests who invited women to celebrate the Eucharist, its intensity was rooted in outrage over the fact that women had seized the initiative, claiming and exercising power to bring about change on their own timetable.

Each of the events leading to the ordination in Philadelphia had carried the activist women further outside the boundaries of conventional behavior and eroded the ability of ecclesiastical authorities to control the situation. Publicity drew more supporters to the cause and stimulated various opposition groups, so that bishops and other institutional leaders were put on the defensive, reacting to an agenda they no longer directed. The ugliness of some of the opposition, such as the scratching incident during Archbishop Michael Ramsey's visit, increased supporters' sense of righteous indignation. The women enjoyed a powerful sense of liberation and validation, free to pursue their goal on their own terms instead of being dependent on others to legitimate their strategies. The importance of this experience of autonomy is captured in a journal entry written by Carter Heyward the week before serious planning for the Philadelphia ordinations began:

> June 14 [1974]....We expend so much energy "asking permission."...And when "they" say "no," we begin making demands. A movement is in process—from "May I please be who I am?" to "Dammit, let me be who I am!" to "I am who I am."[26]

Sue Hiatt recalled her shift in attitude in these terms:

> When I owned my call, I tried in very ladylike and reasonable ways to convince the church that women could be and, indeed, were called. Finally it became necessary to act on the call despite the church's desire to delay.[27]

The activists gave up the rewards of playing by Julia Emery's rules of feminine self-effacement and deference, of passivity and obedience. They discovered that they could step outside the system and survive, and the possibility of changing the system by deliberately breaking its rules became thinkable. This was a generation well acquainted with the civil disobedience tactics of both the civil rights and antiwar movements, actions widely viewed as justifiable means to bring about change within an unwieldy or resistant system. When the duly constituted authorities of the institutional church, in the form of both the General Convention and subsequently their individual dioceses and bishops, refused to do what the activists believed was right, some felt justified in proceeding without authorization.

Others did not. Although by the summer of 1974 some forty women deacons had met all the qualifications for ordination to the priesthood and all who could be contacted were invited to participate, only eleven were ordained in Philadelphia. Among those who chose not to participate were some who had been part of earlier confrontations and protests, but who did not wish to step further outside the conventional process. Alla Bozarth-Campbell's account of the invitation she received to be ordained in Philadelphia makes it clear that the risks were spelled out as clearly as possible:

> Katrina [Swanson] told me the sequence of events which had led to the decision and reminded me that if I accepted the call and presented myself at the Church of the Advocate on July 29th, I risked being deposed and being punitively deprived of all the functions of my ministry.[28]

Bozarth-Campbell and the other ten felt they could take that risk; reasons others had for not joining in the ordinations included financial dependence on a job that would almost certainly be lost; commitment to the conventional processes for change within the church; belief that women's ordination would soon be approved without such a dramatic action, which might even jeopardize approval; uncertainty about whether uncanonical ordinations would be valid; unwillingness for personal or family reasons to risk alienating or disobeying a bishop, or to become subject to adverse publicity and disciplinary action. Not everyone was willing or able to take the step of claiming a higher authority; some believed it inappropriate to do so.

Those who chose to be ordained in Philadelphia, and their supporters, were very clear about their intention to seize the initiative and set the framework within which the issue would henceforth be treated. The goal was to move the priesthood of women from being a theoretical debating point into reality. The church could, and would, oppose the ordinations of these eleven women, but after 1974 it could no longer assume that women would wait for legislative permission to respond to God's call to priesthood.

Violations of Collegiality

Reaction to the Philadelphia ordinations was like reaction to the November 1973 walkout, though on a much larger scale: those who participated in the unconventional action felt empowered and liberated, while the authorities were shocked and angry. In the rest of the church, opinion was sharply divided. Condemnations came from opponents to women's ordination and from some supporters who feared this tactic would hurt the cause. Many others rejoiced, and letters of thanks and support poured in from Episcopalians and from religious and secular women's groups around the country.

On August 14, the House of Bishops met in emergency session in a motel at Chicago's O'Hare Airport, decrying the actions of the four bishops in Philadelphia. That meeting revealed the internal workings of authority and its relationship to women within the church, and manifested the depth of the outrage felt by the senior ordained leadership over the "service" (they would not call it an ordination) in Philadelphia. Many of them had interrupted vacations to attend the meeting, which was characterized by all present as a gathering of very angry men.[29] Emotions were running high, though they were generally cloaked in the language of reason. The bishops were angry because, at the request of eleven women, four men had done what other men had told them not to do, ignoring proper procedures, violating territory, and defying the authority of other bishops.

The meeting focused on condemning the Philadelphia bishops for their "violation of collegiality." Although nine of the women priests were also present, they were studiously ignored, and the discussion was pointedly not about ordaining women but about law and order within the church. The tone was set by a lengthy opening statement from Presiding Bishop Allin, who had held office for only a few weeks. It began, "I have called you together for the express purpose of evaluating our corporate responsibility to the Constitution and Canons of the Episcopal Church."[30] The statement finally adopted at the end of the meeting reflected this preoccupation with order, and also made the theologically indefensible declaration that procedural irregularities rendered the ordinations not merely irregular but actually invalid. Organizers knew from the start the ordinations would be canonically irregular because retired or resigned bishops lack jurisdiction, and the women's dioceses and bishops had not given consent (their hand-inscribed ordination certificates omit the customary assurance of canonical correctness). But the efficacy of the sacrament and the validity of the priestly orders therein conferred could be denied theologically only by those holding that women by nature were not proper "matter" for ordination, as, for example, a stone would not be proper "matter" for the sacrament of baptism.

At the regularly scheduled meeting of the House of Bishops in October 1974, a theology committee report reiterated the assertion that the Philadelphia ordinations were invalid, and the House of Bishops never formally retracted the O'Hare statement. Most members, however, came to admit that it was in error, accepting the conclusions of an international group of Anglican theologians that the ordinations were, as its participants had claimed, "valid but irregular." On the question of proper "matter," they concluded:

> There is no ground whatever for supposing that women are intrinsically incapable of entering into the role of the person who sacramentally represents to the Church its identity in Christ. Indeed, it seems

that to make this assertion would be implicitly to deny or to qualify the meaning of women's baptism.[31]

But at O'Hare in August 1974, the bishops had come together to solve a problem, defined it as one of law and order, blamed their brother bishops for it, refused to recognize or speak with the women themselves, and declared that nothing had really happened. Bishop Bennett Sims later described the way his own attitude, shared by most bishops present, affected his conduct:

> The most unfortunate thing about the Chicago meeting was our cold failure to reach out pastorally....I arrived in Chicago so angry with the four [bishops] that I didn't even think about trying to hear from the eleven [women].[32]

The bishops' action escalated the conflict while exposing the fragility of their power within the church. Charles Willie resigned as vice-president of the House of Deputies in protest. The first black man to hold such a high position in the church's government, he was a highly-regarded lay leader whose denunciation of the O'Hare meeting reminded everyone that bishops seldom have the last word in the Episcopal Church. The bishops' own statement urged resolution of the women's ordination question at the next General Convention, and called on everyone to "wait upon and abide by" whatever happened there—tacit admission that statements by the House of Bishops are not binding. The fact that the O'Hare meeting even took place points to the tentativeness of the bishops' authority, especially that of the Presiding Bishop, when dealing with extraordinary situations.

The bishops may have hoped their O'Hare statement would settle the matter, but it did not. The response of the women priests to the bishops' attempt to make an authoritative judgment about their ordination demonstrated the real crisis of authority:

> We must further ask by what authority the House of Bishops rules on such a weighty question [as the validity of the ordinations]....We cannot accept the decision of the House of Bishops. Each of us will make her own decision as to how and when to affirm the priesthood she knows to be hers.[33]

In organizing their ordinations, the women had appealed to an authority outside the boundaries of the church's polity, in the hope of altering those boundaries. When the bishops responded by pointedly ignoring the women and reinforcing the boundaries, the women announced that they, in turn, would ignore the bishops' action.

This exchange of statements completed the rupture between the Philadelphia ordinands and the House of Bishops. The women's statement explicitly challenged the bishops' collective authority, but for the bishops to have acknowledged it would have been to grant women a status in the dispute, a role in the church's life, which they had never before held. The bishops were unwilling to deal with a group of women who dared to challenge them, and so they refused to respond to them as group. Instead, in a letter from John Allin, the women were offered free individual counseling and pastoral care for help in coping with "what to do, how to feel and how to plan personally and professionally," indicating just how far the bishops were from taking women seriously as colleagues in the church's ministry or peers in its leadership. The two-page letter was full of irony: "Facing this dilemma [of communication], the House of Bishops would like to do something about it," wrote Allin, who four days earlier had led his brothers in refusing to communicate with the women.[34]

No disciplinary action was taken against the ordinands, but charges were filed against the ordaining bishops shortly after the O'Hare meeting, and a Board of Inquiry was appointed to consider whether they should be brought to trial. At their regularly scheduled meeting in October, the bishops reaffirmed 95 to 35 (with 6 abstentions) their earlier support of the principle of ordaining women, but continued to condemn those who had acted without full church authorization.[35] Several of the newly-ordained women celebrated the Eucharist in public services, and ecclesiastical charges were brought against the male priests who had invited them to do so, though not against the women themselves. As a "matter of conscience," Bishop Allin returned the offering from an ecumenical Eucharist celebrated by three of the women, which had been sent to the Presiding Bishop's Fund for World Relief.

The clumsy legal machinery of the Episcopal Church ground to a halt in the spring of 1975, when the Board of Inquiry refused jurisdiction, reporting that although the ordinations did seem to involve constitutional and canonical violations, the underlying doctrinal issues had to be resolved before the legal situation could be clarified. When the House of Bishops met that fall it expressed its acute frustration by censuring bishops Corrigan, DeWitt, and Welles for their Philadelphia actions. They also voted to decry a second irregular ordination two weeks earlier on September 7, 1975, when E. Lee McGee, Alison Palmer, Elizabeth Rosenberg, and Diane Tickell were ordained to the priesthood by retired Bishop George Barrett at the Church of St. Stephen and the Incarnation in Washington, D.C.[36] But neither institutional prohibitions nor the bishops' pleas for collegiality and delay until Convention action proved able to contain the situation. Despite legal actions against male clergy supporters, women priests continued to celebrate the Eucharist in private settings and in some twenty public services in churches throughout the east and midwest, and the Rev. Jane Hwang Hsien Yuen from Hong Kong toured the United States, preaching and celebrating.

Two different versions of reality were before the church. One said that women were now priests and the church ought to affirm that and move on. The other said that women were not priests and the church would decide in 1976 whether they could be or not. Proponents of the first view—the Philadelphia and Washington ordinands and their supporters in Women's Ordination Now—felt validated by their experience of "church" and the power of community during the ordination itself and in the "church-in-exile" where they continued their campaign of witness and civil disobedience, acting as priests instead of asking to be priests. Those who accepted the second view pursued conventional politics to influence the outcome of the 1976 General Convention vote, buoyed by the authorization of women's ordination by the Anglican Church of Canada in June 1975.

Serious threats to institutional unity appeared from both sides. Some bishops who favored ordaining women declared they would delay only until the 1976 Convention and would then proceed regardless of the vote. The second irregular ordination, in 1975, had given weight to this probability, raising the specter of anarchy and chaos. Opponents vowed to leave the church en masse if women's ordination was authorized, raising the equally dread specter of schism. Among the leadership, concern about keeping the church in one piece grew.

Tension, suspense, and anxiety were high on all sides as the 1976 General Convention began in Minneapolis. The proposal to ordain women took the form of a change in the canons, which could become effective right away, rather than an amendment of the constitution, which required a second reading at the subsequent Convention. There was no doubt that the House of Bishops would approve, but no certainty about what the deputies would do. The stakes were high and lobbying on both sides was intense.

On the fourth day, following a two-hour debate, the House of Bishops voted on a measure to add a new section to Title III, Canon 9 on Ministry: "The provisions of these canons for the admission of Candidates, and for the Ordination to the three Orders: Bishops, Priests and Deacons, shall be equally applicable to men and women." On a roll call vote, the bishops approved the change, 95 to 61 with two abstentions. Bishop Stanley Atkins, president of the American Church Union, read a statement of protest on behalf of thirty-seven bishops.

The next afternoon, September 16, 1976, the matter came before the House of Deputies. President John Coburn introduced it with grave remarks about the importance of the issue and the "decorum necessary" in dealing with it. The debate lasted four hours, with twenty-nine deputies speaking on each side of the issue. Finally, after five minutes of silent prayer, the vote by orders was taken. While it was being tallied, various parliamentary housekeeping tasks were performed, and the hall filled with people. The drama and suspense of the moment were intense:

> There was absolute silence in the large, crowded room as deputies, visitors and reporters waited to hear the outcome. No one was breathing in my section of the gallery. The presiding officer read out the tally: "In the clergy order, 114 votes cast, 57 needed for affirmative action, Yes, 60; No, 39; Divided, 15; In the lay order, 113 votes cast, 57 needed for affirmative action, Yes, 64; No, 36; Divided, 12. The motion is passed."...
>
> All around us people were weeping, silently reaching, touching each other. No one spoke.[37]

The legislative process had concluded. The General Convention of the Episcopal Church had acted to make women eligible for ordination to the priesthood and the episcopate.

Chapter 11

Reaction and Response

The ordination and consecration of women priests and bishops will raise for us the gravest of questions—that is, how far this Church can accept such ministrations without fatally compromising its position as a Catholic and Apostolic Body. We ask our brothers in this House to take to heart our resolution....

— Dissenting bishops, 1976[1]

The 1976 vote in Minneapolis to ordain women did not put an end to controversy. As soon as the totals were announced in the House of Deputies, President John Coburn called on the chaplain to lead them in prayer and recognized a deputy from Milwaukee to read a protest similar to the one that had been presented in the House of Bishops. Those wishing to affirm the statement of protest were invited to sign it, and the president adjourned the session. What would happen next?

First, the church had to decide what to do about the fifteen women ordained in Philadelphia and Washington. The depth of the continuing anger about the irregular ordinations was manifested in the fact that the House of Bishops, after hours of rancorous debate, at first voted to recommend to their respective diocesan bishops that these women participate in a service of "conditional ordination." This suggestion had first been offered in a May 1975 report of the House of Bishops' Committee on Theology, as a pastoral response to reassure the faithful that these women were "authorized channels for divine grace" now, regardless of what had happened in Philadelphia. It was also an attempt to appear consistent with the O'Hare invalidity statement, which the report attempted to downplay by noting, "We observe that quite different meanings are ascribed to the word 'validity.'"[2]

This action by the bishops, once again refusing to deal directly with what had happened in Philadelphia, recalled for many the frustration, grief, and anger of the O'Hare nonconfrontation. While everyone recognized that some form of reconciliation between the institution and the fifteen women was needed, the women priests and their supporters were outraged by the proposal for conditional ordination, which was theologically dubious (either they had been ordained in Philadelphia, or they had not) and clearly implied that their priestly acts in the intervening two years were invalid. Finding a grace-filled way to heal the ruptured relationships was extremely difficult. As Alla Bozarth-Campbell recalled:

> Our diocesan bishops knew us well enough to realize that we could not submit to conditional ordination with integrity—it would be a betrayal of the communities we had served as priests suddenly to throw doubt on the actuality of our priesthood....The Minnesota Committee for Women's Ordination Now called an emergency meeting to discern a way of saving the Church from the betrayal of its own priesthood....The Presiding Bishop's words of the opening session were recalled: "We must stand for reconciliation." At one in the morning, signs were made to be posted in the House of Bishops: "Conditional Ordination is Not Reconciliation."[3]

The next day, after urgent midnight consultations, surrounded by protest signs and in response to a statement of conscience presented by most of the women priests' bishops, the House of Bishops reversed itself and accepted the theology committee's entire report, including the alternative of a "public event" of recognition and regularization.

For the majority of the church, these services of recognition completed the task of reconciling the two perceptions of reality that had been in conflict since the Philadelphia ordinations. At the heart of that conflict had been a debate over the conditions necessary for authoritative action within the church, and the conflict was fueled by the profound emotions evoked when a group of women stepped outside the church's law in order to force the issue. Now the law had been changed. By permitting a "public event" instead of conditional ordinations, the House of Bishops acknowledged that women had been priests since 1974; by participating in these services the women acknowledged the power of the church to permit or deny the exercise of their priesthood within the institution. They could now be properly licensed; they could now be employed as priests in good standing in the Episcopal Church.

Thus began a new stage of adapting to the presence of women in its ordained leadership. From the period of broad educational activity, intense political maneuvering, and the symbolic actions of the Philadelphia Eleven and the Washington Four, the church entered a transitional stage of adjustment, implementation—and resistance. Even before the 1976 General Convention ended, opponents sought authorization for noncompliance with the Convention's action. While the debate over conditional ordinations was still going on, a statement from bishops who opposed women's ordination was distributed in the House of Bishops, and the Council of Advice introduced a "conscience clause" resolution to protect those who rejected Convention's action. After considerable debate and parliamentary maneuvering, it was tabled on a vote of 70 to 53, so the 1976 Convention ended with the question of noncompliance unresolved.

Among those who opposed the ordination of women were some very influential people, including the Presiding Bishop, John Allin. In the fall of 1977, in his opening address to the House of Bishops' meeting in Port St. Lucie, Florida, Allin compared the present situation with that of the first American bishops' meeting in 1789 in terms of the gravity of the problems to be resolved. He reported on his participation in a meeting of opponents to the ordination of women and the revised prayer book who had formed the new Anglican Church of North America. He then stunned the House by offering to resign if they could not accept the leadership of one who did not believe "that women can be priests any more than they can become fathers or husbands." After two days of discussions on this and a host of related issues, the bishops adopted a statement of conscience: no one should be "coerced, harassed or caused to suffer canonical impediment" because of opposition to—or support of—the action authorizing women's ordination. Two days after that, they also adopted a resolution affirming Allin's leadership and his right "to hold a personal conviction on this issue, trusting him to uphold the law of this church and the decision of General Convention in his official actions."[4]

Allin's statement caused consternation among supporters of women's ordination throughout the church. Twenty-seven lay and ordained women signed a mailgram asking the bishops to accept Allin's resignation if he could not accept the decisions of General Convention, but like the women of the Triennial attempting to influence the House of Deputies prior to 1970, they had no direct access to the decision-makers. Their message was not brought to the attention of the whole House, and the Council of Advice to which it was referred responded blandly after the meeting: "Thanks to you for sharing your concern."[5] Though women now sat in the House of Deputies and were ordained as deacons and priests, it was still quite possible for bishops to refuse to hear their voices.

During the same Port St. Lucie meeting, the bishops debated the subject of homosexuality at considerable length, including marriage between homosexuals and the desirability of ordaining them. The ordination of Ellen M. Barrett, a lesbian, by Bishop Paul Moore of New York had provoked a furor, confirming traditionalists' dire warnings (and tapping liberals' secret fears) that to ordain women was to undermine the entire familiar framework of social and personal relationships. The bishops also publicly deplored the actions of retired Bishop Albert Chambers, who had confirmed and ordained members of schismatic congregations against the wishes of the local bishop, a clear violation of territorial jurisdiction upon which all could agree regardless of the issues involved. Chambers's action led them to wrestle yet again with the meaning of collegiality within the House of Bishops, and the tension between the authority of individual bishops and that of the whole group:

> Collegiality must sometimes take into account matters involving sharp differences of conscientious conviction. There are those who for one reason or another cannot endorse a majority view or even a fairly impressive agreement. There will be bold spirits who feel called by God to words and actions of an innovative sort which go further than any present consensus; there will be those who are not able to endorse agreement already achieved. Collegiality involves a sensitivity to such persons and a patience and forbearance....On their part, persons holding minority views will need to give whatever agreement has been achieved its due weight by remaining as open as possible to

whatever truth and conviction such agreement represents. Error and scandal are less likely to prevail if this principle of collegial action and decision is observed.[6]

The depth of the conflict was revealed when the bishops voted against adopting this diplomatically phrased statement from their theology committee. The tortured mood of the Port St. Lucie meeting, the sense of crisis, and the bishops' mode of operating were neatly characterized by an observer:

> As gentlemen's societies go, the House of Bishops is one of the more genteel. While this quality has some real benefits in fostering bonds of brotherly affection, it does tend to introduce an element of unusual reticence when serious matters involve members of the club....The specter of the head of the church asking to be excused from some of its legitimate laws added an element of incredulity that almost paralyzed the bishops....Bishop Allin, known to have difficulties in communication, quickly tried to assure reporters that he never really meant [to resign]. If that is the case, the gesture represented an empty ploy and a back-handed reach for a pat on the back....The Allin affair set the tone for further confrontations.[7]

The "Allin affair" set the tone not only for that House of Bishops' meeting but also for the church's approach to the issue of women's ordination for years to come. The pastoral letter issued by the Port St. Lucie meeting, reporting on Bishop Allin's opposition and the bishops' adoption of the statement of conscience, asserted that "Convention sought to permit but not to coerce." This interpretation would be used again and again to exclude women from the ordination process in practice despite their canonical inclusion, and even despite the plain language of the statement of conscience itself, which was supposed to provide protection for those who supported the Convention's action as well as those who opposed it. The phrase "or support of" had been inserted at the last minute, and was virtually ignored thereafter. The Port St. Lucie statement, modeled after the conscience clause adopted by the Anglican Church of Canada the year before, was conceived as protection for those who opposed the ordination of women, and was thenceforth cited to justify the refusal of some bishops, dioceses, and parishes to ordain women or recognize those ordained elsewhere. It was never ratified by the General Convention, and therefore actually bound no one—except perhaps those bishops who voted for it.

Though cloaked in pastoral and theological language, the statement of conscience was a political action expressing the balance of power in the House of Bishops on the issue of women in the church. It seemed to the bishops to offer a way to stay together despite major disagreement, in the midst of widespread concern that the church was disintegrating after the prolonged controversies of the late 1960s and 1970s. Yet the clause papered over the fact that within the structure of the church two groups existed who were no longer fully in communion with one another. Further, it legitimized as a matter of conscience the opponents' disregard of the church's canons, although a similar disregard by the women who were ordained as a matter of conscience had been condemned. Those who for the sake of conscience had defied the authority of the General Convention before 1976 were decried and censured; those who defied it after the vote were fully protected. This inconsistency was intertwined with concepts of collegiality, whose claims were redefined again and again as they came into conflict with the claims of conscience.

The Meaning of Collegiality

As an American institution, the Episcopal Church lives by the principles and myths of democracy, which interact in sometimes interesting ways with the hierarchical framework of holy orders. The General Convention structure and the deputies' vote by orders are examples of this, in which equal legislative weight is given to the votes of some two hundred bishops representing themselves, about four hundred clergy representing twelve thousand others, and about four hundred lay deputies representing almost three million others. This imbalance in favor of the ordained is offset by the fact that the authority of the clergy, including that of bishops, is limited to the boundaries of their own jurisdictions to which they are generally elected, not appointed, and there is no single person at the top. Thus the hierarchical pyramid in the Episcopal Church is short and flat.

This flat top of the authority pyramid gives immense importance to collegiality among the "brotherhood" of the House of Bishops whenever there is a major controversy. Collegiality had been an underlying theme throughout the 1966 proceedings resulting in censure of Bishop James Pike, since many bishops felt that his investiture of Phyllis Edwards as a deacon had violated informal "collegial" agreements reached at the Glacier Park meeting. Pike died in 1969, but memories of the anger over his blithe refusal to play by the rules of the brotherhood added intensity to the bishops' desire for conformity within the House over the issue of women's ordination to the priesthood. After the 1973 Louisville defeat of women's ordination, the House of Bishops tried quite explicitly to use the ideal of collegiality to control the possibility of dissident action. A resolution put forward near the end of the Convention expressed it plainly:

> It has been said that individual Bishops have expressed their intention to ordain women to the priesthood in spite of the action of the House of Deputies; therefore be it *Resolved*, That the House of Bishops put these rumors to rest by a public affirmation of its adherence to the principles of collegiality and mutual loyalty, as well as respect for due constitutional and canonical process.[8]

Many bishops had already departed and those remaining were sharply divided: the resolution passed by a vote of 53 to 40, hardly a clear consensus on "principles of collegiality and mutual loyalty." Nevertheless, at O'Hare the following summer the bishops' strongest language was in judgment against their fellows for acting independently, while the canonical violation is treated almost as an afterthought: "We decry their acting in *violation of the collegiality of the House of Bishops* as well as the legislative process of the whole church." The next year's vote to decry retired Bishop George Barrett's ordination of four more women continued the emphasis on conformity within the brotherhood. A portion of the report presented by the Advisory Committee on that occasion articulated the importance of not breaking ranks:

> The overwhelming *majority of us have remained true to each other* and loyal to the democratically constituted authorities of this Church. Our *ranks have not been broken by the few*. We, therefore, are in a position to move with honor, dignity, and in statesmanlike fashion toward the discovery of means by which the present brokenness of our Church may be bound up.[9]

Episcopal authority is, in fact, authority derived from consensus. No one becomes a bishop except with the consent of both houses of the General Convention or, between Conventions, the consent of a majority of diocesan standing committees and diocesan bishops. To acquire the authority of the episcopate, one must be voted into the club, which carries an implied expectation of maintaining its traditions in cooperation with other members. The breakdown of consensus represented by the Philadelphia and Washington ordinations was decried because it symbolized a challenge to the authority of the House of Bishops and hence to every member of it.

Those who stay within the bounds of collegiality, however, can claim the full support and authority of the House. Pressure to conform to the norms of the brotherhood is intense, and the norms are enforced by resolutions of disapproval or censure against those who act on their own. Members protect their own authority by guarding the authority of the group, both by conforming to its norms and by swiftly isolating and punishing those who challenge them. Mechanisms for accomplishing this were elaborated in the controversies surrounding Bishop Pike in the 1960s, and employed repeatedly in the struggle over women's ordination in the 1970s. This coercive aspect of collegiality becomes apparent only when controversy strikes, because the norms and boundaries of acceptable behavior within the House of Bishops (and the Episcopal Church as a whole) are very broad. Toleration and pride in the *via media* are practically articles of Anglican faith; they are certainly hallmarks of Episcopal identity. But when the authority of the brotherhood has been challenged because someone has broken "the rules" in some previously unthinkable way, collegiality is invoked and bishops are censured.

In both the Pike and Philadelphia censure actions, official statements focused on the challenge to authority rather than on the substantive issues that called for redefining the system's rules and boundaries. Bishop Pike's primary offenses involved expressing unconventional theological views and pressing the issue of women in the diaconate, but the censure in 1966 was justified in terms of the effect of his behavior on the perceived authority of the church: "We would disassociate ourselves from many of his utterances as being irresponsible on the part of one holding the office and trust that he shares with us." To most of the bishops, Pike's affirmation of "loyalty to the Doctrine, Discipline and Worship of this Church and expressed concern for the *episcopal brotherhood he shares with us*" meant he would play by the familiar rules in the future. They felt betrayed and deeply resented the fact that he continued to act independently, even provocatively.[10]

One result of the Bishop Pike affair was that fresh attention was paid to the legal limits on bishops' actions. An Advisory Committee on Theological Freedom and Social Responsibilities—chaired by Bishop Stephen Bayne and generally know as the Bayne Committee—was set to exploring issues the Pike controversy had raised. The primary focus was on the church's response to concerns about theological orthodoxy and heresy, but the Bayne Committee report dealt with authority issues as well. Presented to the 1967 Convention along with legislation making it very difficult to initiate "heresy trials," it articulated a framework for collegial behavior and for the bishops' response to those who moved beyond prevailing norms in actions as well as words. Of particular importance for the future was its recommendation distinguishing between censure and disassociation:

> Without censuring or condemning any individual for his ideas, the Church may find it necessary, on occasion, to disassociate itself publicly from theological views which it considers to be seriously subversive of essential Christian truths.[11]

This distinction drew on the language and concepts of the 1966 resolution about Bishop Pike and demonstrated a typically Anglican aversion to theological dogmatism. Although the 1967 Bayne Committee report referred solely to theological teaching, disassociation became an additional strategy for enforcing broad norms of episcopal behavior.

Reacting to the Philadelphia ordinations in 1974, the bishops again focused not on what had been done but on the authority (or lack thereof) for such action. The primary offense was ordaining women to the priesthood, but the censure related to violations of collegiality which "deprived others in the Church of their proper and appointed functions."[12] This focus on order and shared authority, made as explicit in the 1975 statement of censure as it had been implicit in the O'Hare statement decrying the bishops' actions in Philadelphia, was also given clear expression in the intervening report of the Board of Inquiry:

> The basic doctrinal question is not simply whether women should be ordained...but rather whether this Church's understanding of the nature of the Church and the authority of the episcopate permits individual bishops, by appealing solely to their consciences, to usurp the proper functions of other duly constituted authorities in this Church.[13]

In both the Pike and Philadelphia cases, the censure statements attempted to distinguish between the primary offense and the challenge to order and authority implicit in the violation of collegiality, asserting that it was only the latter which was being censured. The Pike statement was careful to acknowledge the value of reinterpreting traditional doctrines in contemporary forms, while the Philadelphia statement began with a reaffirmation of the bishops' majority support for ordaining women. The statements seem to be saying, "We're working on these same issues, but the tactics you have chosen are unacceptable because you are not acting in concert with the rest of us." Both documents disclaimed any intent to make a legal statement (which might prejudice a future ecclesiastical trial), but nevertheless focused on a legalistic concern for order, not on the issues of theology or the place of women which gave rise to the offending bishops' actions. These crises in the life of the church were defined as challenges to the collective authority of the bishops. On the surface, the problem seemed to be the challenge to their authority, not the substantive *nature* of the challenge.

In the absence of a formal hierarchy among bishops—the Presiding Bishop has authority only over national church staff—any challenge to authority is experienced as threatening to all. The pattern of reaction to such challenges demonstrates the degree to which the authority, power, and status of individual bishops is perceived as being dependent upon the authority, power, and status of the group. Consequent upon this relationship is the importance of consensus within the church's ordained leadership. On any matter of controversy, democratic majorities are not enough and unanimity is sought. Bishops who "break ranks" by departing from the prevailing standard, however conscientiously, are disciplined—informally through isolation and personal pressure, or formally by disassociating from their views, decrying their actions, voting to censure, or pursuing legal action.

Even the apparently inconsistent toleration of bishops who refused to accept the church's decision to ordain women actually confirms this theory of authority by consensus. The Port St. Lucie statement on conscience signified a consensus among bishops that on this particular point the church's canon law, though duly enacted by the General Convention, need not be honored: "It is oversimplifying to demand obedience to the canon [on women's ordination] just as one does for every other canon," declared the bishops in 1977.[14] Bishops who defied this canon for reasons of conscience, and thus departed from the new norm about ordaining women established by the whole church, would not be considered as violating the collegiality of the House of Bishops. The interpretation and exercise of authority and collegiality, therefore, was fluid; the same behavior decried in one instance could be warmly tolerated in another. Collegiality became a convenient screen behind which to act on perplexing matters, especially those issues—such as the place of women—which directly challenged traditional power arrangements and authority structures of church and society. Consensus and collegiality could be used to legitimize otherwise inconsistent actions. Those bishops who participated in the Philadelphia ordinations did so as a matter of conscience, but in their case conscience was not considered a valid reason for acting individually in disregard of canonical process; their actions were condemned as invalid and a violation of episcopal collegiality. After 1976, collegiality was invoked again as a bulwark against schism and a delaying tactic in the expansion of the ordained ministry, this time by linking collegiality with a toleration of the refusal of some bishops to ordain women for the reason of conscience.

The Traditionalist Resistance

"Tradition" has several meanings within the context of the church. Anglicans have long agreed that Scripture, tradition, and reason (reason sometimes understood as incorporating experience) together constitute the source of authority for their faith. Defining and interpreting tradition is necessarily a complex and never-ending process, and the conflict over the ordination of women is a major contemporary example of this process: proponents hold that the tradition supports this development because of the gospel's promise of freedom and wholeness for all, while opponents believe the maleness of the twelve disciples named in the New Testament establishes an unalterable tradition of male priesthood. Proponents of women's ordination resent the use of the term "traditionalist" by opponents, with its implication that only the latter value the historic faith. For the sake of convenience, however, "traditionalist" is used here as shorthand to designate those who adhere to interpretations of that historic faith which have been "traditional" (in the sense of that which is usually practiced) in the past, of which a central feature is a male priesthood.

The political struggles in the Episcopal Church surrounding the ordination of women, first to the priesthood and later to the episcopate, were the catalyst that brought together several traditionalist organizations in the early and mid-1970s, and again in the late 1980s. A number of organizations had served those dissatisfied with the direction of the Episcopal Church in the 1970s, some of whom eventually left it altogether. The subsequent experience of those potentially schismatic groups—of continuing conflict and further splintering—suggests that they were united in their opposition to what was happening in the Episcopal Church, but not in their vision of an alternative.

Opposition to the ordination of women was the major unifying force for traditionalists in the 1970s, but they were troubled by other issues also. Church historian Donald Armentrout has assembled information about many traditionalist groups and publications in that period; for eleven of them, his data is complete enough to identify and compare the issues that concerned them. Eight distinguishable contemporary issues appeared in differing mixes for each group: the ordination of women, the revision of the Book of Common Prayer, religious orthodoxy and the authority of Scripture, divorce, abortion, sexual morality, homosexuality, and secular politics. All eleven groups opposed the ordination of women. Eight explicitly opposed any liberalization of teaching or practice about abortion or divorce. Seven opposed the direction and scope of the prayer book revision process. Six opposed liberal tendencies in theology, particularly in relation to biblical authority. Five were concerned with changes in traditional sexual morality, while three explicitly opposed homosexuality. Two expressed a nationalistic political conservatism with racist overtones.[15]

This cluster of issues characterized traditionalist groups in the 1970s. The numbers should not be taken as a rank ordering of issues, because there is considerable overlap: many would subsume issues of divorce, abortion, and homosexuality under the general rubric of sexual morality, while some would assume opposition to liberal theology to be implicit in opposition to prayer book revision. Women's ordination, however, holds a clearly distinguishable position in the agenda of all eleven groups and traditionalist publications detailed in Armentrout's study. In fact, it was also opposed by the other twenty organizations and splinter churches he studied—a remarkable consistency given the fact that it was not a study about women and the church, but about schism. Clearly, changes in women's place do upset traditional church structures. The ordination of women proved to be a very concrete issue around which traditionalist coalitions could be formed, functioning as a lightning rod for dissent, a rallying symbol around which resistance to change might gather.

No study such as Armentrout's has yet been done of traditionalist groups functioning in the Episcopal Church in the 1980s and 1990s, but a brief look at three of the most prominent reveals the same cluster of issues. Two were continuations of groups established in the earlier period of controversy: the Prayer Book Society and the Evangelical and Catholic Mission; the third, Episcopalians United for Revelation, Renewal, and Reformation, was organized in 1987.

The Prayer Book Society is the oldest and most extreme of the traditionalist groups.[16] Founded in 1971 as the Society for the Preservation of the Book of Common Prayer, it continued through the 1980s and into the 1990s as an aggressive, well-financed organization opposing changes to the 1928 prayer book, championing political and theological conservatism, and challenging Episcopal Church leaders on issues ranging from ecumenism to Nicaragua to homosexuality. After the revision of the prayer book was approved in 1976, it lobbied for the continued use of the 1928 book in the Episcopal Church and in the "continuing churches" which broke away after the 1976 Convention.

Although the ordination of women was not officially on its list of issues, in practice the Prayer Book Society joined other traditionalists in opposing this development. Long-time president Jerome Politzer described the ordination of women as "a violation of the intention of the sacrament to confer the order of priesthood or episcopacy in accordance with instructions of our Lord and the teachings of the scripture,"[17] and it launched a major effort to block consents to a woman in the episcopate in 1988. A sustained project in the late-1980s was a campaign against Bishop John Spong of Newark, attacking his liberal theological views and approach to sexual ethics and attempting to bring him to trial for heresy.

The Evangelical and Catholic Mission (ECM) existed for fifteen years, from 1976 until 1990, as "a fellowship of orthodox clergy and laity." Bishop Stanley Atkins was chair from its founding until his retirement in 1981; he was succeeded by the next bishop of Eau Claire, William C. Wantland, who was followed in turn by bishops Robert E. Terwilliger of Dallas, William Stevens of Fond du Lac, and Clarence Pope of Fort Worth. ECM was organized soon after the 1976 General Convention to create a "supportive ecclesial entity *within* the Episcopal Church" for those who opposed the church's decision to ordain women to the priesthood and episcopate. Its organizing statement also pledged to maintain "the standards of the New Testament and the universal Christian tradition in matters of behavior and morality." This involved opposition to the church's "relaxed" interpretation about abortion, its "watered-down" regulations for divorce and remarriage, and its failure to require "high moral standards." It was evangelical in its emphasis on scriptural authority, and catholic in its veneration of "universal Christian tradition" and the teaching authority of bishops.[18]

This group was intentionally not schismatic; it sought instead to preserve within the Episcopal Church aspects of the apostolic tradition which seemed to its members to be endangered. Like other early traditionalist groups, the Evangelical and Catholic Mission organized around the issue of the ordination of women to the priesthood and the episcopate, but had other concerns as well. In a 1988 statement from its bishops, most of the issues identified at their 1976 founding were cited again as signs of the "final crisis" of the church:

> At the root of the present crisis is the rejection of the authority of God's revelation of Himself and His will...[expressed in] the challenge to the central authority of Holy Scripture, the denial of Jesus Christ as the full, perfect and sufficient self-revelation of God,...proposals to rewrite the language of the Bible and liturgical prayer, decay of marital discipline,...pressure to abandon the received standards of chastity,...the purported admission of women to priestly and episcopal orders.[19]

Although it officially accepted the 1979 prayer book, the creation of supplemental liturgies using inclusive language was seen as a threat to traditional formulations of Scripture and theology, in which the masculinity of language and imagery, especially the metaphors of God as father and king and Jesus as lord, were understood to be essential aspects of revealed truth. Opposition to the inclusive language movement was consistent with the commitment to a masculine priesthood and episcopate, and was soon part of the agenda of other traditionalists as well. The Evangelical and Catholic Mission dismantled itself in 1990 to make way for another traditionalist entity, the Episcopal Synod of America.

In the fall of 1987 another group of traditionalists announced the formation of a new organization to be called Episcopalians United for Revelation, Renewal, and Reformation.[20] Its purpose was avowedly political—"to influence the structures of the Episcopal Church"—and in its first year it expended considerable energy and money in lobbying activities related to the 1988 General Convention in Detroit.

Episcopalians United was evangelical in focus, lacking the heavy influence of Anglo-Catholic attitudes that characterized the Evangelical and Catholic Mission. Its founding chairperson was Harry Griffith, then head of the Anglican Fellowship of Prayer and founder of the Bible Reading Fellowship; board members were connected with the renewal movement and the newly-accredited evangelical seminary in Pittsburgh, Trinity Episcopal School for Ministry. Within this evangelical coalition there were both opponents and proponents of the ordination of women. Episcopalians United formally supported ordaining women to the priesthood, but did express opposition to the consecration of women as bishops.

Except for the compromise position on ordaining women, its agenda coincided almost exactly with the cluster of traditionalist issues that had concerned earlier groups: the authority of Scripture, sexual morality, abortion, divorce, homosexuality, inclusive language, and a general political conservatism. These issues were presented in evangelical terms, as five affirmations and five developments to be opposed. Affirmed were the centrality of Jesus Christ, revealed in Scripture and confessed in the creeds; winning the world for Christ; the primacy of scriptural authority; the sanctity of marriage; and the sanctity of all human life. The group opposed the ordination of non-celibate homosexuals; normalization of homosexuality as an alternative lifestyle; sexual relations outside marriage; liberalization of the Episcopal Church's position on abortion; and inclusive language that "changes the nature of God."[21]

Like the Prayer Book Society and the Evangelical and Catholic Mission, Episcopalians United often expressed its views in dramatic rhetoric designed to alarm readers and encourage financial contributions. A typical recruitment letter echoed other traditionalists' declarations about the crisis facing the church:

> The future of the Episcopal Church in this country is at best uncertain and at worst in grave danger....Our Church has been under constant assault for more than twenty-five years from a steady stream of radical groups who have forced change after change.

They were quick to assign the blame for this state of affairs, identifying the "radical groups" assaulting the church as follows:

> Social activists in the '60's. Liberal liturgical thinkers and radical feminists in the '70's. Today gay and lesbian lobbies are trying to take control.[22]

In a book review discussing the abortion issue, the newsletter of the National Organization of Episcopalians for Life (an anti-abortion group with ties to Episcopalians United) made similar charges:

> Since the end of the Second World War...the foundational values upon which we base our most important moral decisions have disappeared. The process has been insidious and gradual, taking many by surprise. The Civil Rights Movement, the upheaval of the 60's, the

Sexual Revolution, and the Feminist Movement have caused many to reject the moral constraints which governed past generations.[23]

Traces of racism appear here, in pejorative references to the civil rights movement and "social activists" of the 1960s. Blatant racism was no longer acceptable among Episcopalians, but it persisted below the surface in combination with fear of other groups promoting social change.

Declaring war on all such enemies of the faith, Episcopalians United and fellow traditionalists—linked by their acute distress over changing roles and relationships—manifested the polarization in the church and in the rest of American society, which deepened as the twentieth century neared its end. The complex foundations of this distress would become even more visible when women moved from the priesthood into the episcopate.

Chapter 12

The Struggle for Unity

J n 1985, a major transition in Episcopal Church leadership occurred which had vital implications for women and the ordained ministry. After a dozen years under the conservative Presiding Bishop John Allin, the bishops were apparently ready to return to the liberal tradition of his two predecessors. At the General Convention meeting in Anaheim, the House of Bishops elected Edmond L. Browning to succeed retiring Allin as Presiding Bishop, and the House of Deputies promptly confirmed that choice. Although the Presiding Bishop has no executive powers outside the staff of the Episcopal Church Center, the position carries great moral authority as the "first among equals" and its incumbent does much to set the tone for the church as a whole. Browning was as staunch a supporter of ordaining women as Allin had been an opponent, and his election marked a new stage in the acceptance of women's ordination. The House of Bishops continued to honor its "conscience clause," but a new era of active support had begun within the House of Bishops and indeed throughout the church, and the pace of developments quickened.

Leaders throughout the Anglican Communion were trying to brace for the disruption sure to follow the ordination of women to the episcopate. When the Lambeth Conference met in 1978 it had to face the fact of women priests and the likelihood of women bishops, since four provinces of the Anglican Communion (Hong Kong and Macao, Canada, New Zealand, and the United States) had already begun ordaining women to the priesthood. Lacking the structural authority to allow—or disallow—the ordination of women as a communion-wide practice, the Lambeth Conference instead sought mechanisms for maintaining relationships between provinces despite opposing views and practices.

While calling for acceptance of churches which ordain women, Lambeth urged "that they respect the convictions of those provinces and dioceses which do not." It also recommended consultation with other provinces and "overwhelming support" within the province and diocese concerned prior to consecrating a woman as bishop, "lest the bishop's office should become a cause of disunity instead of a focus of unity." Like the authority of the Lambeth Conference itself, that of its member bishops is chiefly moral and symbolic (a "focus") rather than structural or juridical (an "instrument").[1]

Responding to the Lambeth recommendation about consultation, the House of Bishops in 1985 voted 112 to 31 not to oppose the consecration of a woman as a bishop, and the Convention as a whole authorized a committee to study the issue of women in the episcopate and to "make recommendations concerning the ecumenical and ecclesiological considerations."[2] The following year Presiding Bishop Browning raised the issue while attending his first meeting of the primates of the Anglican Communion. From that 1986 meeting, the primates issued a statement interpreting the recommended consultation with other provinces as a dialogue rather than as a seeking of permission to ordain women and asked the Archbishop of Canterbury, Robert Runcie, to appoint a working party to study the matter further.[3]

As the institutional processes leading to women in the episcopate gained momentum, traditionalists became increasingly alarmed. Shortly after the primates' meeting, three Evangelical and Catholic Mission bishops met with Bishop Browning to discuss ways of accommodating traditionalist concerns if and when a woman became bishop. At the next House of Bishops' meeting, in San Antonio in September 1986, Bishop Clarence Pope of Fort Worth made an impassioned plea for the protection of traditionalists. Following his remarks and extended discussion of their study materials on women in the episcopate, the bishops voted 78 to 50 to reaffirm their earlier resolution on not withholding consent to the consecration of a woman as bishop, but noted the need for restraint until after the 1988 Lambeth Conference.[4] The intention of the majority to proceed was clear, but a number of bishops who supported the principle of ordaining women were hesitant in view of the traditionalists' strong opposition.

The threat of an international incident colored this meeting. A conflict between a traditionalist parish in Tulsa, Oklahoma and the bishop and council of that diocese had resulted in the deposition of the priest and civil litigation over the church property. Bishop Graham Leonard of London, an opponent of women's ordination, announced that he was "in communion" with this parish and would send a suffragan bishop to confirm some of its members, leading to a flurry of alarmed consultations among the diocesan bishop, Presiding Bishop Browning, and Archbishop Runcie.

During the 1986 House of Bishops meeting, the problem of such renegade churches was discussed alongside women in the episcopate. On the last day, echoing their response to retired Bishop Chambers's 1977 forays into schismatic congregations, the bishops adopted a statement of episcopal jurisdiction condemning the performance of episcopal functions in any but one's own diocese without the expressed invitation of the diocesan bishop.[5] For all their confusion over how to deal with divisive issues, the bishops revealed no ambiguity on the subject of protecting their territory: the vote was unanimous.

In May 1987, the Anglican Consultative Council met in Singapore in a climate of increasing urgency. Since the process of accepting women in orders was proceeding at dramatically different rates in different provinces, members questioned how long the Anglican Communion would be able to live with its disagreements. They identified two major theological issues in the struggle: Can women properly exercise "headship," representing Christ in the church? How is the historical development of the church's faith and order to be discerned, tested, and accepted?

That summer the Primates' Working Party began circulating its own report, "Women and the Episcopate" which went more deeply into the question of provincial autonomy and interdependence and the theological principle of "reception" as a process in the development of the church's faith and order. Reception, a concept fraught with potential for misinterpretation, refers to the historical reality that new developments in the life of the church go through a process of being received and accepted; some are ultimately rejected, and until acceptance is complete, at least within a discrete ecclesial entity, any new development has a "provisional" quality about it. The concepts of reception and provisionality would assume great importance in future discussions concerning the ordination of women.

The Potential for Schism

The nature of the conflict was shifting, because the focus had changed. It had moved away from whether women should be priests and bishops to the problem of unity: some parts of the church were ordaining women while others were firmly against it. Although provinces that did not yet ordain women continued to debate its legitimacy, the committees appointed to study it concentrated most of their attention on unity rather than on women's ordination, on polity rather than theology. Following the 1978 Lambeth principle of respect for the convictions of both sides, they sought structural and pastoral mechanisms for containing the conflict within the institution.

The 1977 formation of break-away traditionalist groups in the United States and Canada and the 1986 Oklahoma incident had already demonstrated that the ordination of women was so divisive an issue that it could lead to schism, a prospect Anglicans abhor—for financial as well as theological reasons. Schism invariably leads to protracted disputes about ownership of church buildings and other property, and to questions about continued pension coverage and other benefits for clergy who separate themselves from the church which administers the pension and insurance funds. With segments of the church straining in apparently opposite directions, keeping the conflict within the family assumed a high priority for those charged with maintaining the unity of the church.

In effect, strategists on both sides struggled to press the Anglican image of the *via media* to new limits, yet a dignified middle way seemed out of the question when church members held mutually exclusive positions about its ordained ministry. Since theological accommodation appeared impossible, structural and pastoral compromises were needed, and the *via media* image was invested with new significance as an all-embracing inclusivity and toleration for contradiction. This approach was inherently problematic, however, because the ministry had so many structural and pastoral ramifications. Disagreements over the nature of the "real presence" of Christ in the Eucharist need not prevent people from joining together at the altar rail, but differences over the validity of the ordination of the person at the altar do. In relation to ordaining women, theology and practice are so intertwined that tolerance for diversity of belief entails confronting practices that threaten the unity of the church. Like the ritualist controversies of the nineteenth century that wrenched the fabric of Anglicanism, the ordination of women placed profound pressure on the institutional structures of the church and the outcome was unpredictable.

As these conflicts intensified, it became more difficult to sustain dialogue and the appearance of unity. Within the Episcopal Church, as more people experienced and warmed to the ministry of ordained women, the shrinking minority in opposition redoubled its efforts to halt what it regarded as destruction of the church's historic ministry. Positions hardened as supporters of women's ordination grew impatient with the recurrent opposition which drained energy from other more urgent concerns, while traditionalists felt themselves increasingly isolated and powerless to reverse the process. The 1977 House of Bishops' statement of conscience, with its 1978 Lambeth corollary calling both sides to respect mutually exclusive convictions, had poured oil on troubled waters without eliminating the cause of the trouble.

After ten years, the looming prospect of a woman bishop in the United States threatened finally to shatter the smooth surface of seeming unity. When the House of Bishops met in St. Charles, Illinois in 1987, the study committee on the episcopate created by the 1985 General Convention recommended that "this Church proceed to ordain women as bishops as soon as they are duly elected and approved." The bishops voted to approve and recommend the report to diocesan standing committees and the Lambeth Conference "as a statement of the mind of the majority."[6] When a few bishops protested vigorously, not only to the report and its approval but also to the fact that the study committee had consisted entirely of supporters of women's ordination, they were permitted to prepare an "alternate view" which would be distributed along with the study committee's report.

This "Alternate View" was prepared by leaders of the Evangelical and Catholic Mission, then chaired by William C. Wantland of Eau Claire, and was eventually endorsed by twelve diocesan bishops (David Ball of Albany, William Wantland of Eau Claire, William Stevens of Fond du Lac, Clarence Pope of Fort Worth, Harry Shipps of Georgia, Robert Witcher of Long Island, Donald Parsons of Quincy,

Victor Rivera of San Joaquin, Calvin Schofield of Southeast Florida, Luc Garnier of Haiti, Bernardo Botero of Colombia, and A. Donald Davies of the American Convocation in Europe) and by twenty-three retired bishops.[7] Their report was candid in acknowledging two points of view among those opposing the ordination of women to the priesthood and episcopate. One allowed for the possibility at some time in the future, when there was a consensus of the whole church in support of such an innovation, perhaps determined by an ecumenical council; the other regarded ordaining women as impossible now or ever because the male priesthood was part of the "divinely given Order of the Church" and no mortal could alter it. While proponents of these differing views could make common cause in opposing the imminent prospect of a woman bishop, the fact that their foundational arguments were contradictory signalled the same potential for future fragmentation that had plagued the potentially schismatic groups in the 1970s.

Nonetheless, this "Alternate View" boldly articulated a traditionalist alliance, building on the message Bishop Pope had brought to the 1986 meeting about the traditionalists' need for a permanently protected position within the church. Its most significant statement from a strategic point of view was a promise and warning of continued resistance and ecclesiastical disobedience:

> Adherents of both points of view are seriously distressed by the current situation in the American Church and are at one in their loyalty to the Order of the Church, to the point of a willingness, albeit somewhat reluctant, to engage in conscientious disobedience to the institutions of the Episcopal Church should that become necessary to preserve the Order of the Church....The patience of many with the crisis has been strained to the breaking-point.[8]

In response to this threat of disruption if their position was not afforded special protection—a threat raised by Bishop Pope in 1986 and articulated even more intensely by Bishop Wantland in 1987—the bishops authorized Presiding Bishop Browning to seek a pastoral resolution of the apparent impasse. He appointed a committee of four bishops, four priests, and four lay people, which included three women (one a priest, the Rev. Gay Jennings) and nine men, evenly divided between proponents and opponents of women's ordination.

In describing the work of the committee, which was to prepare rec-ommendations to the next General Convention, Jennings observed that the Evangelical and Catholic Mission agenda—the creation of a separate enclave for traditionalists within the Episcopal Church—dominated because it took time for the supporters of women's ordi-nation to get to know one another and develop an effective method of negotiating with the opponents. She believed the work of the sup-porters was hampered as a result.[9]

The Episcopal Visitors Controversy

The dialogue committee's report triggered a major controversy. It was mailed to bishops and deputies, with a letter of endorsement from Browning, just two weeks before the Convention assembled. Consequently, almost no one was prepared for it, there was no op-portunity for study or consultation with parish or diocesan leaders, and many deputies had not even read it before leaving for Detroit. As its contents became known, the Presiding Bishop was deluged with calls, telegrams, and letters of protest; additional protests from indi-viduals and groups of clergy and laity continued to be delivered to bishops and deputies throughout the Convention week, as news of the proposal filtered back home. The House of Bishops had been wrestling with the traditionalists' insistent requests at its interim meetings, but members of the House of Deputies had no such back-ground, and no pressure of collegiality to encourage accommoda-tion.

The heart of the controversy was a proposal for "episcopal visi-tors," who were to be traditionalist bishops permitted to minister to like-minded parishes in any diocese whose bishop was either a woman or a man who had consented to the consecration of a woman as bishop. Supporters of the ordination of women objected strenu-ously that this called into question the validity of women's orders and amounted to a form of discrimination that would not be toler-ated in the case of, for example, a bishop of color. Others objected to compromising the principle of geographical jurisdiction by permit-ting "alien" bishops to function in other bishops' dioceses.

It became clear that the resolutions as proposed had no chance of passage in the House of Deputies, and a drafting committee was as-signed to revise them. The results were presented, first to the bishops and then to the deputies, as Substitute Resolutions B22s and B23s. The first addressed the jurisdictional problem by making the appointment of a "visitor" dependent upon a request from the local bishop, and set a time limit of six years; it easily passed the House of Bishops (138-28 with 5 abstentions) but barely survived a vote by orders in the House of Deputies (with a three-vote margin in the clergy order and only one in the lay order).[10]

The companion resolution on ordination and deployment, B23s, meant to provide some protection for individuals experiencing discrimination in the ordination or deployment process, was also approved by the bishops. But it was complex and ambiguous, trying to handle two very different problems with one solution: the difficulties faced by women seeking ordination or employment in the few remaining traditionalist dioceses, and the pressures experienced by traditionalist men in parishes and dioceses supportive of the ordination of women. To protect women in traditionalist dioceses, it recommended the so-called Montgomery Plan, named for its originator, Bishop James Montgomery of Chicago. This approach enabled women whose bishops were traditionalists to be ordained by other bishops, and it had been affirmed by the 1987 House of Bishops as "an appropriate model for bishops who cannot yet in conscience ordain women."[11] But it was a proposal most traditionalists found abhorrent, since it would facilitate the ordination of women in dioceses where the bishop was opposed to it.

To deal with the problems experienced by traditionalists outside their own enclaves, B23s contained language so reminiscent of the statement of conscience that many supporters of women's ordination *and* of due process and canonical discipline were adamantly opposed. Disagreements were sharp and feelings ran high on all sides. The situation was exacerbated by tense debate during concurrent hearings on the Convention's consent to the election of an outspoken traditionalist, John-David Schofield, as bishop of San Joaquin. When the election of a bishop occurs within three months prior to a General Convention, the usual consent process is set aside and the two houses of Convention simply vote instead. Because of Schofield's opposition to women's ordination, his affiliation with an Orthodox monastery, and charges of impropriety in the election process, the vote in the House of Deputies was preceded by several days of rancorous hearings, which heightened many traditionalists' sense of being isolated and besieged and fueled their desire for structural protection within the church. In the end, the second resolution was so heavily amended, each side trying to protect its own interests, that it was resoundingly defeated.[12]

Ever since the 1977 Port St. Lucie meeting, the statement of conscience had symbolized the divide between traditionalists and supporters of women's ordination, and between the bishops and the rest of the church. It contained phrases that might theoretically have been used to protect supporters as well as opponents of women's ordination, but in practice it had only been invoked on behalf of the opposition. Many people rejected its authority as an attempt by the bishops to undermine the clear canonical intent of the 1976 General Convention decision. Traditionalists, on the other hand, as well as many bishops anxious about averting schism, used the statement to claim that the canonical change allowing women's ordination was only permissive, not mandatory. This interpretive strategy enabled them to assert that conscientious refusal to recognize the ministries of properly ordained women, or to admit women to the ordination process at all, did not actually violate the discipline of the church.

The episcopal visitors proposal was initiated by traditionalists in an attempt both to guarantee and to expand this area of exemption from the church's discipline. The dialogue committee's report had begun by citing the conscience statement as the basis for its work and recommendations, and the guarantee sought by traditionalists would have been a Convention resolution legitimizing a conscience clause. Resolution B23, even in its substitute form, would have had this effect, directing that "where clergy and people cannot accept the decision of the Church to ordain women, their position be respected by those who do accept this Church's decision." Its resounding rejection by the House of Deputies signalled the growing impatience of the rest of the church over the House of Bishops' willingness to compromise the church's discipline and witness about women for the sake of collegiality and superficial unity. As their numbers declined, traditionalists became understandably more and more anxious about their position and more insistent in their demands for protection, but accommodating them seemed to supporters to be holding the rest of the church hostage to the convictions of a few.

Traditionalists sought to expand their exemption from the ordination canon by establishing mechanisms that would insulate them from the actions of the rest of the church. So long as women were ordained only to the diaconate and the priesthood, traditionalists could avoid conflict either passively by staying away from places where ordained women were ministering or actively by excluding ordained women or women seeking ordination from the life of traditionalist parishes or dioceses. But a woman bishop would have a place in the ecclesiastical authority structure that would make avoidance impossible—how would one know, for example, whether a male priest celebrating the Eucharist had been ordained by a woman bishop, which to a traditionalist would make his priesthood and that Eucharist invalid? Traditionalists sought structural protection from this uncertainty, which to them represented a contamination of the historic ministry.

The possibility that there would soon be a woman bishop had been the original catalyst for the episcopal visitors measure, but it was designed to apply to dioceses with male bishops as well. It authorized traditionalist congregations to request episcopal services from a bishop who shared their views if their diocesan bishop did not. This was to be done through the Presiding Bishop, and in the final version of the resolution the permission of the diocesan bishop was explicitly required. In wording apparently meant to appeal to supporters of women's ordination by reiterating the church's commitment to women in ministry, the resolution also specified that "this provision is only to be used for the transition and incorporation of women into all ordained ministries and is not otherwise applicable." It could not be applied, for example, to avoid a visitation from a bishop whose liturgical style or politics did not please a congregation, or to discriminate on the basis of race or ethnicity. But it did sanction a psychological and spiritual transfer of pastoral allegiance away from the diocesan bishop, and the breaking of fellowship such a move entails, and it plainly implied that continued discrimination against women was permissible.

Technically, the resolution in its final form was completely redundant and unnecessary; psychologically, however, it had immense importance. Congregations have always been free to seek their diocesan bishop's permission to invite a visiting bishop to perform episcopal functions such as confirmations and ordinations, and such visits are commonplace for a wide variety of reasons. The significance of the resolution was that it would tie this freedom directly to the conflict over ordaining women. Those supporting episcopal visitors hoped it would serve to sanction their dissent from the principles and their noncompliance with the canons regarding ordination, creating a special enclave within the church in which opposition to the inclusion of women in its ministry could be fostered without interference.

The proposal also presupposed that traditionalists would never change their minds, and "pastoral concern" took preeminence over theological debate. The traditionalists were not looking simply for a grandfather clause to protect a dwindling few, but also for a means to promote their views from within the church. In 1986, Bishop Pope had asked the bishops for "a mode of accommodation for our position...which will allow for the *nurturing and growth* of those who are called to our position."[13] The episcopal visitors resolution was thus a faulty attempt to respond to the minority's request without doing violence to the structures of the church or the convictions of the majority of its members. In pursuit of the ideal of unity, and despairing of resolving the conflict through theological debate, bishops on both sides of the issue spoke increasingly of the need for a "pastoral" solution, a way to live together in Christian fellowship despite a fundamental contradiction.

A pastoral solution was certainly a noble ideal, but it collided repeatedly with the church's structure and polity. The search for mechanisms to allow diversity of belief and practice regarding the ordination of women was repeatedly frustrated, and the term "pastoral" appeared to take on the chameleon quality of "collegiality" in the bishops' debates. Moreover, a system which encouraged conformity to the canons in some places but not in others created a confusing patchwork in which no one felt safe. Women felt ill-treated in traditionalist strongholds where aspirants were denied access to the ordination process and those wishing the ministry of ordained women were constantly thwarted; traditionalist clergy felt ill-treated elsewhere, passed over for appointments, with few employment prospects. The 1988 attempt to institutionalize a "pastoral" solution through the episcopal visitors resolution simply didn't work.

As a result, no one was happy. Despite the well-intentioned efforts of church leaders to accommodate the minority, traditionalists' needs were fundamentally opposed to those of the majority in ways that rendered true compromise virtually impossible. As at O'Hare after the Philadelphia ordinations and in Detroit in 1988 as the prospect of a woman bishop loomed, two different perceptions of reality were still in conflict: either women could be (and had been) ordained or they could not be (and would never be). The institutional structure was stretched to its limit in trying to contain both perceptions, and few believed this situation could continue indefinitely. While bishops struggled to maintain structural unity, clergy and people on all sides were losing patience. In a gloomy commentary on the defeat of B23s, the General Convention newsletter of the Evangelical and Catholic Mission offered its reading of the signs of the times:

> General Convention of the Episcopal Church has now demonstrated convincingly its unwillingness to insure a permanent place for those clergy and congregations unable to accept the ordination of women. This is the clear message that has emerged from the lengthy deliberations over proposals designed to prevent possible schism in the wake of future consecrations of women bishops.[14]

Most supporters of the ordination of women were also discouraged and angry about the passage of episcopal visitors measure; to them it seemed to signal a retreat, institutionalizing discrimination against ordained women and thus diluting the church's witness to and about all women. In practice, nothing ever came of the resolution; as adopted, the measure was administratively vague. An effort by members of the Episcopal Women's Caucus to develop an implementation process that would protect women and promote dialogue also came to nothing, and the continued scattered conflicts between traditionalist parishes and their bishops were handled informally. The resolution called for annual reports from the Presiding Bishop to the House of Bishops, but this was quietly ignored. There was, in fact, no way to provide the kind of structural protection the traditionalists sought, and the 1988 Convention demonstrated that the division symbolized by the ordination of women was still deep.

The Lambeth Conference, 1988

The Lambeth Conference of 1988 followed immediately after the General Convention. Some bishops flew directly from Detroit to London; few had had time to analyze what the Convention had finally done about episcopal visitors or to gauge the response of people in their dioceses. The unworkability of the compromise was not yet apparent. Consequently, most American bishops approached the deliberations at Lambeth with an optimistic view of the possibilities for maintaining church unity across the great divide of opinion about women's ordination. They were able to report that the conflict, severe as it was, had not rent the American church asunder, and such reassurances certainly contributed to Lambeth's ability to take the next tentative steps in support of ordaining women.

The 1988 Lambeth Conference could not have been a source of much satisfaction to traditionalists. This conference of over five hundred diocesan bishops from the world-wide Anglican Communion is neither a governing body nor a legislative gathering, but its deliberations have always had considerable influence on the participating bishops and their home churches, and Lambeth 1988 included several features that increased the visibility and advanced the position of women in the church.

One of these was the unofficial presence of a "women's witnessing community," an international gathering of Anglican women organized by the Episcopal Women's Caucus in the United States with help from Australian, English, and other women's groups supporting the ordination of women. It provided educational programs, hospitality, and alternative worship for bishops, wives, and observers from around the world, keeping real women—including ordained women—before the bishops as they debated policy about women. As Vida Scudder and her Companions had witnessed unofficially from the sidelines, pressing the General Convention to attend to the needs of the poor, so women gathered outside Canterbury in an unprecedented public attempt to influence the Lambeth Conference. Unlike Scudder, the women who witnessed at Lambeth 1988 were deliberately raising the concerns not of the poor, but of themselves. As resistance to changes in women's roles intensified within traditionalist strongholds, more and more women found their voice, and their language was no longer deferential. As some gathered in England, others around the world joined them in prayer:

> God of our mothers, hear our prayer on behalf of the women witnessing at Lambeth to your love for all, to the needs of women throughout the world who seek justice, equality and peace, and to your call to women to serve you as laity, bishops, priests and deacons.[15]

In addition to this unofficial presence, there was also, for the first time, official participation of a few women within the conference structure. Bishops' wives were welcomed, housed with their husbands (at previous conferences they had had to sleep elsewhere), and provided with their own program during the conference—separate and unequal, but present to share daily impressions and comment on developments. Nine lay women from the Anglican Consultative Council were full participants in the conference, including Pamela P. Chinnis, the first female vice-president of the American House of Deputies and a long-time advocate of the ordination of women. Seven of twenty-six consultants to the conference were women, making a total of sixteen women who were official participants, along with the over five hundred bishops.

One of the official consultants, the Rev. Nan Arrington Peete, then a priest from the diocese of Indianapolis, was invited to address the conference session devoted to the ordination of women. Peete described her traditional Anglo-Catholic upbringing and ministry as rector of a large, inner-city parish; when she finished, she was given a standing ovation. The first person to rise was the Most Rev. Desmond Tutu, Archbishop of the Province of Southern Africa, who in earlier years had expressed the opinion held by many African bishops that the ordination of women was a peripheral issue diverting attention from the "real" work of the church. His shift to active support for women influenced many others, because of his international standing as a leader of the struggle against apartheid, a Nobel Peace Prize winner, and a universally beloved and revered spiritual leader.[16]

In an environment no longer totally masculine, Lambeth took some tentative steps to further the process of incorporating ordained women throughout the Anglican Communion. A resolution introduced by traditionalists asking provinces to refrain from ordaining women as bishops lost, while a resolution stating that women bishops would not destroy the unity of the Communion was overwhelmingly approved. It asked provinces to respect one another's differences while "maintaining the highest possible degree of communion," and asked Archbishop of Canterbury Robert Runcie to appoint a commission to monitor and encourage the process, and to devise principles for maintaining unity when a woman became bishop. Drawing on the American experience of trying to accommodate the traditionalists, the commission was to give particular attention to providing pastoral services for traditionalist clergy and congregations, using the episcopal visitors approach as a possible model.[17]

In 1988 Lambeth also wrestled with several other questions about authority raised by the conflict over the ordination of women. What relative weight should be given to the sources of Anglican authority—Scripture, tradition, and reason—in decision-making about women in the ordained ministry? Whose interpretations of these authorities is authoritative? In a communion of autonomous provinces, with no communion-wide mechanism for making binding decisions, what kind of authority do local decisions carry? What should be the balance between the individual and the collegial authority of bishops, and how does this relate to the role of other clergy and laity in church governance? Is an all-male group of primates truly representative of the whole communion? Is there any structure for appeal or ultimate authority for resolving intractable conflicts?

None of these questions had obvious answers, though the questions themselves reveal much about the peculiar identity of Anglicans. But a key to understanding the church's preoccupation with such questions lies in the link between women and the church's authority structures. Why was it that ordaining women, and particularly the prospect of a woman bishop, seemed to shake those structures to their foundations?

Part Four

Shaking the Foundations

T he schismatic potential of ordaining women, especially to the episcopate—what the traditionalists would call the church's "final crisis"—demonstrates that the subordination of women had been fundamental to the life of the Episcopal Church and its parent Anglican Communion. As women began to move out of their traditional places at the bottom of the hierarchical system, its institutional framework—the doctrinal, moral, and political structure of the church—was profoundly shaken.

Challenged to its foundations, the institution responded by trying to strengthen the structure. It used all the stabilizing tactics of bureaucracy: study commissions and tasks forces, international guidelines and consultations, definitions and redefinitions that might transform new problems into something the old structure could handle. Bishops and international commissions worried over who had the power to make what decisions, and cast these discussions in terms of collegiality, communion, autonomy, and authority.

The movement of women out of subordinate roles in church and in society challenged the hierarchical structures of both, in ways that everyone found difficult to address directly. At O'Hare the bishops had refused to speak with the women ordained in Philadelphia. Fifteen years later, the threat of schism precipitated by the consecration of a woman bishop would again be handled by closed-door bargaining among men. Though often unnamed and unspoken, even unspeakable, it was the steadfast refusal by women to remain in their "proper place" that precipitated each stage of the crisis. This difficulty in naming what was happening was compounded by what Presiding Bishop Browning would call a "great divide of consciousness," two world views in which contradictory meanings could be assigned to a common heritage of faith and practice. By keeping the focus on authority instead of talking about and with women, male church leaders and traditionalists could concentrate on stabilizing the existing male-dominated structures of power, instead of opening up those structures to women. Yet the pressure to incorporate women fully into the church's life proved irresistable.

Chapter 13

Women in the Episcopate

J ust weeks after the 1988 Lambeth Conference adjourned, a woman was called forth to join the long procession leading back to the apostles and forward into a new era in the church's life. On September 24, 1988, the diocese of Massachusetts elected fifty-eight-year-old Barbara Clementine Harris as suffragan bishop, to assist diocesan bishop David Johnson with administration and pastoral oversight of the large Boston-area diocese.

The election of any woman as bishop would have caused a stir; the election of this particular woman was a sensation because Barbara Harris did not match any previous norms for the American episcopate. An African American in an overwhelmingly white church, she had no college degree and had read for orders instead of attending seminary in a church that prided itself on a highly-educated clergy. Her primary pastoral ministry had taken place in a prison, in a church that considers the parish to be the primary locus of Christian life. She was divorced, in a church dismayed over the apparent collapse of traditional family structures. An outspoken advocate of the right to choice regarding abortion, and of the civil and ecclesiastical rights of gay men and lesbians, she preached boldly about oppression and economic injustice for the marginalized at home and abroad, in a church long identified with the affluent power structure of American society. And she had been the crucifer leading the procession at the Philadelphia ordinations in 1974, in a church that wanted very much to forget that pivotal event. The idea of this diminutive, elegant, gravel-voiced, sharp-tongued, funny, iconoclastic, professional radical joining the Anglican gentleman's society that was the House of Bishops stretched everyone's imagination.

Many women and men throughout the church—and in the wider society too, where the news was prominently carried in newspapers and television reports—rejoiced at her election; others shared John Throop's prediction that she "will demonstrate all the worst nightmares of what women in the episcopate will be like to the traditionalists."[1] The traditionalists immediately launched a campaign to try to prevent Harris's consecration. Consents were necessary from a majority of diocesan standing committees and diocesan bishops, and since so many people found something to criticize about Harris even apart from her gender, the outcome was uncertain.

The most vocal opposition came from the Prayer Book Society and from Episcopalians United, who criticized Harris's politics and support for women's issues. There were also attempts to discredit her personally through efforts to dredge up details about a youthful marriage and divorce, and the common anti-feminist tactic of labelling an independent women a lesbian. This label did not appear explicitly in print, at least in mainstream church publications, but it was the subject of widespread gossip and rumor, fueled by columns supporting lesbian and gay rights written while Harris was with *The Witness* magazine. The next year an English newspaper article demonstrated that such gossip had crossed the Atlantic. Discussing the decision of the Church of Ireland to ordain women to the priesthood, the traditionalist author described four deacons who would soon become priests, concluding—in a thinly-veiled allusion to Harris—that at least "there is not a black, lesbian or divorcee among them."[2] Some standing committees voted not to give consent for Harris's consecration, as did some bishops, but well within the canonical time period consents were received from the necessary majorities and planning for the service went forward.[3]

"The Final Crisis"
Anticipating this outcome, the leadership of the Evangelical and Catholic Mission reserved most of its energy for taking the next steps to secure a safe enclave for traditionalists. Four days after Harris's election, these bishops issued a statement echoing Bishop Clarence Pope's 1986 appeal to the House of Bishops. It was signed by six diocesan bishops (David Ball of Albany, William Wantland of Eau Claire, William Stevens of Fond du Lac, Clarence Pope of Fort Worth, Ed-

ward MacBurney of Quincy, and Victor Rivera of San Joaquin) and three retired bishops, all supporters of the 1987 "Alternate View" statement, and declared their commitment to defend the church which they felt to be under attack:

> The election in Massachusetts is a direct assault upon the unity of the Church....The historic faith of Anglicanism will have been irreparably compromised should Ms. Harris undergo the rite of Consecration....We will be unable to consider ourselves in communion with her as a bishop or accept any episcopal actions performed by her....Other practical consequences of this are not yet clear but consultations within the U.S. and internationally are underway at this time.[4]

The structural challenge to the Episcopal Church had escalated. This refusal to be in communion with Harris (or by implication anyone ordained by her) demonstrated that the traditionalists' commitment to the unity of the church was limited by their opposition to ordaining women. Obviously the episcopal visitors resolution for which they had worked so hard earlier in the year did not, in the form adopted, satisfy their desire for a safeguard for their "consciences and convictions." In fact, the September statement seemed to dismiss that model completely, and its final sentence about "practical consequences" and international consultations had an ominous ring.

By early November, the Evangelical and Catholic Mission had set itself on a course somewhere between rebellion and schism. Describing themselves as "a college of bishops," its leaders issued a pastoral letter declaring this to be "the final crisis of the Episcopal Church" and calling for a synod of like-minded people to meet in Bishop Pope's diocese of Fort Worth the following June. Rejecting the model of a break-away or schismatic group, these bishops sought to call the Episcopal Church back to what they considered the divinely-given order of the historic faith. Thus they proposed a gathering "to consider how we shall be the Church within the Episcopal Church and to...plan for active witness in the face of the institution's present disintegration." Excerpts from the letter were included as part of an advertisement placed in church periodicals, which also included a "Declaration of Common Faith and Purpose" to be signed by all attending the synod.[5]

The rhetoric of the letter was harsh, critical, and inflammatory. It accused the church of rebellion against a God-given order and rejection of the authority of divine revelation by admitting women to the episcopate and the priesthood. It claimed an obligation to maintain the historic faith by pursuing the "reformation, replacement, or transcendence" of the institution; in a veiled reference to the Presiding Bishop, it attacked Browning's commitment to inclusivity as "a thin velvet glove sheathing the mailed fist of intolerance." Its language revealed how deep-seated were the emotions stirred up by the entry of women into the inner sanctum. This characteristic was to reappear again and again as the Anglican Communion struggled to reinterpret its traditions and include women as full participants in its life.

Defining the Historic Episcopate

Because of the role which the episcopate plays in the life and historical continuity of the Anglican Communion, the controversy about women as bishops had much greater institutional significance than the question of women as priests. One of the four marks of the Anglican Communion is the "historic episcopate," passed from one generation to another through apostolic succession—a presumably unbroken line of bishops ordained by other bishops stretching back to the apostles of the New Testament. Priests and deacons are connected to this succession through the bishops who ordain them, as are church members when they are confirmed by a bishop. Apostolic succession anchors the church in its history, and is understood to guarantee the adequacy of its teaching and the wisdom of its decision-making, while ensuring the validity of its sacramental life. The succession is continued through a ritual laying on of hands: the ordination and consecration of a bishop at which at least three bishops must gather to bestow episcopal authority on another.

Succession as guarantor of the validity of the ministry is one essential for communion, but by itself it is not enough. Anglicans recognize the validity of the orders of all ministers in the apostolic succession—Roman Catholics, Orthodox, and some smaller groups such as the Old Catholics—and thus of the sacraments administered by those ministers, whether priests or bishops. But because of other doctrinal or ecclesial differences, Anglicans are not "in communion" with most of them—that is, they do not share communion in the

Eucharist, nor are their ministries interchangeable. Yet even though "communion" does not exist, Anglicans do not question the validity of the ordained ministry or the efficacy of the sacramental life of those churches.

The Anglican tradition has long understood itself to be a broad *via media*—a middle way—in which a common worship and theology has been given many cultural forms. The ministry, guaranteed by the apostolic succession, has been one of its unifying characteristics, an institutional structure supplying continuity across continents, oceans, and centuries. As cultural adaptations, liturgical forms, and ecclesial patterns have diversified in the late twentieth century, acceptance of a common ministry has assumed greater importance in binding together the far-flung provinces, dioceses, and peoples of the Anglican Communion. Thus the limitation placed on the interchangeability of clergy by disagreements concerning women posed a serious threat to both the fragile structures and the bonds of good will that unite them.

In addition, while the validity of a priest's orders is significant chiefly for his or her congregation, the validity of a bishop's orders affects the whole church—those confirmed, those ordained to the priesthood, and those consecrated as bishops, together with all their future confirmands, ordinands, and successors in the episcopate. To those who believed a woman was by nature simply not able to be ordained—the way a tree or a truck, for example, could not become a bishop no matter how correct the canonical process and the ceremony—a woman bishop would break the apostolic succession and thus jeopardize all that flows from it. This was the prospect from which traditionalists recoiled, which drove them to break communion with others who, in their view, had already abandoned the communion by compromising its ministry.

To address this question, Robert Runcie, the Archbishop of Canterbury, appointed a Commission on Communion and Women in the Episcopate. Called the Eames Commission after its chair, Robert Eames, the Archbishop of Armagh and Primate of Ireland, members of the commission were balanced between proponents and opponents of women's ordination, and included one American bishop, Mark Dyer of Bethlehem, and one woman, the Church of England's ecumenical officer, Mary Tanner. The commission held its first meeting in London soon after Barbara Harris's election; its preliminary report attempted to define the essential elements of episcopal ministry (preacher, pastoral caregiver, administrator of the sacraments, symbol of unity, teacher of the faith), affirmed the principle of respect for diocesan boundaries, and promised to deal with the pastoral needs of traditionalists.[6]

The Eames Commission had a difficult task. The bishops at Lambeth had committed themselves to maintaining the highest possible degree of communion, and the commission was to seek structures that might promote this ideal. Yet some structures and practices already limited communion between dioceses and provinces: women priests visiting in England or Fort Worth, for example, could not be licensed to celebrate the Eucharist, and individual traditionalists habitually stayed away if a woman priest was at the altar. The Evangelical and Catholic Mission statement made it clear that this *de facto* impairment to communion would increase with the consecration of a woman to the episcopate, and in November the Archbishop of Canterbury, Robert Runcie, himself raised this issue. In response to the Harris election, he outlined for the Church of England General Synod the legal situation in that province, in which not only the Synod but also the Parliament would have to authorize such a change in the ministry:

> The Church of England does not *canonically* accept the ministry of either women priests or bishops of other churches, unless and until the ecclesiastical law is changed...nor are we able to accept clergy ordained by a woman bishop as long as her episcopate is not officially accepted.[7]

Did this put the Archbishop in the same category as the Evangelical and Catholic Mission in rejecting the consecration of a woman as bishop? If so, it would seem that the Eames Commission had been given the impossible task of maintaining communion when the church's own laws appeared to prevent it.

But this was not what Archbishop Runcie was saying in his carefully-worded statement to the English Synod. He spoke of canonical acceptance, not validity. The ministry of women priests, women bishops, and male priests ordained by women bishops could not be accepted in England because of legal differences, as the ministry of Roman Catholic or Orthodox clergy could not be accepted, but this did not imply that their ordinations were invalid or the sacraments administered by them incomplete. His phrase "unless and until the ecclesiastical law is changed" clearly implied that the barrier was technical rather than doctrinal. Thus his statement left the way open for future acceptance and the restoration of full communion.

Bishop Barbara Clementine Harris

On February 11, 1989, before a jubilant crowd of eight thousand people in the Hynes Auditorium in Boston, Barbara Clementine Harris was consecrated suffragan bishop of the most populous diocese in the American church. It took half an hour for the procession of distinguished guests (including Anglicans from around the world, ecumenical leaders, and government officials), several choirs, hundreds of vested clergy and members of religious orders, dozens of bishops, and one small woman to take their places. At the appointed moment early in the service, two protests were lodged, one from the Prayer Book Society and one from an individual priest, to which Presiding Bishop Browning responded that the issues they raised had been extensively debated throughout the church, which had then chosen through due canonical process to proceed. Continuing with the ordination rite, he asked the congregation, "Is it your will that we ordain Barbara a bishop?" "That is our will," came the joyous reply, a moment so filled with powerful emotion that Browning had to pause and swallow hard before continuing. "Will you uphold Barbara as bishop?" "We will!" The three-hour service combined solemn ceremony with hand-clapping gospel music, deep silence as Harris was surrounded by sixty-two bishops for the laying on of hands, and prolonged, thunderous applause when the new bishop put on cope and mitre and turned to face the congregation.

Everything about the service testified to the fact that the old order was changing. The preacher was Harris's mentor, Paul Washington, rector of the Church of the Advocate which had hosted the Philadelphia ordinations fifteen years earlier. Joining Bishop Harris around the altar to concelebrate the Eucharist were Florence Li Tim-Oi, the first Anglican woman ordained to the priesthood in 1944, and Carter Heyward, one of the Philadelphia Eleven and a tenured faculty member at the Episcopal Divinity School in Cambridge, Massachusetts. Racial and ethnic diversity marked the entire assembly, and those playing special roles in the service were male and female, gay, lesbian, and straight, young and old, lay and ordained. The entire service was telecast live by a Boston television station, and accounts appeared on the evening news and in many secular newspapers as well as the church press. A woman had become a bishop, and the episcopacy had been transformed: no longer a male preserve, it had become an image of human leadership within a community of diverse men and women united in Christ's service.[8]

Chapter 14

Adapting to a New Reality

A fter Barbara Harris's consecration, institutional energy both within the Episcopal Church and in the Anglican Communion focused chiefly on dealing with the traditionalist reaction. The following month, the Eames Commission gathered on Long Island, holding separate meetings with Bishop Harris and three women priests from the United States and Canada, and with Bishop Pope and three other representatives of the Evangelical and Catholic Mission, which was preparing for its June synod in Fort Worth. A major portion of the commission's subsequent report was devoted to a theological discussion of *koinonia* (Christian community) and the process of "reception" by which developments in practice and doctrine are accepted throughout the church. The report also included a number of specific recommendations responding to traditionalists' concerns.[1] At their April meeting in Cyprus, the Anglican primates received the commission's report and endorsed all but one of its recommendations. In a major defeat for traditionalists, the heads of the Anglican Communion's provinces rejected as neither "practical or theologically appropriate" the commission's recommendation that for the time being a male bishop share in all episcopal acts performed by a female bishop.[2]

In May, Presiding Bishop Browning sent his first pastoral letter to the whole church, calling for ongoing dialogue and prayer for the church and its mission. While he disputed the traditionalists' view of the situation, Browning supported their right to gather and affirmed his commitment to an inclusive church broad enough to encompass all points of view:

I want to affirm the June gathering in Fort Worth....There is value in the coming together of those in our Church who disagree with the majority decision... [but] I reject the ECM's characterization of our Church as in "disintegration" and "crisis."...The Eames Report insists that we see our present tensions and disagreements in the context of our history as a Christian community [in which communion has always been maintained] "through mutual acceptance and respect and the toleration of a diversity of practice."...What we have in common is more important than what divides.[3]

Browning's letter calling for an inclusive church was read in Episcopal congregations on Sunday, May 28, 1989, just a few days before the Fort Worth synod brought together about fifteen hundred people—bishops, clergy, lay men and women—who voted to form the Episcopal Synod of America and elected Bishop Clarence Pope as Synod president.[4] Participants were drawn mostly from the ranks of the Evangelical and Catholic Mission, but the meeting was also supported by Episcopalians United and the Prayer Book Society, and its resolutions reflected the full range of the traditionalist agenda. The primary organizing focus, as with earlier groups, was the issue of women's ordination: the new Synod sought to create a structure for providing pastoral services to traditionalists in dioceses with a woman bishop, or a male bishop who supported women in the episcopate, and to insulate its members from the ministry of women priests.

The Eames Commission's work was regarded with ambivalence by those in attendance, particularly those who believed that revelation was permanent and unchanging. Although the commission's emphasis on the process of reception, with its implicit possibility that developments such as the ordination of women might ultimately be rejected by "the whole church," offered some hope to the traditionalist position, the implications for practice posed particular difficulties. In his opening address Bishop Pope spelled out this dilemma:

We are not living with an idea. We are living with an idea which has been institutionalized and given flesh and bones. Many hundreds of women have undergone the rite of ordination....How is it possible to take the theory of "reception" seriously in the face of such institutionalization, even though the process is said to carry with it the possibility of rejection?...The Eames Commission has succumbed to the American concept of progressive revelation.[5]

Amid veiled threats of schism, Bishop Pope called on dioceses, parishes, and individuals to affiliate with the Synod as the "Church within the church" that would resist this institutionalization of an expanded ministry.

Synod bishops divided the whole country into regions for which they would assume pastoral oversight, declaring that if they were denied permission for episcopal visitations by a diocesan bishop they were ready as a matter of conscience to perform ecclesiastical disobedience in order to minister to traditionalist congregations within their regions. They were ready, in other words, to violate the long-standing Anglican principle of the geographical integrity of individual dioceses, despite the House of Bishops' unanimous reaffirmation of that principle in connection with the Oklahoma incident in 1986, Lambeth's endorsement in 1988, and the Eames Commission's reiteration just weeks before the Fort Worth meeting.

The leadership of the Synod overlapped with that of the Evangelical and Catholic Mission, but the Synod was a new organizational entity designed to appeal to a broader coalition of traditionalists. Their structures were similar and the emphasis on the authority of bishops was a distinctive characteristic of both organizations, but the Synod's ethos and structure gave bishops an even more prominent place. Instead of a national council of bishops, priests, and laypeople, the Synod's constitution established separate houses of bishops and deputies like those of the Episcopal Church's General Convention; though they were to meet and vote together on most matters, separate voting could be called for, giving the bishops veto power over deputies. The final statement of the "Declaration of Common Faith and Purpose," which all members were required to sign, emphasized the authority of bishops within the organization: "I will be guided in this endeavor by the Godly counsel of the Bishops who share this common faith and purpose and of the Synod convoked by them."[6]

Intent upon not breaking away from the Episcopal Church, the synod was a kind of shadow church that described itself in press releases and promotional materials as a "Church within the Episcopal Church." A statement adopted at Fort Worth acknowledged a "baptismal unity" which joined all Christians, but put sharp qualifications on the extent of the Synod's communion with others, including other Episcopalians. Taking a very different approach to communion than the Eames Commission, the declaration identified four areas—faith, moral principle, worship, and ministry—in which communion might or might not be shared. The nuances of this statement, like that of the other resolutions adopted at the Fort Worth meeting, suggest that considerable negotiation took place in the course of building a broad coalition of conservative Episcopalians. The key paragraph reads:

> [We] share a *communion of faith* with all who accept the supreme authority of Scripture and the truth of the Creeds; a *communion of moral principle* with all who defend the rights of the unborn and the sanctity of all human life, the sanctity of marriage as our Lord defined it, and with all who reject proposals to approve homosexual unions by liturgical services and blessings; a *communion of worship* with all who worship God according to His revelation of Himself, including all who worship according to the Book of Common Prayer, understood in a biblical and traditional way; a *communion of the ministry* of the word and sacraments with all who maintain the historic threefold ministry, recognizing that the episcopate and the presbyterate are limited to males.[7]

These requirements for being in communion with the Synod presented in quasi-theological garb the full cluster of traditionalist issues: biblical authority and doctrinal orthodoxy, opposition to abortion, divorce, and homosexuality, preservation of traditional forms of worship (including masculine terminology for God), and an exclusively male ordained ministry. Using these criteria, the declaration clearly stated that Synod members were not in communion with the majority of the Episcopal Church: "We are in communion with some in the first three ways with whom we are not at present in communion in the fourth way." Coupled with the Synod's own version of episcopal visitors, which set forth its bishops' willingness to violate the church's canons if denied permission to perform episcopal acts in other dioceses, this declaration established the Episcopal Synod of America as an entity openly challenging the unity and discipline of the Episcopal Church.

From Fort Worth to Philadelphia: A Test of Collegiality
The issue of the ordination of women was now openly cast as a matter of territoriality. The House of Bishops met in September 1989 in Philadelphia, on the two-hundredth anniversary of the adoption of the Episcopal Church's constitution and prayer book in that City of Brotherly Love. For the first time, a woman was seated as a member of the House of Bishops. It was nineteen years after women's admission to the House of Deputies and forty-three years after Elizabeth Dyer's brief appearance there; fifteen years had passed since the first American ordinations of women to the priesthood in that same city.

In accordance with traditional practice, new bishops were presented to the House during a dinner the night before the meeting officially began. Barbara Harris of Province I was the first new bishop to be welcomed, receiving enthusiastic greetings from most of those present. When the House formally convened the next morning, however, her presence was overshadowed by the fear of Synod bishops raiding their neighbors' dioceses. Many bishops were angry and impatient with Synod tactics and intemperate press releases, and were no more prepared to tolerate unauthorized bishops in their dioceses now than they had been to tolerate the interference of Graham Leonard, the bishop of London, in Oklahoma in 1986, Bishop Albert Chambers's forays to confirm and ordain in schismatic congregations in 1977, or the retired bishops' irregular ordinations in Philadelphia in 1974. Once again the territorial imperative proved inseparable from the bishops' ideal of collegiality.

Nevertheless, a dogged insistence on unity dominated the proceedings. From the House of Bishops' perspective, the Synod situation differed in important ways from that of the Oklahoma or Chambers incidents, or the ordinations of the Philadelphia Eleven and the Washington Four. The Synod bishops presenting this new challenge to collegiality were neither from overseas nor retired, but active bishops with jurisdiction in their own dioceses, full membership in the House, and a well-funded following outside. They were colleagues who could not be censured without seriously disrupting the conventional power structure. To move against a sitting bishop would have grave consequences; even James Pike had not been actually censured until after he had resigned his jurisdiction as the bishop of California.

The House was also stymied by the terms of its own statement of conscience, which had been echoed and elaborated by Lambeth and the Eames Commission's encouragement of respect for opposing positions. In late June, Presiding Bishop Browning had reiterated his own deep commitment to maintaining the unity of the church:

> With regard to the meeting in Fort Worth, I cannot overemphasize my belief that those who disagree with the majority must not be marginalized in our Church and will not be. This is not a political strategy. This is a theological necessity.[8]

Led by Browning and with the ideals of Lambeth lingering in their collective consciousness alongside the threat of schism, the House of Bishops was looking for peace. They plunged into eight days of meetings carefully orchestrated to promote dialogue and harmony, with presentations from Mark Dyer and Mary Tanner about the Eames Commission report dealing especially with its discussion of the theology of reception and the provisionality of new developments in the life of the church. They heard an impassioned plea for understanding from Synod bishop William Wantland, whose deft address managed to smooth over many concerns raised by the Fort Worth meeting. They heard daily homilies from the Presiding Bishop on the theme "Beyond Anger." They met in small Bible study groups to identify issues and react to drafts of a statement responding to the Synod situation prepared by a team chaired by Bishop Richard Grein, then coadjutor of New York, which consulted with Bishop Pope and Bishop Wantland but not with Bishop Harris.

The fact that Harris's only access to the drafting process of a statement related to women in the episcopate was *via* the small group reporting process suggests that an old pattern was still in place, rendering women virtually invisible and men incapable of hearing their voices. The team reported to a press briefing that the two Synod bishops had been consulted by the drafting committee because of their special interest in the outcome, but Bishop Harris had not because it would not have been fair "to put her on the spot." The response to a question about whether Harris had been given the opportunity to decide that for herself was, "No, but she'll be satisfied with the results because Bishop Johnson [the diocesan bishop of Massachusetts] was involved." Apparently Harris was not completely satisfied, and offered a suggestion for improvement during the floor debate, which was ignored. Analyzing this incident in a report for the Episcopal Women's Caucus, Martha Blacklock wrote:

> The bishop behind her in line, very excited by what he had to say, stepped right up and went ahead with his suggestion before hers had been dealt with. Bishop Browning, in the chair, didn't interrupt. Which left Barbara in the position of having to come up later and say that her contribution had not been considered....Men overtalk women without noticing that it's happening.[9]

It was certainly not the first time men had debated issues directly affecting women without inviting their participation, nor would it be the last.

On the final day in Philadelphia, after lengthy debate and one successful amendment from the floor, the bishops unanimously passed a "mind of the house" statement of "our intention to live together." Billed as a "formula for peace with the traditionalists," the four-page statement was conciliatory in tone and tried to mark out within the company of bishops the common ground which had eluded the previous General Convention in its struggles over episcopal visitors. It began by noting the seating of Barbara Harris at that meeting and affirming the ministries of women in the church. Within the context of the Anglican Communion's divided state on the question, it then expressed the bishops' commitment to continuing dialogue and fellowship with the traditionalists:

> Within the Anglican Communion and indeed even within our own church, there is not a common theological mind or agreed practice on the matter of the ordination of women....We acknowledge that within Anglicanism those who believe that women should not be ordained hold *a recognized theological position*....We have heard the voices of those...of the Episcopal Church who hold that view and we affirm them as loyal members of the family.[10]

Citing Lambeth and the Episcopal Church's own constitution, the statement also reaffirmed the inviolability of diocesan boundaries and the necessity for invitation and permission before one bishop entered another's territory. After the unanimous vote, Clarence Pope of Fort Worth and David Johnson of Massachusetts were called to the platform to be photographed in a fraternal embrace. Bishop Harris remained quietly in her seat—unheard and unseen as the brotherhood celebrated its unity.

The Aftermath of Peace

Like the episcopal visitors resolution, the House of Bishops' attempt at compromise also proved a source of discontent. The bishops, immersed in the theological intricacies and political negotiations that had resulted in the highly-nuanced Philadelphia document, were satisfied, but many clergy and people on both sides were unhappy with the statement. Immediately after the meeting, Bishop Pope issued a press release discussing complaints he had received from Synod members and attempting to explain away the concessions he and Bishop Wantland had made in the drafting process. Despite the House of Bishops' decisive reaffirmation of the inviolability of diocesan boundaries, statements issuing from the Synod after the meeting made it clear that at least some of its bishops, responding to anxious and angry supporters, were still committed to visiting in other dioceses without permission "if forced to," so the territorial question remained unresolved.[11]

On the other side, to ordained women and their supporters the Philadelphia statement seemed to be another retreat from the church's authorized position. The major stumbling block for them was the use of the phrase "recognized theological position" to describe opposition to ordaining women. The draft had actually used the even stronger phrase "accepted theological position," but this was amended on the floor. The vigorous debate on several proposed amendments indicated that many bishops were reluctant to appear to endorse a position that contradicted the Episcopal Church's canons, but in the context of the whole Anglican Communion the revised statement was technically accurate: opposition to ordaining women *was* a position held by many and recognizing it was simply to acknowledge a fact.[12] Yet it could be (and subsequently was) used by the Synod to imply that the House of Bishops had approved their position, and the intricate theological discussion of reception and provisionality was easily twisted into the suggestion that ordained women's orders were provisional and hence not quite real or valid. Much confusion and distress resulted.

To some it appeared that the bishops, in an excess of their wonted collegiality, were "crying peace" in the midst of an escalating conflict. Brother Tobias Haller, head of the pro-women's ordination Catholic Fellowship of the Episcopal Church, observed caustically:

> As I read the varied interpretations of the bishops' statement, I am reminded of three things: Neville Chamberlain and his little piece of paper; a line from the collect for the commemoration of Richard Hooker: "not as compromise for the sake of peace, but comprehension for the sake of truth"; and Jeremiah's comments about prophesying peace when there is no peace....To "agree to disagree" about matters as fundamental to polity as the validity of orders raises questions about the nature and structure of the Episcopal Church.[13]

Martha Blacklock also captured the feelings of many in her Episcopal Women's Caucus report:

> The bishops wanted to come out of their meeting in harmony, so that they could model the possibility for the rest of the Anglican Communion. If we can do it, they said, we can lead others into the same unity....If by "modeling" they hoped to demonstrate how to replicate their achievement, the effect was more like magic...[since] the essentials took place out of sight. What I actually heard and saw were outrageous statements by ESA [the Synod]...cheerfully not challenged by the House. And maybe that IS how you do it—carefully not listen to what is being said, as long as nothing against the rules is being done. Well, why not, if it makes everybody happy? Is everybody happy?[14]

Furthermore, most clergy had had neither the time nor the motivation to study the hundreds of pages of reports issuing from study committees, working parties, and international commissions. Even fewer lay people were following the complex arguments and political maneuvering. They saw only the bishops' Philadelphia statement, and many were not happy.

There were strong parallels between the 1989 and 1977 House of Bishops meetings. The bishops had met in Port St. Lucie a year after the 1976 General Convention approved the ordination of women to the priesthood and episcopate, and a few weeks after traditionalists gathered in St. Louis to oppose that decision and initiate a schismatic church body. The bishops met in Philadelphia a year after the 1988 Convention had reaffirmed the 1976 decision by preparing for the ordination of women to the episcopate, and a few weeks after traditionalists had gathered in Fort Worth to oppose that step. Each time, the bishops tried to maintain unity by reaching out to traditionalists in their own ranks, with the statement of conscience in 1977 and the Philadelphia statement in 1989. Each time, ordained women and their supporters felt betrayed while their opponents remained unsatisfied.

A Question of Authority

Traditionalists could more easily avoid conflict with a woman bishop who served in a suffragan (assistant) role, but a woman diocesan bishop would have direct authority over all parishes and clergy in her jurisdiction. In addition, diocesan bishops are automatically eligible for participation in the Lambeth Conference, and some bishops had threatened not to attend the next one, scheduled for 1998, if a woman bishop were present. These fears came to a head in November 1989, when the Anglican Church in New Zealand quietly announced the election of Penelope Ann Jamieson as diocesan bishop of Dunedin.

Few could take exception to Jamieson's credentials—conventionally educated, married, with solid parish experience—but she shared with Barbara Harris a deep commitment to the marginalized of church and society, and was equally plain-spoken about the place of women in the authority structures of the church. At her consecration the following summer, with Barbara Harris as a co-consecrator and visitors from around the Anglican Communion in attendance, Jamieson was ritually called into the cathedral by a ninety-two-year-old Maori woman in a ceremonial feather cloak, and later a group of lay and clergy women surrounded her singing a Celtic blessing, "May God hold you in the hollow of her hand."

Jamieson's elevation to the episcopate demonstrated that Harris's election had not been a one-time fluke, and that women in the episcopate was not a phenomenon confined to the church in the United States. It also seemed to confirm the promise implicit in Harris's episcopate, that women might approach the exercise of episcopal authority in a different way. "I'm more interested in working in or on the ragged boundaries of the church than being at the center," Jamieson told an interviewer.[15]

In the spring of 1990, the Eames Commission met for the fourth time, its first gathering with an ordained woman as member (Julia Gatta of the Berkeley Divinity School faculty at Yale University). To those moving forward with the incorporation of women into the epis- copacy, the commission advised wide consultation, sensitivity to the distress of traditionalists, and meticulous adherence to the canons. Traditionalists were urged to acknowledge the canonical legitimacy of the consecration of a woman even if they could not accept her sac- ramental ministry; not to break fellowship or withhold financial sup- port; to recognize and accept a woman bishop within the province's collegial structure (synod or house of bishops); and not to "actively oppose" her episcopal ministry. Discussing this restriction, the report came close to prescribing a limit for what Anglicans might believe— or at least say—about the ordination of women:

> Such congregations and clergy would not go as far as to say that a woman could *never* be a bishop. Their position might simply be that of uncertainty in the matter or of waiting for a consensus either way to emerge in the Anglican Communion or ecumenically.[16]

The commission thus allowed room for one of the two schools of thought held by traditionalist American bishops, but seemed to ex- clude the position that the male priesthood and episcopate were part of an eternally unchangeable God-given order. It was the rigidity of the latter view, held by some influential members of the Episcopal Synod of America, that contributed to the Synod's political volatility and rhetorical intemperance. The 1990 Eames report constituted an international rebuke of such behavior, the more weighty because it came from a body that included a number of traditionalists.

The report also expressed disapproval of bishops like Graham Leonard of London who were making pronouncements concerning who was or was not "in communion" with whom. Earlier the com- mission had asserted that "no Province or individual bishop, priest or lay person could meaningfully declare themselves to be out of com- munion with another";[17] now, retreating slightly from that blanket prohibition, it simply insisted that the authority to make statements about ecclesial communion resided only with each province, not with any single bishop or diocese. The commission plainly suggested that no province ought to do so, even though nothing could actually prevent them from taking such action. These recommendations had no binding force, but they had a powerful influence on the consensual decision-making processes of the provinces and contributed to a gradual shift in the emotional and theological climate surrounding the question of women's ordination.

The burning question, ultimately, was one of authority. Who could decide and pronounce on the matter of being in communion, or, for that matter, on anything else? This authority had become bound up with issues of meaning: what did it actually *mean* to be in or out of communion within the Anglican Communion? Did saying it was so in fact make it so? The Eames Commission insisted that individuals could not "meaningfully declare themselves to be out of communion," despite the fact that traditionalist bishops and clergy had already made such declarations and were behaving as though they were true. Who was defining reality, or determining what was "meaningful" in the church?

In the absence of a pope or other ultimate arbiter of disputes, Anglicans have always had to endure periods, often stormy, in which opposing meanings compete for acceptance. This sometimes lends a certain *Through the Looking Glass* quality to debates:

> "When *I* use a word," Humpty Dumpty said in a rather scornful tone, "it means just what I choose it to mean—neither more nor less."
>
> "The question is," said Alice, "whether you *can* make words mean different things."
>
> "The question is," said Humpty Dumpty, "which is to be master— that's all."[18]

The ordination of women to the priesthood had crystallized this question of "mastery" in the American church in the 1970s. By 1990 the ordination of women to the episcopate had carried the struggle into the international arena. Mutually exclusive definitions of being "in communion" epitomized the struggle, making "words mean different things" for opposing groups.

As traditionalists slowly lost ground on the ordination issue, they became more and more articulate about other concerns in an attempt to define and defend the traditions of the church. In this context, Humpty Dumpty's retort about definition and meaning captures the crisis of authority which the church was experiencing. Who is to be master? Who has the authority to determine how we order our ministry and common life as a church, to interpret the Word of God, to instruct us in the faith, to guide us in making decisions about our lives, to bless us or call us to repentance? This crisis took on curious new forms as the consequences of opening up authority structures to women unfolded.

Chapter 15

Two World Views

The 1988 General Convention and the election of Barbara Harris to the episcopate moved the conflict between traditionalist groups and the rest of the Episcopal Church into a new stage. Most Episcopalians considered the question of ordaining women long since settled, but developments related to the rest of the traditionalist agenda, especially controversy around the issue of homosexuality, sustained a sense of crisis. The rejection of traditional authority on all fronts became the rallying point, as Clarence Pope showed in his address to the Fort Worth synod:

> The vexing symptoms of our problem [are]: the ordination of women to the presbyterate and episcopate, problems relating to practicing homosexuality, the dangerous and seemingly unstoppable influence of radical feminist theology, questions relating to how we shall address God, the authority of the Bible, the nature of tradition, marital fidelity and personal morality....The underlying problem from which these florid symptoms erupt is the loss of respect for the authority of Holy Scripture and the embracing of a world view which ignores history....The ordinations of women to the presbyterate and episcopate were not the root problems but signs of a breakdown in authority.[1]

The inseparability of these issues was also noted by an English commentator in the wake of Barbara Harris's election:

> The real and serious opposition to Ms. Harris comes from those who believe that the ordination of women is all part of a package "secular in origin and thought," as the Bishop of London [Graham Leonard] put it. It is the whole package they object to, not just the women in it.[2]

This secular package was in conflict with all that traditionalists valued. In an article opposing Harris's consecration, English columnist William Oddie, who wrote for traditionalist Anglican publications on both sides of the Atlantic before becoming a Roman Catholic, set forth a common perception of the polarization of the church:

> Within the Episcopal Church there are two worlds, hermetically sealed from one another...[and] women's ordination is seen as a key symbolic issue defining the line of separation. There are others: the right to use the old Book of Common Prayer; sexual ethics; the authority of biblical revelation and two thousand years of Christian tradition....If you are against women in the episcopate, the likelihood is that you will be in favour of the right to use the 1928 American Prayer Book, against homosexual "marriages" in church, and in favour of upholding biblical authority in matters of doctrine and morals. If you are for women priests and bishops, you are more likely to believe in social activism and a generally radical political stance.[3]

The connection with secular political issues in the waning days of the Cold War was drawn even more dramatically by the Prayer Book Society's president, Jerome Politzer, who described Harris's election as the work of "a left-wing cabal...[a] radical junta now destroying the church."[4]

From the other side of the conflict, Presiding Bishop Browning described the competing world views in similar terms:

> The search for *koinonia* is made more difficult by that great divide in consciousness that is the hallmark of our time...between those who tend to see tradition as a dynamic reality and who, therefore, accept the possibility of continuing revelation...[and] those who tend to see a once-for-all-ness in the divine dispensation....The divide in consciousness threatens our Communion most severely today over issues of authority, sexuality and ordination of women.[5]

Feminist social theory generally supports this traditionalist analysis of the present crisis challenging systems of authority in the Western world. The two groups often ascribe quite different meanings to the same terms and feminist evaluations of the ultimate significance of the crisis would be diametrically opposed to the judgments of traditionalists, but most feminist analyses would draw the same connections among issues facing the church. Feminists would name these as the foundations of patriarchy and seek to dismantle their structure, even as traditionalists seek its preservation.

The Great Divide

All societies develop a framework of relationships and conventional behavior that provides predictability and security for its members and continuity from generation to generation. This framework sets the limits of acceptable behavior and defines how power is distributed—who has what kinds of power over whom: kings over subjects, lords over serfs, owners over workers, parents over children, priests over people, and so on. Such hierarchies of power, in the church as in the society, depend on the attribution of greater value (older, stronger, wiser, holier) to one group, which is then entitled to dominate the others for the ostensible good of the community. Such hierarchies depend, in other words, on the ability to distinguish categories of people from one another: male or female, rich or poor, black or white, strong or weak.

From this perspective, each issue on the traditionalist agenda can be viewed as one of the structures which keeps in place a hierarchy based on the attribution of greater value to men than to women. Most of the contemporary changes regarding reproductive and sexual behavior, for example, have had the effect of increasing women's independence from men in determining whether and when to bear children. The availability of contraceptives and education about family planning make pregnancy no longer an automatic consequence for sexually active women, and the legalization of abortion further limits male control over female bodies by giving women a share in the life-or-death decision-making of society. In keeping with a theology which regards companionship and mutual joy rather than procreation as the chief purpose of matrimony and sexual relations, the Episcopal Church and Anglicans generally have promoted responsible family planning for decades. The prominence of the traditionalists' concern about the church's progressive policy regarding abortion can be seen as one aspect of their wider resistance to changes in women's roles in the areas of sexuality and childbearing.

Consider also the recent changes in attitudes toward divorce and work outside the home. For generations of middle-class women, divorce was so scandalous and financially ruinous that it was not really an option. Almost every family can point to some female member who remained in an emotionally or physically abusive relationship for decades because she could see no safe way out for herself and her children. In twentieth-century America, more tolerant attitudes toward divorce and expanding employment opportunities have benefitted women by weakening the psychological authority and financial power of men over women in the marriage relationship. But the prolonged exclusion of Episcopal women from discussions of the marriage canon, the resistance to permitting remarriage within the church, and the continued opposition to divorce on the traditionalist agenda all testify to the role the church has played in perpetuating the traditional male-dominant model of matrimony.

The increased acceptance of premarital sexual activity that was one result of the middle-class sexual revolution of the 1950s and 1960s has reduced the traditional double standard, extending to heterosexual women the tolerance for early experimentation long granted to men. For good or ill, society—and most clergy—no longer expect brides to be virginal while "real" men come with experience to the marriage bed, and living together without benefit of marriage has become a common practice for couples of all ages and social classes, including many Episcopalians. As the sexual revolution plays itself out in the age of AIDS, standards of responsible sexual behavior within a context of care and commitment are beginning to be applied to both men and women, increasing the potential for real mutuality in intimate relationships. At the same time, the proliferation of family models is often confused with the exploitation of casual or violent sex which dominates advertising and the mass media, and conservative Episcopalians join other critics in blaming the collapse of the 1950s-style nuclear family on the loss of an absolute "no sex outside marriage" ideal.

That concern is multiplied many times over in reference to homosexuality. The increasing visibility and recognition of gay and lesbian relationships directly challenges the norm of male-dominated heterosexual marriage as the basic unit of society. Gay men do not cooperate in perpetuating that norm, while lesbian relationships explicitly defy social and religious assumptions about women's dependence on men. Responses to this situation mark the cleavage in attitude between conservatives and progressives in the church as well as society. On the one side are those who believe lesbian and gay partnerships can be healthy and life-giving, offering a model of mutuality among peers as an alternative to the pattern of traditional marriage and ultimately strengthening the institution of marriage by reserving it to heterosexual men and women who freely chose to share their lives with one another. On the other side, because same-sex partnerships violate fundamental cultural assumptions about masculinity and male/female relationships, considered by many to be ordained by God, they elicit intensely negative, often hate-filled, sometimes violent reactions.

The importance of the connection between sexuality and the place of women in church and society cannot be overestimated. It was no coincidence that in 1977 the House of Bishops wrestled with—and disapproved of—homosexual marriages at the same Port St. Lucie meeting where they agreed not to enforce the canon on women's ordination. Nor is it accidental that the Episcopal Synod of America increasingly emphasized its opposition to the ordination of homosexuals as support for its opposition to the ordination of women dwindled. Because those admitted to ordained leadership are understood to be models of virtuous and godly living, the ordination of gay men and lesbians challenges the single standard of marriage-or-celibacy and thus appears to threaten the entire framework of social, familial, and ecclesiastical relationships.

The polarization within the church over these societal and religious issues marks that "great divide in consciousness" of which Presiding Bishop Browning spoke. To traditionalists, all are part of the "secular package of radical feminist theology" which threatens the authority of Scripture and violates the integrity of the historic faith. From another perspective, the changes begin to address centuries of injustice and distorted relationships between men and women—in the home, in the church, and in the society at large.

Order, Authority, and Women

From a feminist perspective, the notion of a God-given order for the church gives to traditionalist thinking a particularly inflexible attitude toward authority. It fosters an inability to distinguish between the medium and the message, between the human institutions and texts that bear the faith from age to age, and the dynamic, redemptive reality of divine love for humankind. Those who are satisfied with the distribution of power and privilege in existing social and religious structures have no incentive to question traditional interpretation, and indeed risk losing much in the process. Most traditionalists simply regard existing structures as inseparable from God's self-revelation. Reaffirming traditional patterns and sources of authority, therefore, seems to them the only faithful response, a necessary aspect of obedience to God's will.

Theologian Letty Russell has pointed out how the link between feminism and problems about authority lies in the often-unconscious patriarchal assumption that authority is a masculine attribute:

> Whatever feminist theologians take up transforms itself into an authority problem.... [Women] find that their words, actions and being tend to raise questions of authority within a society and church that assumes authority only comes in the male gender....Whatever women do in a role that claims academic or ecclesiastical authority tends to be interpreted as a threat.[6]

Confirming this observation, many women going through the process toward ordination have quickly learned that women are far more often told they have a "problem with authority" than are male applicants.

Threats to the religious status quo are perceived by traditionalists as rising from a rejection of the authority of God "himself"—God implicitly and often explicitly understood as a patriarchal figure whose nature manifests an eternal and essential connection between authority and the masculine. Most Christian feminists would respond that it is not the authority of God—the author of all creation—which is being questioned, or even the derivative authority of the texts and traditions through which God's Word comes to each new generation. Rather, it is the authority of traditional interpretations and interpreters of the texts and traditions, and of the ecclesial and social structures which have embodied those interpretations, which is now being challenged.

As in the conversation between Humpty Dumpty and Alice, the feminist/traditionalist controversy hinges on who has the power to define religious meaning, to interpret significance, to draw authoritative conclusions—in Humpty's words, who is to be master. In the Episcopal Church and the Anglican Communion as a whole, which lack either an individual office or a centralized body with authority to pass ultimate judgments about meaning, the struggle for mastery becomes a protracted interaction of political maneuvering and theological debate. This struggle is particularly complex and poignant for feminists, who generally reject mastery itself as one of the structures of domination. Can women break free of patriarchal control without creating new forms of domination? As Audre Lorde has observed, "The master's tools will never dismantle the master's house."[7]

The subordination of women is such an integral part of religion and culture that most of the time it goes unrecognized. The majority of Episcopalians would probably deny any necessary theological or institutional connection between ordaining women and homosexuality, abortion, or prayer book revision, because those connections are so integral to our world view that we literally cannot see them. Many who accept the idea of women's equality hold "traditional" views on other issues. It is politically risky for supporters to admit that the ordination of women is an integral part of some "radical feminist package." But the breadth of the traditionalist agenda, its historical and psychological foundation in opposition to new roles for women, and its consistency across the spectrum of other party divisions (high church/low church, catholic/evangelical/renewal) cannot be ignored. One of the most important things that traditionalists teach the rest of the church is that these issues *are* connected.

Chapter 16

Women, Sex, and Sexuality

A s acceptance of the ordination of women spread throughout the Episcopal Church and the Anglican Communion, the links among the questions of women, authority, and sexuality—especially homosexuality—became even more apparent. When the House of Bishops in 1977 faced potential schism over the 1976 decision to ordain women, it was also dealing with outrage over the fact that one of the first women to be ordained priest was a lesbian, Ellen Barrett, of the diocese of New York. Similarly, in the 1990s the traditionalists' horror at assaults on the old order dwelt on the sexuality question, and nowhere was this more sharply demonstrated than in the controversy stirred up by an ordination in the diocese of Newark.

In December 1989, Bishop John S. Spong ordained Robert Williams to the priesthood. Spong was a long-time supporter of women's ordination and had become an outspoken theological iconoclast through such books as *Living in Sin* and *Rescuing the Bible from Fundamentalism*. Like Bishop Pike, he seemed to enjoy playing the maverick, and had a similar ability to grab the attention of the secular media. Williams—employed as the first director of the Oasis, a new diocesan ministry intended to serve the lesbian-gay community—was openly gay and had lived for years with another man. The ordination was billed as a first in the Episcopal Church, since, ironically, many seemed to have forgotten Ellen Barrett, and it was widely publicized by secular and church press, provoking an intense outcry. At a national conference soon after, Williams made more headlines by questioning the value of monogamy and ridiculing celibacy, which precipitated a painful confrontation with Spong and the Oasis Board.

At the end of January Williams resigned and later renounced his orders in the Episcopal Church.

The issue was by no means laid to rest by his resignation, however. At its February meeting, the Presiding Bishop's Council of Advice issued a statement "disassociating" itself from the ordination of Williams, implying that ordaining openly gay persons violated church discipline and harshly criticizing Spong. Then the Executive Council, which acts on behalf of the General Convention between its triennial meetings, issued its own statement, calling for moderation and dialogue, and implicitly criticizing the bishops' statement for its emphasis on the murky legal situation.[1]

The "legality" of ordaining gay men and lesbians in the Episcopal Church is ambiguous. At this writing there is no explicit constitutional or canonical language either permitting or prohibiting such ordinations, as there had been nothing explicit about ordaining women prior to 1976. Though seldom documented, it is tacitly recognized that many priests and bishops throughout the church's history have been gay men, of whom only some have remained celibate, but the subject was never openly discussed until the ordination of women was authorized. Then in January 1977, Bishop Paul Moore of New York, with the support of his diocesan standing committee, ordained Ellen Barrett. Barrett was a co-founder of Integrity, the Episcopal organization supporting lesbians and gay men, and, though she was not living with another woman, she chose not to lie about her sexual orientation.

When the House of Bishops met in Port St. Lucie that September Moore was harshly criticized, and discussions about homosexuality were woven throughout that crisis-driven meeting. In the end, Moore was not actually disciplined. The only rule he had broken, after all, was an unwritten one—"don't ordain homosexuals if they tell the truth about themselves"—and since the House was simultaneously preparing a statement of conscience permitting people to ignore the canons about women, it was in a weak position to criticize the canonically-impeccable New York ordination. But a statement on collegiality adopted at that meeting, aimed primarily at retired Bishop Albert Chambers for his support of the schismatic Anglican Church of North America, also implicitly criticized the "unilateral" New York action:

Error and scandal are less likely to prevail if this principle of collegial action and decision is observed. This indicates the importance of consultation among bishops whenever a bishop anticipates the need to act apart from the agreed position of the House of Bishops, or in a situation where no collegial guidelines have been set.[2]

The bishops also endorsed a report saying "our present understanding of biblical and theological truth would make [ordination of an advocating and/or practicing homosexual] impossible," and resolved that "no Bishop of this Church shall confer Holy Orders in violation of these principles."[3]

The next General Convention, in 1979, adopted a resolution recommending that sexual orientation in itself not be a criterion for judging fitness for ordination, but declaring that it was "not appropriate" to ordain anyone who was sexually active outside of marriage. This recommendation, though weighty, carried no canonical or constitutional force.[4] Twenty-one bishops dissented, noting that the resolution against ordaining "practicing" homosexuals was "recommendatory and not prescriptive" and giving notice that they did not intend to be bound by it; and a group of deputies endorsed the bishops' statement.[5] Thus it was common knowledge that the church would continue to ordain gay men and lesbians, some remaining celibate while others were living in committed relationships, or "practicing." Some were open about themselves during the ordination process while others chose to remain silent. Supportive bishops generally advised secrecy, since few congregations were willing to employ an openly lesbian or gay priest.

Attempts were made at subsequent General Conventions to amend the canons by including sexual orientation as a given which, like race and gender, could not be used to exclude people from ordination. Patient lobbying by Integrity brought such a change within one vote of passage in 1988. It was approved by the House of Bishops, and by the clergy in the House of Deputies on a vote by orders, but vehement opposition coordinated by Episcopalians United and other traditionalists brought its defeat by a single lay vote.[6] Thus the 1988 General Convention ended with a precarious compromise on the ordination of women (the narrow endorsement of half the episcopal visitors proposal) and another stalemate, complete with contradictory manifestos, on the subject of homosexuality.

It was in this context that Bishop Spong, the Newark standing committee, and Robert Williams chose to do publicly what others had been doing quietly, and found themselves in the midst of a fire-storm of protest. Conservatives had been unhappy with Spong for years because of his liberal theology, provocative style, and challenging approach to sexual ethics in general. Many drew parallels between Spong and James Pike, who had played the same iconoclastic role in the House of Bishops in the 1960s that Spong seemed to play in the 1980s, and responded to Spong as an earlier generation had to Pike: with attacks in the press, attempts to try him for heresy, and censure motions even before the controversy regarding the Williams ordination.

After the trauma and institutional embarrassment of the attempts to try Bishop Pike, however, Episcopalians had little taste for heresy trials. Many appreciated Spong's willingness to tackle vexing contemporary issues, and believed that his witness helped the church to maintain credibility (or at least to gain a hearing) in an increasingly secular world. The intemperate nature of some traditionalist attacks, particularly those from the Prayer Book Society, even drew some sympathy for Spong, who became a test case for how much authority and independence a bishop had—to administer, to teach, to "be a bishop."

The Williams incident revealed where the limits of that independence were. In the months that followed, the church struggled to cope with the challenge to the norms of authority and sexuality which had been violated by the Newark ordination. Parallels with the Philadelphia ordination were drawn. Some sought to bring the bishop to church trial, while others were preoccupied with trying to repair the damage done to the lesbian/gay community. Petitions were circulated opposing the ordination of gay men and lesbians, and other signatures were collected supporting the continuation of such ordinations. Following several months of negotiations with Presiding Bishop Browning's office, Spong announced that he would postpone the ordination of Barry Stopfel, another gay men living with a male partner. In September the House of Bishops met, and debated the matter at length. Although seven of the ten signatories to the Council of Advice statement—including the Presiding Bishop himself—now distanced themselves from their February action, the

House voted narrowly to affirm the Council of Advice's "disassociation," and then listened to a ringing defense from Bishop Spong who chastised them for hypocrisy and exercising a double standard of collegiality and autonomy. Two weeks later Stopfel was ordained by Spong's assistant bishop, Walter Righter, and Bishop John Howe of Central Florida announced he would bring a canonical amendment to the 1991 Convention prohibiting the ordination of "practicing" homosexuals and their advocates.

Two aspects of this extremely complex incident are worth noting here. First, the most sustained and organized opposition to the events in Newark came from the three major traditionalist organizations: the Prayer Book Society, Episcopalians United, and the Episcopal Synod of America. Second, a different standard of conformity to the church's discipline was applied to Newark than was being applied to members of the Synod and others opposed to women's ordination. History was repeating itself, as the web connecting authority, gender, and sexuality became more visible, and once again ordination was the catalyst exposing the connections.

Echoes from the Past

The Williams ordination revealed where the outer limits of episcopal autonomy lay in 1990. Reminiscent of the O'Hare response to the Philadelphia ordinations and Episcopal Synod statements on the effect of women bishops, the sharply-worded statement from Browning and his council had also been written in the heat of crisis. It drew on language and concepts (especially "disassociation") developed in the Bayne Committee report following the Pike heresy controversy of the 1960s. Moreover, the rebuke demonstrated the three factors which can limit a bishop's autonomy: the conformist pressures of collegiality, the symbolic power of ordination, and the deep connection between traditional gender norms and the authority structure and sense of order in the church.

Collegiality was invoked throughout the statement. It claimed to be the result of extensive discussion, and quoted repeatedly from comments by regional groups of bishops—a fascinating textual example of collegiality, in which the authoritativeness of the statement is enhanced by suggesting that many groups arrived at the same consensus. It referred to bishops' responsibility for the unity of the church and to "orderly process." One quotation even seemed to hold all bishops accountable for the controversial actions of each, as a way of justifying their decision to repudiate Spong's action: "We do not believe any of us is being responsible to the duties of this office and the polity of this church when one of us acts in such public disregard."[7] Then, with echoes of the Bayne Committee report and the censure statement that followed the Philadelphia ordinations, the Council of Advice proceeded to "decry" and "disassociate" themselves from the ordination in Newark.

At O'Hare the bishops made an ill-advised declaration that the Philadelphia ordinations were not valid; in February 1990 the Council of Advice made a similarly ill-founded assertion that the 1979 General Convention recommendation was "authoritative." Like Humpty Dumpty and Alice, the church expressed its conflict through opposing definitions—was the resolution a "recommendation," or was it "authoritative"? The Episcopal Synod was quick to pick up on the council's statement: "The word 'authoritative' is crucial. It undercuts the position held by Spong and supporters of the Williams ordination—namely that the resolution is merely advisory."[8] A lack of consensus about the issues led to a lack of consensus about sources of authority in the church.

Another echo of the reaction to the Philadelphia ordinations was the very limited nature of the "extensive consultation" which produced the statement. When the bishops met at O'Hare in 1974 they spoke only among themselves, refusing to talk with the ordained women. In 1990 Browning and his advisors took counsel only among an inner circle of other bishops, denying Spong's request to meet with his accusers, and refusing to include representatives from Integrity in discussions leading to the statement. In September, the House debated the matter for two hours, voted to reaffirm the February statement, and only then listened to Bishop Spong. There was no open dialogue with those whose actions were being decried. The closed-door nature of much of the negotiations, the shifting positions of key participants (including Spong, who chose to delay Stopfel's ordination), and the closeness of the House of Bishops' vote (80-76 with two abstentions, one of them Spong) demonstrated just how dangerous the intersection of sexuality and authority was perceived to be by the church's leaders.

In this volatile context, the symbolic power of ordination can be seen undergirding the entire statement, and indeed every aspect of the incident. One is ordained to the priesthood for the whole church, not merely for a local ministry or diocese. As the statement pointed out, the prayer book expects every ordinand to be "a wholesome example to all people," and the criteria for ordination have served *de facto* as the church's model for "godly living." Just as the ordination of women served as the pivot around which opposition to women's changing roles revolved, so the ordination of gay men and lesbians became the focus of the church's struggle with the whole topic of sexuality. To ordain or not ordain people on the basis of their membership in a particular group makes a profound statement about the church's attitude toward all members of that group—whether defined in terms of race, gender, sexuality, physical ability, language, culture, or any other category which societies have used as a basis for discrimination. If some members of a group can be ordained, all are implicitly recognized as full members of the church; if not, all are not. The 1990 Council of Advice statement had tried to soften the rejection of gay men and lesbians by distinguishing between their action and the people it affected:

> We must stress that our "disassociation" is not from the many members of our church who are gay and lesbian....[We] value their presence and their service within the church.

But such reassurance sounded hollow in the context of the bishops' actions, as meaningless as earlier votes of thanks for women's missionary labors and United Thank Offering dollars coupled with repeated denial of seats in the House of Deputies.

"Great Fear and Prejudice"

In fact, the church's leadership was profoundly divided and ambivalent about homosexuality. Two days after disassociating themselves from Spong's action, the bishops adopted a pastoral statement on human sexuality which made explicit the lack of consensus:

> We begin by acknowledging that on the issues of human sexuality, wide diversity and confusion mark our church and most Christian communities....We are not of a single mind....We urge you to pray for patience.[9]

Like their ambivalence about women's ordination, the bishops' confusion about homosexuality was rooted in cultural patterns and taboos which protected the traditional power structures of church and society. Traditional concepts of order and authority in the church paralleled secular concepts about the family, both of which were challenged by changing attitudes toward women and toward sexuality. Feminist analyst Rosalind Petchesky notes in her study of the relationship of the anti-abortion movement and the political New Right to women's rights:

> Male homosexuality is even more dangerous than female...because it signals a breakdown of "masculinity" itself....At stake in the New Right campaign against homosexuality is the very idea of what it means to be a "man" or a "woman," and the structure and meaning of the traditional family. [10]

The ordination of Robert Williams, symbolic of a breakdown of masculinity within the very sanctuary of the church, confirmed the traditionalists' worst fears about what would happen if women were released from their subordinate places. It unnerved the liberals too, because it seemed to prove that the traditionalists were right—all the old structures were coming under attack. In that context, the bishops' attempt to regain control by focusing on questions of order is not surprising.

Most significant in the Council of Advice statement was the way it chose to define the offense committed in Newark. Although it referred to "scandal," it did not explicitly mention the ordination of a gay man, as the censure of the Philadelphia bishops did not explicitly refer to their having ordained women. It referred instead to order, discipline, and process, and the balance between individual action and decision-making in the larger church. Despite the fact that—as in the 1977 ordination of Ellen Barrett—all applicable canons had been observed, this exercise of conscience in ignoring the 1979 Convention's recommendation was treated as a major offense.

The response of the bishops to the Newark ordination was consistent with their attitude to the Philadelphia ordinations in expressing outrage when people outside the existing norm were admitted to the church's ordained ministry, but it was completely inconsistent with their response to traditionalists' refusal to accept the church's decision to ordain women. In the latter case, it was not merely a "mind of Convention" recommendation but the canon law of the church being set aside by individual bishops, dioceses, and parishes. Why condemn ignoring the canons in Philadelphia, tolerate the traditionalists' disregard of the canons regarding the ordination of women, and condemn a canonically unassailable action in Newark? As Spong observed in his stirring *apologia* following the House of Bishops' endorsement of the Council of Advice statement, "Permissive canons and binding recommendations—my sister and brothers, only great fear and prejudice would enable one to talk this way."[11] Yet inconsistent as they were, both responses tended to stabilize the institution by minimizing the redistribution of power to the margins, thus slowing the rate at which straight women, lesbians, and gay men were permitted to share with heterosexual men in the full life of the church symbolized by its ordained leadership.

Sexual distinctions—of gender and orientation—proved crucial to the exercise of authority in the church. Sex and power have long been bound together in the church's institutional structures, in which the subordination of women is treated—in practice if not in theory— as though it were essential to maintaining ecclesiastical authority. Women's exclusion from lay and ordained leadership and their domination in daily life through religiously-sanctioned norms of sexual and reproductive behavior and a single standard of heterosexual family life have been perpetuated and reinforced by male-dominant religious language and imagery. The system is so pervasive and interlocking that it is practically invisible, and is extremely difficult to describe or analyze because it is imbedded in our very thought patterns and language.

The traditionalist agenda has identified the interlocking issues that connect the "woman question" with questions of authority in the church and that create the ecclesiastical and spiritual framework within which we perceive and enter into relationship with God. When one piece of this framework is changed, all are affected. It is not possible, therefore, to ordain women without realigning concepts and practices about language, sexuality, authority, and God, because all are linked psychologically, emotionally, theoretically, and historically. As the twentieth century draws to a close, the Episcopal Church remains deep in the throes of this examination, evaluating inclusive language liturgical texts, studying reproductive issues and sexual behavior, debating the sanctioning of lesbian/gay relationships and the ordination of gay men and lesbians, and among traditionalists still debating the ordination of women.

Because of the deep divisions within the church on these unresolved issues, the question of who has authority to make decisions regarding them is fraught with significance. The Humpty Dumpty problem of definition, "who is to be master," shows itself in struggles among the various institutional entities with the constitutional power to make decisions for the church. The House of Bishops, the Presiding Bishop and his Council of Advice, the General Convention, the Executive Council, diocesan conventions and standing committees, and individual bishops all act for the church in varying capacities. But the consensus necessary for their actions to be received as authoritative is fragile, easily broken by the profound contradictions between the traditionalist view and the "radical feminist package."

Washington and Phoenix

In June 1991, a year after the ordination of a gay man in Newark, another diocese also chose not to follow the 1979 General Convention recommendation. Ronald Haines, then suffragan bishop in the diocese of Washington (the diocesan bishop, John Walker, having died a few months earlier) ordained to the priesthood Elizabeth Carl, a lesbian who lived openly with her life partner. Carl's ordination to the diaconate had taken place quietly during the summer between Spong's ordination of Williams and the House of Bishops meeting, but news of her impending ordination to the priesthood was leaked to the press and provoked another firestorm of protest.

The General Convention met the next month in Phoenix, Arizona, and the conflict became so intense that the House of Bishops was literally paralyzed. Even before the convention opened controversy had erupted over whether to move it to another city in the wake of Arizona's rejection of the Martin Luther King, Jr., holiday, and so tension over racism combined with conflicts over gender, sexuality, and authority. Proposals to censure bishops Haines and Righter (who had ordained Stopfel after the bishops' "disassociation" from Spong), to establish a local option for diocesan decisions on ordaining homosexuals, to add a canon forbidding sexual relations outside marriage for clergy, to study the blessing of same-sex unions—all were debated furiously.

Proceedings in the House of Bishops became so heated that legislation was suspended and the House met several times in executive session, attempting to restore civility. The bishops finally adopted a substitute resolution restating traditional teaching restricting sexual expression to heterosexual marriage, but noted a "discontinuity" between this teaching and the experience of many Episcopalians. It called for dialogue throughout the church and preparation of a pastoral teaching on the subject for the next Convention. A telling clause indicated the depth of the stalemate: "This General Convention confesses our failure to lead and to resolve this discontinuity through legislative efforts based upon random resolutions directed at singular and various aspects of these issues."[12]

In fact, it was the House of Bishops which had lost its ability to lead. Its resolution was amended in the House of Deputies, where voting on related issues had been much more decisive, and deputies insisted on including six of their own members in the preparation of the pastoral teaching—a distinct challenge to the teaching authority of the bishops. On the next to the last day of Convention, recognizing the unlikelihood of support from the House of Deputies, the bishops adopted a tortured "mind of the House" resolution recognizing "the pain and damage to the collegiality and credibility of this House and to the whole Church when individual bishops and dioceses ordain sexually active gay and lesbian persons," and acknowledging that there was no clear consensus on these ordinations in the House of Bishops.[13] An attempt to add a call that bishops refrain from such ordinations until further notice was defeated.

Continuing conflict over the ordination of women was a running counterpoint to the sexuality debates in Phoenix. The Episcopal Synod of America continued its effort to create a protected enclave for those who did not recognize the validity of women's orders, and joined forces with the Prayer Book Society to lobby for the full range of traditionalist issues. In the House of Deputies, larger and much more diverse than the House of Bishops (half the deputies are lay, and in 1991 thirty percent were women), the traditionalists' concerns were vehemently presented but generally voted down by significant margins. Conservative forces then seemed to concentrate in the House of Bishops, but met with only a little more success there. The lack of consensus, the damage to collegiality, the certainty that individual bishops and dioceses would follow the lead of Newark and Washington, and the bitterly acrimonious personal exchanges between bishops in both public and executive sessions demonstrated the extent to which their perception of authority had depended on unity, and unity had depended on a uniform approach to matters of gender and sexuality.

While the bishops wrangled, the House of Deputies took an historic step: they elected as their president Pamela P. Chinnis. The first woman to hold that post, Chinnis had filled virtually every other position open to laywomen in the Episcopal Church and the Anglican Communion, including presiding officer for the Triennial Meeting in Minneapolis in 1976, when she scandalized some by observing that the church was still sexist despite approval of women's ordination. A remarkable mixture of intellect, rapier wit, and disarming, lady-like decorum, Chinnis succeeded David Collins as president of the nearly nine-hundred-member legislative body. Collins had been a popular presiding officer because of his gentle humor and impeccable fairness. He was also well known as a conservative leader, associated with the renewal movement and Episcopalians United, whereas Chinnis's liberal credentials were extensive, including years of campaigning for the ordination of women and forthright support for gay men and lesbians. Her uncontested election testified to the growing momentum for change in women's roles, and the six deputies appointed to work with bishops on a sexuality statement were chosen by her. Charming she may have been, but to traditionalists her assumption of presidential powers could not have boded well.

Schism appeared to be drawing closer. At the end of the 1991 Convention, the Episcopal Synod declared: "There are now two religions in the Episcopal Church. We worship two Gods...[and we] must recognize the radical theological divorce between us."[14] At its November meeting, the Synod announced the formation of a "Missionary Diocese of America" headed by its most provocative leader, retired bishop A. Donald Davies. This new diocese appeared to be a unilateral attempt to establish the nongeographical "doctrinal province" proposed by the Synod to no avail the year before. The original plan for inviting like-minded Episcopal congregations to affiliate with the missionary diocese was scrapped in the face of heated criticism—it was uncanonical and violated all the principles of Anglican polity and Lambeth resolutions regarding unity—but several earlier break-away groups did affiliate with Davies's group. It was increasingly clear that, even seventeen years after Philadelphia, the ecclesiastical implications of ordaining women had only begun to be realized.

The Balance of Power Continues to Shift

Only one woman had sat in the House of Bishops in 1991, but the following year the diocese of Washington elected a new suffragan bishop: Jane Holmes Dixon, rector of a prosperous suburban Maryland parish and president of the standing committee that had supported Ronald Haines in his decision to ordain Elizabeth Carl. Following her election at the end of May 1992, the Episcopal Synod and Episcopalians United conducted a campaign opposing consent to her consecration, similar to the campaign against Barbara Harris five years earlier. However, the focus of criticism had shifted to Dixon's support of the full participation of gay men and lesbians in the church's life, rather than the fact that she was a woman.

Despite the campaign of opposition, the necessary consents for Dixon's consecration were easily received and in the fall of 1992 the tide turned against the traditionalist wing of the church in the United States and throughout the Anglican Communion. In early November, just before Dixon was consecrated, the Church of England voted narrowly but decisively to authorize the ordination of women as priests. Joining Presiding Bishop Browning and Bishop Barbara Harris as co-consecrator of Jane Dixon was Bishop Penelope Jamieson of New Zealand, representing the global extent of commitment to women in the episcopate; Dixon's concelebrants were Bishop Haines and the Rev. Elizabeth Carl, in silent witness to that diocese's continuing commitment to the ministry of gay men and lesbians. Two days later, years of bitter conflict over permitting the ordination of women in the Anglican Church of Australia were resolved, making a clear majority of the twenty-eight provinces of the Anglican Communion who were in support of women's ordination. When the Anglican Consultative Council met in joint session with the primates of the world-wide Communion in January in Capetown, South Africa, host Archbishop

Desmond Tutu included newly-ordained women priests in the welcoming liturgies. That symbolism was reinforced by decree when the Capetown gathering turned aside proposals from traditionalists in England and the United States seeking a nongeographical province within the Communion for those opposed to ordaining women.

The likelihood of turning back this "novelty" within the Anglican Communion grew faint, and defections and the threat of schism once again dominated the news. The day after Dixon's consecration, the Missionary Diocese of America, with its handful of dissident congregations, severed relations with the Synod and formed the "Episcopal Missionary Church." In accordance with the canons, Donald Davies was warned, quietly suspended, and later deposed for abandoning the communion of the Episcopal Church. A prominent lay leader among English traditionalists, William Oddie, converted to Roman Catholicism, and the now retired bishop of London (Graham Leonard, whose interference in the diocese of Oklahoma had so exercised the House of Bishops in 1987) announced his intention of becoming Roman Catholic, too.

But there were many traditionalists anxious to remain within the church, and their future was less certain. Some became even more intent on forcing an accommodation on their own terms, while the patience of others wore thin. Following the defection of the missionary diocese, the Episcopal Synod of America announced a strategy to force the next General Convention either to provide its members some sort of protected ecclesiastical enclave in perpetuity or to expel them outright.

Shortly thereafter, the diocese of Fort Worth elected another Synod leader, Jack Iker, to succeed Clarence Pope as bishop, and a campaign to withhold consents to his consecration was so nearly successful that the service had to be postponed twice. Six protests were lodged during the service while several hundred silent demonstrators prayed outside and a score of prayer vigils were held around the country to show solidarity with those in the diocese of Fort Worth who were denied access to the ministry of ordained women. Before proceeding with the consecration Presiding Bishop Browning himself urged members of the diocese to join with the rest of the church in welcoming the ministries of women. The Episcopal Women's Caucus announced a campaign to encourage a reconsideration of the conscience statement, and before the Iker controversy had died down, the diocese of Vermont became the first jurisdiction to elect a woman, Mary Adelia McLeod, as diocesan bishop. By year's end the Anglican Church of Canada had become the third province in the Communion to elect a woman bishop, when Virginia Matthews was chosen suffragan of Toronto.

Throughout this period, another, grimmer manifestation of dramatic changes in traditional patterns kept appearing in the news. High walls of protective silence were besieged by an unprecedented series of revelations about sexual misconduct on the part of prominent male clergy, including bishops. Like similar cases involving Roman Catholic and Protestant clergy and secular leaders accused of sexual harassment or abuse, most of these incidents involved past relationships only now being brought to light, and they demonstrated a subtle but profound shift affecting authority, gender relationships, and sexual norms. For generations, centuries even, society had tacitly sanctioned—by remaining silent—the sexual exploitation of women and children, and this unspoken tolerance was practiced within the church as well as the secular society. Gradually the conspiracy of silence, quiet transfers of parochial clergy, and suspicion of those bringing charges broke down, and one of the most sordid, hidden aspects of male privilege began to be exposed. It was not a coincidence that most of the religious leaders naming this evil, giving voice to its victims, and mobilizing the church to promote healing and discipline were ordained women, most notably Marie Fortune and Karen Labecqz of the United Church of Christ, and Margo Maris of the Episcopal Diocese of Minnesota. Power—for good or for ill, to hide or to heal—was no longer held exclusively by men, and the leadership of women called men to a new discipline and responsibility in pastoral relationships. The old rules were changing in unanticipated ways—not to everyone's liking.

The day after Jane Dixon was consecrated suffragan bishop of Washington, she joined bishops Harris and Jamieson on a radio talk show to discuss the situation of women and leadership in the church. The one-hour conversation was wide-ranging, but the exchange which dominated church press coverage and provoked a stream of outraged editorializing occurred when the interviewer, Diane Rehm, asked Dixon why it was important for women to share the episcopate with men. "Authority! And being able to make decisions," Dixon said, to which Rehm responded, "The key issue is power and the operating of power."[15]

The prospect of women assuming power in the church is a catalyst for the struggle between two world views. Women take on this power by moving into leadership positions previously closed to them: in doing so they also—often inadvertently—disturb the power relationships in all aspects of personal, social, and ecclesial life and thereby challenge everyone's sense of identity, ideas about right relationships with each other, and concepts of God. Women who moved beyond their defined roles and began to exercise power as equals with men threatened traditionalists' concept of the church. When the constitutionally and canonically sanctioned authorities within the Episcopal Church "capitulated" to powerful women, opponents looked outside the contemporary institution to ancient tradition and sacred text, seeking an authoritative word of God to sanction their resistance to the redistribution of power within the church. They also became increasingly hostile to those they perceived to be leading the church astray, and resistant to supporting the national church of Presiding Bishop Browning and President Chinnis. Criticism of "the structure" as no longer enabling the proper mission of the church became commonplace, alongside nostalgia for the booming 1950s and acute anxiety in the face of persistent economic pressures in a post-Christian society.

From the establishment of the Woman's Auxiliary in 1872 to Pam Chinnis's election as president of the House of Deputies in 1991 and Mary Adelia McLeod's consecration at the hands of the Presiding Bishop, Barbara Harris, and Jane Dixon in 1993, women had certainly moved into a "higher sphere of usefulness" in the Episcopal Church. But the church they were called to lead was scarcely recognizable as the institution which had for so long kept them on the margins. They had to contend with fear and anger and to invent new forms for authority and leadership which did not depend on the power historically ascribed to males within all social relationships. Traditionalists were apparently willing to bring the church to the brink of schism—and beyond—in order to preserve the male-dominant model of Christian community. The rest of the House of Bishops, theoretically committed to the inclusion of women, had chosen a strategy of accommodation and conciliation which perpetuated women's exclusion in many places. Nevertheless, women's expanding participation steadily brought about profound changes in the polity, liturgy, theology, and ethical framework within which Episcopalians live.

New Wine,
New Wineskins

"But my dear," said the Hatter with a frown, "was there progress?"
"Well," said Alice earnestly, "there was change."
                                        —Anonymous, after Lewis Carroll

C hanges in women's roles in the past twenty-five years have challenged the ecclesiastical structures of the Episcopal Church more profoundly than any other social issue in the two centuries since it was first organized in 1789. During that time women moved from near-invisibility within the church's institutional structures into positions in every area of lay and ordained leadership. These dramatic institutional changes placed immense stress on the church's spiritual framework, threatening its traditional interpretations of authority, morality, and theology and demonstrating that the subordination of women had been a necessary element in traditional ecclesiastical structures. Like old wineskins, those structures threatened to burst with the new wine of mutuality between men and women.

New structures—rules, language, attitudes, interpretations, relationships—had to be created to hold this new wine at every stage. The passage from participation in the Woman's Auxiliary to membership in the House of Bishops and a woman president of the House of Deputies included long periods of gradual adaptation and short periods of sharp conflict. Deeper issues began to emerge with the symbolic completion of women's admission to the church's ordained leadership. The ecclesiastical controversies marking the beginning of the 1990s exposed many connections between women's "place" and the theological and moral framework of patriarchal culture manifested in the Episcopal Church.

The rise of the Woman's Auxiliary illustrated the boundaries within which Episcopal women could operate in the period following the Civil War. Embracing "auxiliary" status and using a rhetoric of submission, they were free to create a quasi-public sphere of activity within the church which conformed to prevailing norms for dependent female behavior. Because deference was built into this structure, women benefitted from men's tendency not to notice what women did as long as their dominant status was not challenged. Even the substantial financial power represented by the United Thank Offering was not perceived as a serious threat to the official power structure because its origins were so lowly (pennies placed in blue boxes on the family table day after day), and because the funds were strategically allocated to the favorite projects of influential priests and bishops throughout the church. Thus women's organized religious work supported the male-defined enterprise of the church without disturbing traditional arrangements of power. In the writings of leaders like Julia and Mary Emery one finds suggestions that they were not entirely content with the limitations imposed on them, but neither they nor their successors on the Auxiliary staff seem to have aspired to power alongside men. Their expressed motivation was to engage women in the mission of the church, the spread of the gospel, and the redemption of the world.

Alongside the Auxiliary structure around the turn of the century, other women created and supported unofficial organizations to foster their own spiritual development, minister in response to a variety of social needs, and occasionally pressure the official church. Some of these groups included men; all were relatively small and on the fringes of the church's organized life. Women in such groups were temperamentally less conventional than those in the Auxiliary, less patient with bureaucratic structures and delays, and often much more radical on social and political issues facing the church. Like Vida Scudder, many held a no-nonsense position that women should share in church government, but their primary commitment was not to campaigning for women's rights.

Both the Auxiliary and the unofficial groups nurtured a new kind of churchwoman who knew how official ecclesial and political structures operated and built personal networks with other women and with men in positions of power within official structures. Women played significant roles behind the scenes prior to World War I in shaping the church's response to rapidly changing social conditions, and in the flux of that period a few women were even permitted to play quasi-official roles on the edges of the General Convention structure. But that structure proved resistant, tightening up its appointment rules immediately after women appeared on an official commission in 1913, and resoundingly defeating measures to include women in church governance in the 1920s. Women could encourage male allies to work on their behalf, but they had no role in the decisions of the General Convention. Their experiences on the margins of the institution had not equipped them to influence its center.

The long campaign for seating women in the House of Deputies demonstrated the bankruptcy of deferential rhetoric as a political tool when equality is sought. So long as the Auxiliary was asking for authorization to conduct its separate and unequal activities, submissive language and "ladylike" behavior were effective in achieving its goals. But the same language fell on absolutely deaf ears when the request was for admission to the House of Deputies. Time after time the women of the Triennial politely petitioned, and time after time the deputies refused—as each Convention duly performed the rituals of deference and power imbedded in the United Thank Offering, modestly presented by the women and magnanimously received by the men. Power does not bow to deference, and it was not until a greater power was exerted, in the form of the increasingly embarrassing distance between secular and church practices highlighted by Presiding Bishop Lichtenberger's sharp rebuke in 1964, that the men of the Convention finally voted to allow women to join them as lay deputies.

The 1970 and 1973 defeat of proposals for ordaining women to the priesthood made two things clear: first, ordination symbolizes access to power in the Episcopal Church far more than either baptism or full voting membership; second, most of the men who held that power were not eager to share it with women. Laymen's votes had delayed the admission of women to the ranks of lay deputies, and it was ordained men whose votes delayed the admission of women to the ordained ministry. Although both campaigns involved the acceptance of women into previously all-male areas of church leadership, the campaign for women's ordination was much briefer, and took a form radically different from the campaign for women deputies. Key leaders in the ordination struggle were able to look back and reflect on the earlier campaign, and on their own failures to persuade bishops and key clergy to take decisive action. Deferential rhetoric and polite requests had not won women seats in Convention, and were even less likely to gain them admission to the sanctuary.

The moment that women priests were a reality instead of a future prospect, the power dynamic within the church underwent dramatic change, producing a period of instability before a new equilibrium could be achieved. While authorizing the inclusion of women, the institution reasserted its right to regulate the ordained ministry through "regularization" services for the Philadelphia and Washington ordinands in 1974 and 1975. Acknowledging that the sacramental power women had claimed was valid, these ceremonies made it clear that women, like men, could only exercise it within the church by submitting to the ecclesial authority of their diocesan bishops. Although a process of reconciliation was begun between the institution and the "outsiders" who had claimed a share of its power, and a disruptive presence was absorbed into what had become a larger framework, these relationships were affected by the persistence of opposition to the original decision to ordain women.

The role of bishop, and the power of the House of Bishops, are central to understanding the persistence of the conflict. Although it had voted in support of women's ordination several years before the deputies approved it, the House of Bishops had lost its ability to provide clear leadership on this issue when it became mired in arguments over collegiality following the Philadelphia ordinations. This set the stage, after the 1976 General Convention vote, for a minority implacably opposed to ordaining women to paralyze the church's normal process by repeatedly threatening schism. Had there not been active bishops among the opponents to women's ordination, the resistance effort within the church would very probably have collapsed within a few years. Eventually the House of Bishops took on a negative function, that of delaying full implementation of the canonical change. The delicate balance between individual episcopal authority and the collegial authority of the whole House prevented the church's chief pastors from dealing with the traditionalists' challenge to General Convention's authority in an unambiguous way.

The question of authority became explicit as regards ordaining women. By what authority did the Episcopal Church depart from the gospel precedent of the all-male Twelve, or the seemingly unbroken tradition of the church? Was it legitimate for the Episcopal Church to act independently of the rest of the Anglican Communion, or of Catholic Christendom? Could a canonical change approved by a single action of the General Convention overturn centuries of deliberate gender segregation in the ministry? From the other side, did the House of Bishops have the authority unilaterally to sanction the exclusion of women in some parts of the church by making obedience to the canons optional? When "consciences" were fundamentally opposed, who had the authority to determine God's will in regard to ordaining women, or in all the related matters of sexuality and of the proper roles and relationships of men and women?

Issues of authority have played a central part in every historical stage of expansion in women's roles in the church. As we have seen, the Woman's Auxiliary was authorized only because it was explicitly subordinated to the authority of the Board of Missions, and authority was a central issue in the resistance to women serving the church as deaconesses, who were finally accepted only because they vowed strict obedience to the bishop. It surfaced again in the Edwards/Pike conflict surrounding the canonical change from deaconess to deacon, when one renegade bishop's support of a less subservient form of women's diaconal ministry was experienced as a challenge to the collegiality of the House of Bishops. This challenge became acute when more bishops broke ranks to participate in the Philadelphia ordinations, enabling women to defy traditional authority structures based on inequality and subordination, by asserting as a higher authority a contradictory norm of equality and mutuality. The actual admission of women to the brotherhood of bishops shattered a powerful symbol of male control over women that the episcopate had represented, and the ascension of Pamela Chinnis to the presidency of the House of Deputies signalled the inclusion of women in the top levels of church government.

For a woman to preside at the Eucharist or the House of Deputies created an uncomfortable cultural dissonance. If women could exercise the authority of government and the episcopate, how was this authority to be understood? The decisions of a legislative body headed by a woman would not benefit from the authority unconsciously ascribed to the actions of men. The episcopate could no longer automatically appropriate the power culturally accorded to men, and where women were bishops they would overturn familiar patterns by exercising both spiritual and jurisdictional authority over men. These developments threatened the entire network of relationships among bishops, other clergy, and lay people, and the familiar patterns of power and control, both recognized and unconscious. They also upset conventional patterns for every human relationship and interpersonal behavior—for good and ill—all built within a male-dominant system of patriarchal religious authority. The changes confounded traditional theological formulations that depended on male-dominant imagery and language, challenging familiar understandings about the very nature of God and God's relationship to humankind.

For years before women were priests or bishops, they were making their way into leadership positions in business, the professions, and government. Women as entrepreneurs, doctors, judges, and prime ministers created valuable new models and weakened the rigid gender-segregation of Western society. Even the most conservative of Episcopalians were accustomed to those changes. But the intensity of resistance to women bishops testified to the power of religious symbols to establish norms for leadership and human relationships. The existence of women bishops says, in ways that a woman professor or cabinet minister could never say, that it is "right"—that it accords with the holy, the sacred—for women to have authority and to exercise power. Perhaps it was not an accident that a woman became a bishop (twelve years after women's ordination to the priesthood was authorized) before a woman became president of the House of Deputies (twenty-one years after women were seated in that House). When Jane Dixon mentioned "authority," feminists nodded but traditionalists took issue, for the exercise of authority and power by women does fundamentally alter the web of social relationships.

Authority and power shape every social system, and they must be in balance for an organization to function smoothly. Each system needs to have the means (power) to establish those conditions specified by whatever it accepts as authoritative, and it cannot function well if there are other powers operating independently of its legitimate authority. When power dynamics change, authority is called into question. Debates about what is authoritative indicate that the equilibrium in the distribution of power within an organization has been disturbed: some people have acquired more, perhaps at the expense of others. This is most readily observed in revolutionary secular politics, when leaders of a military coup (power) suspend a constitution (authority) for reasons claimed to be more authoritative (such as justice for those previously excluded or exploited).

Similar dynamics occur in the perennial process of reforming the church. It was revolutionary for women to share sacramental power with men in the church because the sources of the church's authority—Scripture and tradition as they had long been reasonably interpreted, together with their resulting theologies, liturgies, ethics, and church polity—seemed to dictate the exclusion of women from such power. Challenging women's exclusion challenged the authority of the tradition that had excluded them. Consequently, everything about that tradition seemed open to question, and this was profoundly upsetting for everyone, no matter what their perspective. It was particularly distressing for those who depended on the personal power and sense of security that came from their place in the old order. Cries of alarm and anguish over the threat to the familiar order carried great weight with the bishops, who were responsible for maintaining the peace and unity of the church. Thus a number of social forces were at work, making ordination the pivotal issue in the profound changes in gender relationships occurring in the Episcopal Church in the late twentieth century.

The Symbolic Power of Ordination

Ordination performs several sociological functions within the Episcopal Church. Most obvious of these is the way it structures the exercise of leadership. Through the ordination process, men and women are selected, trained, validated, and granted authority to exercise defined powers within a hierarchical institutional structure. It is a distinctive and deliberately exclusionary process, with a specialized vocabulary and increasingly elaborate rituals marking progress through stages as aspirant, postulant, candidate, deacon, priest, and bishop. People thus initiated into the leadership structure of the institution are identified by special titles and costumes, which signal their right to exercise certain powers and enjoy certain privileges. These include automatic inclusion in the governance system (diocesan conventions) and access to the economic system of the church, whose employment patterns historically presume the placement of ordained persons in leadership positions at each level of the organizational hierarchy (parish, diocese, province, national church). With such placement come corresponding degrees of status, personal security, affluence, influence, and actual decision-making power.

With ordination also comes the authority to preach and teach, to determine for the community its beliefs and morality, to define its reality, and to administer its rites and sacraments. Granting or withholding the sacraments constitutes, in ritual form, the mechanism though which beliefs and morality are maintained and enforced among church members. Ordination confers authority to exercise considerable power within the social system that is the church.

Ordination also functions as a boundary marker between the sacred and the profane. It establishes a religious ideal, marking off those who represent the sacred from the rest of the membership of the church. Anyone may be baptized, but only a select few are ordained. This is almost the reverse of early church practice, in which baptism was conferred only on those who had successfully completed an extensive and rigorous period of examination and preparation, while ordination was a perfunctory rite authorizing some of the baptized to perform particular functions within the community. One of the problems inherent in the current practice was alluded to in the theologians' report on the validity of the Philadelphia ordinations, which noted that to assert that women could not by nature be ordained was "implicitly to deny or qualify the meaning of women's baptism."[1]

Those who are successful in the selection process leading to ordination are those who meet both explicit and hidden standards for belief and behavior. These standards cover such things as education, with all the class and race bias built into educational norms in American society; physical and psychological health, with all the potential for discrimination built into changing definitions of health; doctrinal conformity, whose determination has historically been an arena for political domination and witch-hunting (literal and figurative); and sexual morality, historically understood by Anglicans as a choice between monogamous heterosexual marriage or life-long celibacy (with celibacy regarded somewhat suspiciously).

This approach presupposes that the ordained are to model Christian living for the laity. Standards for ordained members of the church are implicitly held up as the desirable ideal for all members. Changes in the standards represent shifts in the boundary between the sacred and the profane, the whole (holy) and the imperfect, and thus signal changes in the corporate understanding of who can be a real Christian or a real Episcopalian. For example, changing educational requirements to encourage the ordination of Native Americans signalled greater acceptance of all Native Americans; changing requirements about health to permit the ordination of a person with cerebral palsy marked a new level of acceptance of those with physical handicaps; eliminating the gender restriction expressed a new acceptance of women as the peers of men within the community of the church.

Proposed changes in standards for ordination generate considerable debate, because they challenge both the picture of the "ideal" Episcopalian and the boundaries of the sacred. This has been true of changes that have an actual effect, such as permitting nonwhite men or women to be ordained. It is also the case when a proposed change would simply make explicit what has previously been hidden or unknown, such as acknowledging that homosexual orientation and relationships are not incompatible with the exercise of ordained ministry. Ordaining women expressed a new conviction that all women are fully members of the church, redeemed by God on the same basis as men—a position opposed by those whose theology and sense of identity depend on traditions of male domination and female deference.

Ordaining openly gay men and lesbians likewise expressed a growing conviction about the acceptability of all gay men and lesbians within the life of the church, and a shift in ethical focus away from heterosexual rules concerning sexual behavior toward mutuality and care in relationships. Opposition is based on traditional formulations of morality that obscure the fact that heterosexism, like sexism, protects traditional structures of male privilege by enforcing strictly differentiated behavioral norms on all human relationships. The ordination of gay men and lesbians is also resisted because it requires reinterpreting traditional teachings, giving the appearance of undermining the teaching authority of the church by contradicting earlier condemnations of homosexual feelings and relationships. Here again we have an authority problem, as when in earlier generations Christian teachings about slavery and men's right to dominate women were challenged.

As the traditionalist agenda demonstrates, the link between women and sexuality is not coincidental. It is no accident that the women who worked for the ordination of women were frequently accused of being lesbians. Sexual orientation as a factor in the selection process leading to ordination did not become an open topic of debate until women's ordination was authorized, and the most common complaint leveled against the first women bishops was that they were advocates for gay men and lesbians. Both the ordination of women and the acceptance of homosexuality fundamentally challenge the patriarchal order of world and church, undermining male privilege by presenting alternatives to the traditional male/female dominance/submission model for all relationships, whether domestic, political, or ecclesiastical. Ordaining women, gay men, and lesbians violates traditional images of the sacred, crossing the boundary fixed by defining heterosexual males as the norm for ordained ministry and hence the standard for all Christian living. As Clarence Pope said during the debate over Robert Williams's ordination, not holding the line on ordaining gay mean and lesbians would go "a long way toward changing our religion."[2] For traditionalists, the maintenance of the whole ecclesiastical structure depended on upholding that norm through the subordination of women and insistence on heterosexuality.

Powerful taboos are at work. Women are linked with the whole of sexuality, which gay men and lesbians represent in its most uncontrolled form; all must be excluded from the sacred precincts of the church. This was dramatically expressed at the Philadelphia ordinations when a protester characterized the service as offering up "the smell and the sound and the sight of perversion." The symbol of a woman as priest violated ancient notions of religious purity and thus upset the divine order. It was "trying to make stones into bread," and profaning the sacred. In the words of another protester, at Barbara Harris's consecration fifteen years later, it was "a sacrilegious imposture."[3]

In Search of New Wineskins

What lessons might we draw from this historical analysis of the institutional and political processes of the Episcopal Church, its treatment of women since the Civil War, and the relationship between attitudes and practices which relate to women and the theology and polity of the church?

In the Episcopal Church, like most organizations in Western society, control is now shared symbolically with white women and with men and women of color, but white men continue to dominate both legislative and spiritual leadership. As in the larger society, women and people of color in the church have sometimes been able to make common cause and at other times have been pitted against each other, with women of color often caught in the middle. The consecration of an African American as the first woman bishop was for many a symbol of hope that the church was being delivered from the old ways of discrimination against difference.

And like other organizations, the Episcopal Church achieves stability and continuity through bureaucratic structures designed to resist rapid change, such as meeting for legislation only once every three years and the conservative "vote by orders." These structures automatically confer privilege on insiders over those on the outside, so that even when change occurs those who held power under the old order continue to have more influence than newcomers. Leverage from the outside, however, can alter the balance of institutional power in relation to particular issues, and personal connections between insiders and unofficial groups of outsiders (women, traditionalists, gay men, and lesbians) create a shifting outer network of power that may mobilize, counteract, or even paralyze forces within the organization.

Some aspects of this change process are particular to the history and theology of the Episcopal Church. The evolving role of bishops increasingly has an effect on the way this church responds to conflict and change. Its source of legislative authority, the General Convention, can be at odds with its bishops who are collectively its source of spiritual authority, and no outside arbiter or higher court of appeal exists to resolve conflicts between the two. Once consecrated, bishops may sit in the House of Bishops for life, while deputies are elected for one Convention at a time, with anywhere from a third to a half being new each triennium. Because the bishops meet at least once a year, in a much smaller body than the whole Convention, controversial issues receive more of a hearing, and developments in bishops' attitudes can signal changes which may not be accepted by Convention for several triennia. Because they possess broad administrative powers within their own dioceses, bishops can act independently of church mandates—even in opposition to them—so long as they have support from each other. This sometimes enables them to exercise prophetic leadership, but also risks losing touch with the movement of the Spirit in other parts of the Body of Christ.

Collegiality and community took on increasing importance in the House of Bishops in the latter half of the twentieth century. As events challenged traditional authority and power structures, appealing to collegiality became a tool for protecting the status quo. Bishops who broke ranks with their colleagues on controversial issues were subject to reprimand or censure if they were promoting changes which made the church or the ordained ministry more inclusive. Although those who resisted such changes were granted considerable tolerance, those who championed the cause of outsiders were ostracized, which temporarily secured the power of insiders against the outside threat. This made the House of Bishops inconsistent in its attitude toward the church's legal structure, strictly interpreting the rules in some cases and virtually ignoring them in others.

Social change occurs through some combination of rational argument (education), strategic dialogue (politics), and force. In any tradition, certain symbols are more forceful—that is, have more power to change a situation—than education or politics. For Episcopalians, ordination is such a symbol. Whenever we are found arguing over who may be ordained, we will probably be re-forming our sense of identity as the people of God, charting new boundaries for our awareness of the sacred, forging new language to express our experience of relationship to the Creator and all of creation. Until some women could be ordained, all women were second-class in the church; removing the gender test for ordination profoundly altered a central symbol of the tradition.

There is nothing easy about such a transformation. The virulent conflict generated by the ordination of women in the Episcopal Church demonstrated how fundamental sexism and the subordination of women had been to its traditional structures, both political and spiritual. It serves as a warning of what happens when the vested interests of those privileged by the status quo are threatened, and of the spiritual dangers facing those on every side of a changing boundary. Its expansion into conflicts over sexuality, language, and authority reveals the complex network of psychological, social, and moral forces constituting all human communities.

Recognizing these connections is necessary if the divisions resulting from the conflicts are ever to be healed. At the heart of Christian faith is the radical good news of salvation for all, without distinction. As women take this news seriously, they are empowered to challenge patriarchal structures; but it is not merely a matter of women versus tradition. What is promised is the liberation of all creation from the constraints of domination, from the crippling effects of being subordinate to anything less than the Holy of Holies. In our era a new ideal of mutuality struggles to replace the old hierarchical framework, with implications for every aspect of human experience. The bursting of old wineskins is messy and painful, but as we discover the nature of the new wine, we will be able to fashion suitable new containers.

Traditionalists and feminists agree on the relationships among issues of women's ordination, sexuality, and authority. One group views patriarchy as ordained by God in all its particulars, while the other considers sexism the curse afflicting fallen humanity. Both recognize the inseparability of these issues in individual psyches, in theological concepts, in moral codes, and in the ecclesiastical structures of the church. In an odd way, perhaps not surprising to followers of the God of the Scriptures, traditionalists and feminists may inadvertently work together to educate the rest of the church, so that future decisions arise out of a consistent view of human nature, personal relationships, and social organization—created, judged, saved, and empowered by the one triune God.

Notes

Introduction

1. Joan Scott, "Gender: A Useful Category of Historical Analysis," *American Historical Review* 91 (December 1986): 1053-1075.

Part One: Women's "Proper Place"

Chapter 1: From Colonial America to the First Wave of Feminism

1. Joan Gundersen, "The Non-Institutional Church: The Religious Role of Women in Eighteenth Century Virginia," *Historical Magazine of the Protestant Episcopal Church,* hereinafter cited as *Historical Magazine,* 51 (December 1982): 352.

2. Joan Gundersen, "The Local Parish as a Female Institution: The Experience of All Saints' Episcopal Church in Frontier Minnesota," *Church History* 55 (1980): 307-322.

3. Frederic Dan Huntington, as reported by Mary Abbot Twing in her "Report of the Honorary Secretary," Board of Missions Proceedings, 1898: 291; quoted in Mary Sudman Donovan, *A Different Call: Women's Ministries in the Episcopal Church, 1850-1920* (Wilton, Conn.: Morehouse-Barlow, 1986), 125.

4. "Kemper's Journals and Letters," *Historical Magazine* 4 (September 1935): 223.

5. Julia Chester Emery, *A Century of Endeavor, 1821-1921: A Record of the First Hundred Years of the Domestic and Foreign Missionary Society of the Protestant Episcopal Church in the United States of America* (New York: Department of Missions, 1921), 169.

6. "Woman and the Mission Work," *Spirit of Missions* (June 1870): 321.

Chapter 2: Separate and Unequal

1. *Spirit of Missions* (March 1872): 191-192.

2. Margaret A. Tomes, *Julia Chester Emery: Being the Story of Her Life and Work* (New York: Woman's Auxiliary to the National Council, 1924), 23.

3. "Woman and the Mission Work," *Spirit of Missions* (June 1870): 321.

4. Julia Emery, "Jubilee of the Woman's Auxiliary to the Board of Missions, 1871-1921," *Spirit of Missions* (July 1921): 465-471.

5. Tomes, *Julia Chester Emery*, 119.

6. Ibid., 119, 122.

7. Ibid., 22.

8. Ibid., 75.

9. Julia Emery, "Auxiliary Characteristics," *Spirit of Missions* (October 1921): 635.

10. Julia Emery, "26th Annual Report of the Woman's Auxiliary to the Board of Missions," *Spirit of Missions* (November 1897): 630-631. See also Donovan, *Different Call*, 75.

11. From Bishop Lloyd's memorial address after Emery's death, as quoted in Tomes, *Julia Chester Emery*, 125.

Chapter 3: Outside Groups

1. Vida Dutton Scudder, *On Journey* (New York: E. P. Dutton, 1937), 77.

2. Scudder, *On Journey*, 58.

3. Vida Dutton Scudder, "Womanhood in Poetry," *Poet Lore* 1:10 (1889): 449-465, as quoted in Elizabeth Palmer Carrel, "Reflections in a Mirror: The Progressive Women and the Settlement Experience" (Ph.D. diss., University of Texas at Austin, 1981), 249.

4. Scudder, *On Journey*, 168.

5. Miriam U. Chrisman, *"To Bind Together": A Brief History of the Society of the Companions of the Holy Cross* (South Byfield, Mass.: Society of the Companions of the Holy Cross, 1984), 70.

6. Emily Malbone Morgan, *Letters to Her Companions*, ed. Vida D. Scudder (South Byfield, Mass.: Society of the Companions of the Holy Cross, 1944), 102.

7. "SCHC Secretary's Report, 1907," 5; quoted in "For the Ad Hoc Committee on Public Corporate Stands," compiled by Marion Rollins (South Byfield, Mass.: Society of the Companions of the Holy Cross, 1970), 2; SCHC Archives.

8. Spencer Miller and Joseph F. Fletcher, *The Church and Industry* (New York: Longmans, Green, 1930), 116.

9. *Convention Journal 1910*, 110, 177.

10. Vida Dutton Scudder, commenting on Emily Morgan's 1916 letter, in Morgan, *Letters*, 166.

11. *Convention Journal 1916*, 162, 175, 372. Critiquing the 1913 Convention's resolution, Scudder had written, "It betrays a generation in a fog.... One may doubt whether these general adjurations, excellent as they are, would make any difference to the readers of them." (*The Church and the Hour: Reflections of a Socialist Churchwoman* [New York: E. P. Dutton, 1917], 16.)

12. Morgan, *Letters*, 178.

13. Morgan, *Letters*, 208.

Chapter 4: Will a National Church Include Women?

1. I am indebted to Roland Foster for this concept of changing images and myths of identity; see his *The Role of the Presiding Bishop* (Cincinnati: Forward Movement, 1982), 9-11, 35-39.

2. Scudder, *The Church and the Hour*, 21-24.

3. Vida Scudder, "The Church Today," *Anglican Theological Review* 2 (May 1919): 106-107.

4. William B. Spofford, "Talking It Over," *The Witness* (June 24, 1937): 4.

5. *The Living Church* (October 18, 1919): 878.

6. *The Living Church* (November 1, 1919): 11.

7. Scudder, "The Church Today," 107.

8. Guy Emery Shipler, "Side Lights on the General Convention," *The Churchman* (October 25, 1919): 21.

9. Grace Lindley, "From Strength to Strength," *Spirit of Missions* (October 1921): 637-638; emphasis in original.

10. Scudder, *On Journey*, 64.

11. *The Witness* (October 25, 1919): 1.

Part Two: Should Women Vote...Or Speak?

Chapter 5: Double Messages and Rejection

1. *Convention Journal 1913*, 333, 344-45.

2. Ibid., 162.

3. *Convention Journal 1916*, 40, 75, 321.

4. Ibid., 243, 321.

5. Ibid., 41, 76.

6. Ibid., 75-76, 96.

7. Archdeacon Radcliffe of Ridgeway, Pennsylvania, offered his wisdom about "The Effect of Clothes on Church Attendance" in a front-page story in *The Witness* (August 16, 1919). The editor of the *New York Churchman*, the Rev. William Austin Smith, addressed women at the Cathedral of St. John the Divine (*The Witness* [April 12, 1919]: 3). Missionary Bishop Lucien L. Kinsolving of Brazil "charged that the ministry today is bankrupt unless women...assist in the Church recruiting campaign by giving their sons" (*The Witness* [October 25, 1919]: 3).

8. *The Witness* (August 23, 1919): 3.

9. "Would Not Object to Women Archbishops," *The Witness* (June 28, 1919): 1.

10. *The Witness* (May 3, 1919): 1; (May 24, 1919): 3; (June 7, 1919): 1, 7.

11. *The Witness* (May 3, 1919): 1; emphasis added.

12. Ibid.

13. *The Witness* (October 4, 1919): 1.

14. "Franchise Asked For Women in the Church," *The Witness*, editorial (August 30, 1919): 2.

15. *The Witness* (March 8, 1919): 1.

16. *Convention Journal 1919*, 42, 80, 87, 297, 410; Donovan, *A Different Call*, 162-63.

17. *Convention Journal 1919*, 275, 297.

18. Canon 51, Section 4, "amended through 1916," *Convention Journal 1916, Canons*, 132. In the renumbering of the Canons which resulted from the new sections on the Presiding Bishop and Council, the section on provinces became Canon 53. *Convention Journal 1919*, 176-77, 360, 420, 442-43 and *Canons*, 141.

19. *Convention Journal 1919*, 42, 80, 87, 297, 321, 348, 420, 426. "Equal Rights for Women Shelved: House of Bishops Considers Resolution to Let Committee Discuss Subject," *The Witness* (October 25, 1919): 1.

20. *Convention Journal 1919*, 35-36, 139.

21. Canon 60, Sections 5 & 6; *Convention Journal 1919, Canons*, 156-57.

22. *The Witness* (October 25, 1919): 2.

23. *Convention Journal 1919*, 214, 436, 446.

24. *Convention Journal 1919*, 210, 235, 343, 436, 450. "Equal Rights for Women Shelved," *The Witness* (October 25, 1919): 1.

Chapter 6: The Tide Missed, A Movement Founders

1. The report appears as Appendix XVI in the *Convention Journal 1922*, 671-73.

2. *Encyclical Letter from the Bishops with the Resolutions and Reports*, 39. See also Nelle Bellamy's compilation, "Participation of Women in the Public Life of the Church from Lambeth Conference, 1867-1978," *Historical Magazine* 52 (March 1982): 89.

3. *Convention Journal 1922*, 673.

4. *Convention Journal 1922*, viii, 195, 202, 404. *Convention Journal 1925*, 44, 114, 121, 227, 243, 291, 310, 606. *Convention Journal 1928*, 187, 203-204, 297-98.

5. In the Convention of 1931, a House of Bishops' resolution that required the addition of four women as consultants to the Matrimony Commission was watered down by the deputies so that the commission need only "consider the advisability" of such consultation. In 1934, the Matrimony Commission reported rather lamely that it had been unable to consult with women because of a lack of funds. In 1937, to circumvent resistance to appointing women directly to Convention commissions, a resolution requested the Woman's Auxiliary to make its views known to the Matrimony Commission. *Convention Journal 1931*, 132, 380; *1934*, 479; *1937*, 299-300, 311.

6. *Convention Journal 1940*, 476-89.

7. *The Woman's Auxiliary in the Life of the Church* (New York: Woman's Auxiliary to the National Council, 1934), 4, 11, 34.

8. Ibid., 26-27.

9. *Convention Journal 1934*, 239-45.

10. Letter from the Rt. Rev. Ernest Milmore Stires to Mrs. James Ravenel (Isabelle Lindsay) Cain, December 22, 1937. Copy supplied to the author by Mrs. Cain's daughter, Sister Catherine Josephine, of the Order of St. Helena, Vail's Gate, New York.

11. *Convention Journal 1937*, 148; *1940*, xv.

12. *Convention Journal 1931*, 38, 47, 100, 207, 281, 346; *1934*, 312, 463-65; *1937*, 467-68; *1940*, 469-70; *1943*, 242-43.

13. *Convention Journal 1943*, 284.

Chapter 7: Are Women "Laymen"?

1. William Scarlett, *Leah* (privately printed, 1970), 17.

2. *Convention Journal 1946*, 127.

3. Ibid., 219.

4. *Convention Journal 1949*, 102.

5. Ruth Jenkins, "Memories of 1949: I Still Feel Indignant," *The Witness* (November 1983): 13.

6. Scarlett, *Leah*, 18.

7. *Convention Journal 1949*, 118, 121.

8. Ibid., 357. "Women Ask Equal Rights," *The Living Church* (October 9, 1949): 19.

9. "No Voice, No Vote, No Women," *The Living Church* (October 9, 1949): 9. The magazine's firm support for women's representation had been expressed as early as an editorial on October 8, 1944.

10. "Episcopalians Debate Status of Women," *Christian Century* (October 12, 1949): 1188.

11. *Convention Journal 1949*, 358-59.

12. Ibid., xvii, 358-59.

13. *Women in the Life of the Church* (New York: Woman's Auxiliary, Church Missions House, 1951), 4-5.

14. Ibid., 33, 5, 19-21.

15. Editorial, *The Living Church* (October 8, 1944): 16.

16. "Still No Women," *The Living Church* (October 2, 1955): 25.

17. Anne Bass Fulk, *A Short History of the Triennial Meetings of the Women of the Episcopal Church* (Episcopal Church Women Triennial Committee, 1985), 23-24; David Sumner, *The Episcopal Church's History: 1945-1985* (Wilton, Conn.: Morehouse-Barlow, 1987), 36-37.

18. Records of the successive votes taken in General Conventions concerning Article I, Section 4 may be found in the following issues of the *Convention Journal*: *1949*, 227-28; *1952*, 208-10; *1955*, 201-202; *1958*, 247; *1961*, 215-16; *1964*, 125-26.

Chapter 8: Out from the Shadows

1. *Convention Journal 1958*, 345.

2. *Convention Journal 1961*, 179, 194, 256.

3. Ibid., 241-42.

4. Frances M. Young, *Whatever Happened to Good Old "Women's Work"? A History of Change in the Episcopal Church* (New York: Episcopal Women's History Project, Newsletter Special Issue, Spring 1986), 6-7; John Thornley Docker, *Toward a Totally Ministering Church* (New York: Ministry Development Office, Episcopal Church Center, 1987), 49-72.

5. "A Matter of Segregation," *The Episcopalian* (April 1964): 22.

6. *Convention Journal 1964*, 929.

7. Ibid., 127. See also Foster, *The Role of the Presiding Bishop*, 107, and "Women Rejected," *The Living Church* (October 25, 1964): 8.

8. *The Episcopalian* (December 1964): 26.

9. *The Living Church* (October 25, 1964): 20.

10. Cynthia Wedel was a member of this committee of three bishops, three women, and one priest. "Progress Report to the House of Bishops from the Committee to Study the Proper Place of Women in the Ministry of the Church, October 1966," *Convention Journal 1967*, Appendix 35.

11. Aileen Stokes Rucker, Oral History Transcript, Episcopal Women's History Project, interviewed by Mary S. Donovan, January 7, 1989; Archives of the Episcopal Church. See also Robert R. Hansel, *Showdown at Seattle* (New York: Seabury Press, 1968).

12. Mary Eunice Oliver, "Last Woman Not to be Seated," *The Witness* (November 1983): 10-11.

13. *Convention Journal 1970*, 117-18, 256-57.

14. Oliver, "Last Woman Not to be Seated," 10-11.

15. Frances M. Young, Oral History Transcript, Episcopal Women's History Project, interviewed by Joanna B. Gillespie, October 9, 1986, p. 119; Archives of the Episcopal Church.

16. Mary Donovan, "Beyond the Parallel Church," in *Episcopal Women: Gender, Spirituality, and Commitment in an American Mainline Denomination*, ed. Catherine M. Prelinger (New York: Oxford University Press, 1992), 150-53.

17. Rucker interview by Donovan, 103.

18. Young interview by Gillespie, 144.

Part Three: A Question of Ministry

Chapter 9: What Can Women Do?

1. *Convention Journal 1901*, 539; *1904*, 322, 341, 351, 356; *Canons*, 65.

2. *Convention Journal 1925*, 44, 114, 121, 227, 243, 291, 310, 606.

3. *Convention Journal 1961*, 318-25.

4. *Special Convention Journal 1969*, 182-83.

5. *Convention Journal 1952*, 672.

6. See Donovan, *A Different Call*, pages 88-122 for a full account of the origins and development of the ministry of deaconesses in the Episcopal Church through 1920, and pages 29-51 for an overview of the revival of the religious life in the Episcopal Church. See also Harry Boone Porter, Jr., *Sister Anne: Pioneer in Women's Work* (New York: National Council, 1960).

7. Donovan has shown that the statement, signed by the majority of English bishops, became known in the American church that year *(A Different Call*, 92, 195, note 12).

8. *Convention Journal 1871*, 148-51, 172-73, 344; Donovan, *A Different Call*, 95.

9. See *Annotated Constitution & Canons*, 1954 ed., vol. 2, pp. 261-67, especially the quotation on page 266, quoting the 1924 edition; the 1981 edition dropped the entire history of this canon, except for the paragraph crediting Huntington with its passage, 950-51; Donovan, *A Different Call*, chapters 7-8, esp. page 103.

10. *Annotated Constitution & Canons*, 1954 ed., vol. 2, p. 265; Donovan, *A Different Call*, 116-20; *Convention Journal 1931*, 65, 87, 140, 340, 360, 365, 468-70; *1934*, 199-206, 482-86.

11. Donovan, *A Different Call*, 90.

12. "Reunion Highlights," *Episcopal Women's History Project Newsletter* 10 (Fall 1990): 3.

13. *Convention Journal 1931*, 469-70; *1934*, 486. For a summary of canonical changes through 1952, see *Annotated Constitution & Canons*, 1954 ed., vol. 2, pp. 257-67.

14. *Convention Journal 1964*, 247-48, 833.

15. See William Stringfellow and Anthony Towne, *The Bishop Pike Affair: Scandals of Conscience and Heresy, Relevance and Solemnity in the Contemporary Church* (New York: Harper & Row, 1967), 37-40, 48, 142; and *The Death and Life of Bishop Pike* (Garden City, N. Y.: Doubleday, 1976), 315-17; David Sumner, *The Episcopal Church's History*, 15-17; John Booty, *The Episcopal Church in Crisis* (Cambridge, Mass.: Cowley Publications, 1988), 18-21; and *The Living Church* (April 25, 1965): 8-9.

16. Special Meeting of the House of Bishops, 1965, *Convention Journal 1967*, Part 5, 7-8, 24-29; Stringfellow and Towne, *The Death and Life of Bishop Pike*, 317; *The Living Church* (September 19, 1965): 5-7; (September 26, 1965): 8; (October 3, 1965): 6-7.

17. *Convention Journal 1967*, Part 5, 30.

18. *Convention Journal 1967*, Suppl. A, 26-32, 58-60.

19. "Progress Report to the House of Bishops from the Committee to Study the Proper Place of Women in the Ministry of the Church, October 1966," *Convention Journal 1967*, Appendix 35.4-12.

20. *Lambeth Conference 1968*, 39, 105-106.

21. *Convention Journal 1970*, 249, 270-71, 769-70.

Chapter 10: Breaching the Sacred Barrier

1. Ted Harrison, *Much Beloved Daughter: The Story of Florence Li Tim-Oi* (Wilton, Conn.: Morehouse-Barlow, 1985); *Lambeth Conferences 1867-1948*, 92.

2. *Special Convention Journal 1969*, 235-37.

3. *Convention Journal 1970*, 532-33. Appended to the commission's report were three "annexes": the 1966 study committee report, a summary of relevant Lambeth actions, and a discussion of the most expeditious legal route to ordaining women, 533-39.

4. The vote was: Lay (46 needed) Yes: 49-1/4, No: 28-3/4, Divided: 13; Clergy (46 needed), Yes: 38-1/4, No: 31-3/4, Divided: 21. Donovan notes that totals in the *Convention Journal* are inaccurate (*1970*, 159-60),while correct figures come from *The Living Church* (November 8, 1970): 10; see Mary S. Donovan, *Woman Priests in the Episcopal Church: The Experience of the First Decade* (Cincinnati: Forward Movement, 1988), 6, 12.

5. Resolution 28b, ACC-1 Proceedings, *The Time is Now* (London: SPCK, 1971), 39.

6. "The Episcopal Women's Caucus: A Brief History and A Beginning," *Ruach* 1 (May 1974): 1.

7. Donovan, "Beyond the Parallel Church," *Episcopal Women*, 154-155.

8. *Convention Journal 1973*, 1108, 1114-32.

9. "Women Combat Opposition to Priest Status," *Washington Post* (November 3, 1972), quoted in Shirley Larmour Sartori, "Conflict and Institutional Change: The Ordination of Women in the Episcopal Church" (Ph.D. diss., State University of New York at Albany, 1978), 75.

10. *Convention Journal 1973*, 216-17, 222-26.

11. See *Annotated Constitutions and Canons*, 1981 ed., vol. 1, pp. 37-41, for a history of attempts to change this provision.

12. For a discussion of the vote by orders which reflects the perspective and frustrations of supporters of women's ordination following the 1973 Convention, see Henry H. Righter, "The Existing Canonical Authority for Women's Ordination," in *Toward a New Theology of Ordination: Essays on the Ordination of Women*, ed. Marianne H. Micks and Charles P. Price (Alexandria: Virginia Theological Seminary, 1976), 103-104.

13. Carter Heyward, *A Priest Forever: The Formation of a Woman and a Priest* (New York: Harper & Row, 1976), 67.

14. Sartori, "Conflict and Institutional Change," 186.

15. Heyward, *A Priest Forever*, 51-52; emphasis in original.

16. Suzanne R. Hiatt, "How We Brought the Good News from Graymoor to Minneapolis: An Episcopal Paradigm," *Journal of Ecumenical Studies* 20 (Fall 1983): 579-80.

17. Heyward, *A Priest Forever*, 50.

18. The most complete development of this rationale is found in Righter, "The Existing Canonical Authority for Women's Ordination."

19. For participants' accounts, see Heyward, *A Priest Forever,* 54-55, and Hiatt, "How We Brought the Good News," 580; for analysis, see Sartori, "Conflict and Institutional Change," 87-89.

20. "Women Deacons Ask for Priesthood," *Episcopal New Yorker* (January 1974): 1*ff.* Sartori analyzes this event in terms of conflict theory: "Granting or withholding rewards, *i.e.,* loyalty and respect, is akin to threatening coercion, a middle ground between it and persuasion. In this event nothing illegal occurred, although it was a radical break with custom. In refusing the peace those in the subordinate group were withholding the respect formerly given, and taken for granted by the superordinate class, and moving themselves closer to the performance of coercive action" ("Conflict and Institutional Change," 90).

21. Heyward, *A Priest Forever,* 1; Sumner, *Episcopal Church's History,* 23.

22. Betty Medsger, "View from the Press Agent's Pew," in "Daughters of Prophecy: Special 10th Anniversary Issue," *The Witness* (Summer 1984): 22.

23. Medsger, "Press Agent's Pew," 23; for an account of Ogilby's actions, see Heather Huyck, "To Celebrate a Whole Priesthood: The History of Women's Ordination in the Episcopal Church" (Ph.D. diss, University of Minnesota, 1981), 112-17.

24. For complete text and the ordaining bishops' statement, see Alla Renee Bozarth, *Womanpriest: A Personal Odyssey,* rev. ed. (San Diego: Luramedia, 1988), 98-101.

25. Medsger, "Press Agent's Pew," 23.

26. Heyward, *A Priest Forever,* 73.

27. Suzanne R. Hiatt, "Why I Believe I Am Called to the Priesthood," in *The Ordination of Women: Pro & Con,* Michael P. Hamilton and Nancy S. Montgomery, eds. (New York: Morehouse-Barlow, 1975), 42.

28. Bozarth, *Womanpriest,* 94-96.

29. See accounts in Bozarth, *Womanpriest,* 108-109; Heyward, *A Priest Forever,* 93-95; Paul Moore, Jr., *Take a Bishop Like Me* (New York: Harper & Row, 1979), 17, 19, 21-28; Hiatt, "How We Brought the Good News," 581-82; and analyses in Huyck, "To Celebrate a Whole Priesthood," 124-28, and Sartori, "Conflict and Institutional Change," 109-14.

30. *Convention Journal 1976,* B172, B180.

31. *Convention Journal 1976,* B98; "Report on the Validity of the Philadelphia Ordinations," by Richard A. Norris, Eugene R. Fairweather, James E. Griffiss, and Albert T. Mollegen (January 15, 1975): 11, 15; Wittig files.

32. Bennett Sims, Letter "To the Clergy of the Diocese of Atlanta" (September 16, 1974); Wittig files.

33. Statement headed "Released Thursday August 15, 1974, by 10 of the 11 women priests (the 11th is yet to be reached by phone, the Rev. Katrina Swanson)"; Wittig files.

34. John M. Allin, "Dear Sisters" (August 19, 1974); Wittig files.

35. *Convention Journal 1976,* B165-209, B250-59, B285.

36. *Convention Journal 1976*, B287-376, especially B303, B311-32, B341-42, B347, B354-57.

37. Bozarth, *Womanpriest*, 115, amended. The vote totals reported by Bozarth are slightly inaccurate; those given here are from the *Convention Journal 1976*, C51, D66.

Chapter 11: Reaction and Response

1. *Convention Journal 1976*, B57.

2. The 1976 roll call vote on "conditional ordinations" was 87 to 45 with two abstentions; *Convention Journal 1976*, B120-26, B130-31, B322-24.

3. Bozarth, *Womanpriest*, 117-18; *Convention Journal 1976*, B147-48

4. *Convention Journal 1979*, B157-63, B193-96, B202-203.

5. October 1, 1977 mailgram, and October 11, 1977 letter from Bishop Frederick B. Wolf, convener of the Council of Advice; supplied by Marge Christie, one of the mailgram signers; Darling files.

6. *Convention Journal 1979*, B204-205.

7. Kenneth Briggs, "Episcopal Bishops Eke Out a Fragile Peace," *Christian Century* (November 1, 1977): 996.

8. *Convention Journal 1973*, 125.

9. *Convention Journal 1976*, B317; emphasis added.

10. *Convention Journal 1967*, Part V, Suppl. A, 22-23; Suppl. B, 26-32, 58-60; emphasis added. See also Stringfellow and Towne, *The Bishop Pike Affair*, 72-91.

11. *Convention Journal 1967*, Appendix 6.23.

12. *Convention Journal 1976*, B327.

13. "Board of Inquiry, Majority Report," 2-3, undated, submitted to the Presiding Bishop in April 1975; Wittig files.

14. *Convention Journal 1979*, B193.

15. For description of events and documents relating to these initial schismatic organizing activities, see Donald S. Armentrout, "Episcopal Splinter Groups: Schisms in the Episcopal Church, 1963-85," *Historical Magazine* 55 (December 1986): 295-320; and an extended version, "Episcopal Splinter Groups: A Study of Groups which have Left the Episcopal Church: 1873-1985" (Sewanee, Tenn.: School of Theology, 1985), unpublished Ms., 39-48; Darling files. Armentrout examined more than thirty organizations and splinter churches, but data about most were insufficient to make comparisons on all issues. The figures here come from his data on the following: Anglican Orthodox Church, Certain Trumpet, Coalition for the Apostolic Ministry, Committee of Concerned Episcopalians, Evangelical and Catholic Mission, Fellowship of Concerned Churchmen, Episcopal Renaissance of Pennsylvania, Episcopalians United (later Anglicans United, a different group than the Episcopalians United formed in 1987), Prayer Book Society, Society of the Holy Cross, and the "St. Louis Affirmation," the document

produced at the St. Louis Congress in September 1977 which led to the formation of the Anglican Catholic Church and other schismatic groups.

16. Information in this section is drawn from Armentrout, "Episcopal Splinter Groups," 31; a Prayer Book Society promotional brochure and its newsletter, *Mandate*; and an interview with then-president Jerome F. Politzer in "Episcopal Traditionalists Today: Part II," *Christian Challenge* (September 1983): 6*ff.*

17. "Episcopal Traditionalists Today: Part II," 14.

18. Information in this section is drawn from Armentrout, "Episcopal Splinter Groups," 41-44; a 1983 interview with William Wantland, then ECM National Chairman, in "Episcopal Traditionalists Today: Part III," *Christian Challenge* (October 1983): 4*ff*; the ECM newsletter *The Evangelical Catholic* and its *Episcopal Convention Monitor*; *Foundations: A Magazine of Anglican Faith and Life,* published through Fall 1989 by the Dallas ECM chapter; *Synod News,* issued by the Synod in 1989 until replaced by *Foundations: The Newsmagazine of the Episcopal Synod of America* beginning in December 1989; various brochures and press releases issued by the two organizations; and *The Episcopal Synod of America: Speeches, Documents and Pictures from the Founding Meeting at Fort Worth, Texas, June 3, 1989,* ed. by A. Donald Davies (Wilton, Conn.: Morehouse Publishing, 1990).

19. "A Pastoral Letter Convoking a Synod, from the Bishops of the Evangelical and Catholic Mission" (November 11, 1988), in Davies, ed., *The Episcopal Synod of America,* 107-111.

20. "New Coalition Forms to Challenge Church Leadership," *The Episcopalian* (November 1987): 8. This section draws on information in EURRR brochures, tracts, and its newsletter, *The Advocate.*

21. "New Coalition Forms."

22. "Dear Friend" letter signed by director John Throop, undated, used in several mass mailings in late 1988 and 1989, accompanied by a financial solicitation and opinion survey form. Very similar mailings were distributed in 1992 and 1993, including a fundraising letter from Todd Wetzel so intemperate in tone that it provoked an editorial, "Stoking Anti-Gay Hatred No Way to Raise Money" in *Episcopal Life* (January 1994): 20.

23. Sherry L. Shreffler, "Has Choice Become God?", a review of *When Choice Becomes God* by F. LaGard Smith, *NOEL NEWS* (Fall 1990): 8.

Chapter 12: The Struggle for Unity

1. *Lambeth Conference 1978,* 46-47.

2. *Convention Journal 1985,* 198, 605-606.

3. "Statement on Women in the Episcopate, Primates' Meeting: Toronto, March 1986," *Ecumenical Bulletin 77* (May-June 1986).

4. *Convention Journal 1988,* 352, 358, 386-89.

5. Ibid., 376, 383, 387-88.

6. Ibid., 414, 416-18.

7. "Report of the Committee to Study Women in the Episcopate," with "Addendum: Comments on the Five Issues Raised by the Report of the Primates' Working Party" and "An Alternate View," distributed December 15, 1987; Darling files.

8. "Report on Women in the Episcopate, Alternate View," 3-4.

9. Personal observation, October 27, 1988; see also Nancy Montgomery, "Visitors Resolution Stirs Anger at Women's Caucus," *The Episcopalian* (December 1988): 6.

10. *Convention Journal 1988*, 134-37, 232, 574-75, 577, 582, 586. All deputy votes on the subject were by orders. The totals for Resolution B22s on episcopal visitors were: Laity (116 dioceses voting, 59 needed to pass) Yes: 60; No: 40; Divided: 16; Clergy (116 voting, 59 needed to pass) Yes: 62; No: 38; Divided: 16.

11. Ibid., 438-39.

12. *Convention Journal 1988*, 137-38, 586-87, 593-94. The final vote on B23s was: Laity (166 voting, 59 needed) Yes: 36; No: 64; Divided: 16; Clergy (115 voting, 58 needed) Yes: 40; No: 67; Divided: 8.

13. *Convention Journal 1988*, 358; emphasis added.

14. *Episcopal Convention Monitor* (July 9, 1988): 1-2.

15. From the *EWC: Lambeth '88 Worship Book*, quoted in Jean Staffeld Jersey, *Her Daughters Shall Rise Up: The Women's Witnessing Community at Lambeth 1988* (New York: Office of Women in Mission and Ministry, Episcopal Church Center, 1990), 8.

16. *Lambeth Conference 1988*, 262-63; Mary S. Donovan, "The Dimensions of Unity: Women at Lambeth 1988," *Anglican and Episcopal History* 58 (September 1989): 353-63; Nan Arrington Peete, "Reflections of an Episcopal Priest: In the Fullness of Time," *The Witness* (September 1988): 16-17; Jersey, *Her Daughters Shall Rise Up*, 31-32.

17. *Lambeth Conference 1988*, 58-60, 199, 201.

Part Four: Shaking the Foundations

Chapter 13: Women in the Episcopate

1. *Christian Challenge* (November 1988): 7; for an early analysis of the traditionalist response, see my article, "Patriarchy Strikes Back," *The Witness* (April 1989): 9-11. For accounts of the election and consecration process, see "The Mitre Fits Just Fine," a special section of the Massachusetts diocesan paper, *The Episcopal Times* (February/March 1989): 1-13; see also *The Episcopalian* (November 1988): 1 and *The Witness* (October 1988): 4-5, 22-23; (November 1988): 5-9; (April 1989): entire issue.

2. Stan Gebler Davies, "St. Paul defied as Irish hail lady priests," *The Sunday Telegraph* (May 20, 1990): 8.

3. See Louis W. Pitt's analysis of the consent process in the Massachusetts' diocesan paper, "Pain and Promise: Where do We Go From Here?", *The Episcopal Times* (February/March 1989): 9; see also "Harris: Some 'Just Say No' But Consent Appears Assured," *Christian Challenge* (January/February 1989): 16.

4. "A Statement by Bishops of the Evangelical Catholic Mission, September 28, 1988," distributed by the office of Clarence C. Pope, Bishop of Fort Worth, *The Living Church* (November 20, 1988): 9.

5. "A Pastoral Letter Convoking a Synod, From the Bishops of the Evangelical and Catholic Mission, To the faithful in Christ Jesus in the Episcopal Church and in the Anglican Churches throughout the world," November 11, 1988. See *The Living Church* (December 11,1988): 6; "ECM Bishops Respond to 'Final Crisis' by Convoking Synod," *Christian Challenge* (January/February 1989): 10-13; *The Episcopalian* (March 1989): 15; see also Davies, ed., *The Episcopal Synod of America*, Appendices.

6. *Diocesan Press Service* (December 1, 1988): #88259.

7. *Diocesan Press Service* (November 10, 1988): #88243; emphasis added.

8. See *Fresh Winds Blowing: Highlights from the Ordination and Consecration of the Rev. Barbara Clementine Harris as Bishop Suffragan of the Diocese of Massachusetts* (New York: Episcopal Church, 1989), seventy-five-minute video. I am indebted to the Rev. Janet B. Campbell for the observation that Harris's consecration had fundamentally altered the episcopacy.

Chapter 14: Adapting to a New Reality

1. *Diocesan Press Service* (March 23, 1989): #89056.

2. Archbishop of Canterbury's Commission on Communion and Women in the Episcopate, *Report of the Archbishop of Canterbury's Commission... with Response from the Primates of the Anglican Communion* (London: Anglican Consultative Council, Church Publishing House, 1989). For early reports see "Primates Statement on Eames Report," *Diocesan Press Service* (May 11, 1989): #89092; #89093 contains the primates' statement about the Eames report and #89096 provides the full text of the report.

3. Edmond L. Browning, "A Pastoral Letter from the Presiding Bishop" (May 19, 1989).

4. For contemporary news accounts, see *Diocesan Press Service* (June 8, 1989): #89106; Steve Weston, "Traditionalists Form New Synod, Seek to Stay in Episcopal Church," *The Episcopalian* (July 1989): 1ff.; Jan Nunley, "ESA Says Weed 'Em and Reap," *The Witness* (July/August 1989): 114-16; "Fort Worth Synod," *The Living Church* (June 25, 1989): 6-7; and the May, June, and July/August 1989 issues of *Christian Challenge*. Greater detail and the ECM/ESA perspective on the meeting is presented in *Evangelical Catholic* (July, August, and September 1989), *Foundations* (Fall 1989), and Davies, ed., *The Episcopal Synod of America*.

5. See *Evangelical Catholic* (July 1989): 2, and *Foundations* (Fall 1989) for excerpts of Pope's address. An edited version of the entire speech appears in Davies, ed., *The Episcopal Synod of America, 13-19.*

6. Davies, ed., *The Episcopal Synod of America*, 112.

7. All Synod Resolutions appear in *Foundations* (Fall 1989): 6-7; and Davies, ed., *The Episcopal Synod of America*, App. 5, 121-24.

8. *Diocesan Press Service* (June 22, 1989): 14-16, 32-33.

9. Martha Blacklock, "Observing the House of Bishops," *Ruach* (Autumn 1989): 7.

10. *Episcopal News Service* (October 4, 1989), emphasis added. This issue includes interpretive reports on the House of Bishops (#89159-75), together with the full texts of the Presiding Bishop's opening remarks (#89180), Mary Tanner's address on the Eames Commission report (#89181), and the Statement of the House of Bishops (#89183). See also the minutes, "Meeting of the House of Bishops, 1989," 34-35, 41-42.

11. "ESA President Sees Traditionalist Position Strengthened," a September 29, 1989 news release, reprinted as *Synod News 1* (October 1989).

12. "Meeting of the House of Bishops, 1989," 34-35.

13. *Pax Vobiscum* 5 (Advent 1989): 1.

14. Blacklock, "Observing the House of Bishops," 8.

15. Julie A. Wortman, "New Woman Bishop Prefers 'Ragged Boundaries of the Church," *The Witness* (September 1990): 25.

16. See *Episcopal News Service* (May 10, 1990): #90033, for the complete text of the March 1990 Eames Commission report.

17. Archbishop of Canterbury's Commission, "Report, 1989," paragraph 43, p. 21.

18. Lewis Carroll, *Alice's Adventures in Wonderland; and Through the Looking Glass* (New York: E. P. Dutton, 1954/1970), 185.

Chapter 15: Two World Views

1. Davies, ed., *The Episcopal Synod of America*, 15.

2. Editorial, *The Independent* (November 27, 1988).

3. From an article in *The Daily Telegraph*, quoted in "Fresh Wind of Massachusetts: An Anglican Tempest," *Christian Challenge* (November 1988): 22.

4. From an article by Jerome Politzer in *The Houston Chronicle* (December 10, 1988), 3E.

5. Edmond Browning, "Remarks to the Executive Council" (June 16, 1989), and "Browning Addresses Events in Fort Worth," *Diocesan Press Service* (June 22, 1989): #89117 and unnumbered report, 14-16.

6. Letty M. Russell, *Household of Freedom: Authority in Feminist Theology* (Philadelphia: Westminster Press, 1987), 12.

7. Audre Lorde, *Sister, Outsider: Essays and Speeches* (Trumansburg, N.Y.: Crossing Press, 1984), 110.

Chapter 16: Women, Sex, and Sexuality

1. Edmond Browning, "Statement of the Presiding Bishop and Council of Advice [regarding the ordination of Robert Williams], February 20, 1990," distributed with a "Dear Friends" covering letter dated February 16, 1990; Darling files. For full accounts, including the text of the February 20 statement, see *Integrity News and Notes* (Spring and Summer 1990); see also "Foreign and Domestic Events Provoke Lively [Executive] Council Debate," and "Council [of Advice] Steps Back from Ordination Action," *Episcopal Life* (April 1990): 2, 7.

2. *Convention Journal 1979*, B205.

3. *Convention Journal 1979*, B174-75, B177-78, B183-93; see *Take a Bishop Like Me* for Moore's memoir of the circumstances surrounding Barrett's ordination.

4. The legal status of joint resolutions adopted by the General Convention has remained a puzzle for more than a century. In 1877 a report on the "force" of such resolutions concluded that they "have never been deemed to have, and ought not to be construed as having, the force of law, but as being merely the expression of an opinion...of great weight indeed but not obligatory," and recommended that all future legislation be "by Canon." But the next Convention rejected the proposal to restrict legislation to canonical changes, leaving the status of joint resolutions a matter of opinion. As the 1880 constitutional amendment committee pointed out: "These very resolutions [about the 'force' of joint resolutions], if passed, would themselves become joint resolutions, neither more nor less, and...it is difficult to see how any real relief could come to embarrassed minds from our passing them." *Convention Journal 1877*, 141-43, 205; *1880*, 114-15. See also *Annotated Constitution and Canons*, 1954 ed., vol. 1, 357-61.

5. *Convention Journal 1979*: debate and votes appear on B93-96, C88-93, D127-34; the statement of bishops dissociating from the recommendation is on B111-12; deputies endorsing the bishops' statement are listed on D141.

6. *Convention Journal 1988*, 236, 313-14, 669-70, 676, 689-90.

7. Quoted from the bishops of the Province of the Pacific, in Browning, "Statement of the Presiding Bishop...20 Feb. 1990."

8. William Murchison, "The Newark Ordination: Reverberations and Aftershocks," *Foundations* (March 1990): 1.

9. *Convention Journal 1991*, 505-506, 517-18.

10. Rosalind Pollack Petchesky, "Antiabortion, Antifeminism, and the Rise of the New Right," *Feminist Studies* 7 (Summer 1981): 231.

11. John Shelby Spong, "Call to Confront Homophobia," *The Witness* (November 1990), 23.

12. *Convention Journal 1991*, final text of the much amended substitute resolution appears on p. 746.

13. *Convention Journal 1991*, 322-23.

14. "An Open Letter to the People of the Episcopal Church" (July 20, 1991), distributed by the Episcopal Synod of America on the last day of the General Convention in Phoenix, Arizona.

15. "Three Women 'Cutting New Ground,'" *The Living Church* (December 27, 1992): 7-8; see also "A Conversation Among Three Bishops," *Ruach* (Winter 1993): 10-15.

Conclusion: New Wine, New Wineskins

1. Norris, *et al*, "Report on the Validity of the Philadelphia Ordinations," 15.

2. "Bishops' Vote on Spong Sets Stage for Phoenix," *Episcopal Life* (November 1990): 9.

3. George William Rutler (July 29, 1974), from an audio tape of the Philadelphia ordinations; Wittig files. John Jameson, speaking for the Prayer Book Society (February 11, 1989); from the videotape *Fresh Winds Blowing*.

Index